1.-

The Victorian Treasure-House

Shandyism: The Character of Romantic Irony

Romantic Opera and Literary Form

Imagining America

Television: The Medium and Its Manners

The Art of the City:
Views and Versions of New York

The Everyman History of English Literature

A Song of Love and Death:
The Meaning of Opera

BEHIND
THE
MOUNTAIN

Return to Tasmania

PETER CONRAD

POSEIDON PRESS
New York London Toronto Sydney Tokyo

POSEIDON PRESS
Simon & Schuster Building
Rockefeller Center
1230 Avenue of the Americas
New York, New York 10020

POSEIDON PRESS is a registered trademark
of Simon & Schuster Inc.
POSEIDON PRESS colophon is a trademark
of Simon & Schuster Inc.
Manufactured in the United States of America

1   3   5   7   9   10   8   6   4   2

Library of Congress Cataloging-in-Publication Data
Conrad, Peter, date.
  [Down home]
  Behind the mountain: return to Tasmania/Peter Conrad.
    p.   cm.
  Previously published as: Down home. 1988.
    1. Tasmania—Description and travel—1981–   2. Conrad,
Peter, date.   I. Title.
DU186.C66   1989
919.46′0463—dc19   88-26750
                    CIP

ISBN 0-671-67373-4

Contents

Acknowledgements

To Carmen Callil, who sensed that this was the book I wanted and needed to write, and to Andrew Motion, Jeremy Lewis and Jonathan Burnham for their work on it; to Elaine Pfefferblit for her faith in it; to Pat Kavanagh and Gloria Loomis; to the Governing Body of Christ Church, Oxford, for a grant of leave, and to Glenys McGregor for her typing and her enthusiasm; to Kaye Hosking, Julia Clark, Gordon Dean, Ron Banks, and Robyn and Kristen Lopes for their help in Tasmania; and to the old friends who share my memories of the state – John and Louise White, Wayne and Barbara Hooper, Sam and Marilyn Lake, and Peter and Rae Pierce. I am grateful as well to Peter Pierce's *Oxford Literary Guide to Australia* for revealing to me how many literary dreams are hidden on the map of Tasmania.

I

EMOHRUO

Where Am I?

About halfway through my life – at least I hope my sums are right – I began to wonder about what I had lost. At the time, I hadn't so much lost it as thrown it away, with a negligence I considered cool. When I left home at the age of twenty, it was without a backward glance. First went two tea chests, shipping my books to England. What remained I carried, in endless relays, out to the rusted incinerator in our yard, between the fragrant compost heap and the stilted avenues of beans. There, scrutinised by neighbours pausing at their kitchen windows as they did the washing-up, I set fire to all the leavings of my life so far – diaries and exercise books, bundles of letters tied by string; anything that might incriminate me by attaching an identity to me. The cruel cleanness of it now amazes me, but at that age it's easy to cremate a portion of your life: you don't believe in memory, and so can have no affections. Thus I loaded the funeral pyre with the attributes of a self I was to regard from now on – I thought – as irrelevant, the discarded first draft of a person. The two tea chests contained all I wanted to salvage. Their cargo was academic; being good at exams had earned me my second chance. Home was where you started from, not where you stayed. It was more than ten years before I saw it again.

Only now, when it is irretrievable, has it acquired value for me. The thing I had lost was childhood, youth: the two decades before you control your own life, when you are tussled and twisted into the being which you helplessly remain. And for me, that time was a place. I was born in Tasmania.

Where? you may ask: so did I, as soon as I was capable of asking questions. The answer was disorienting. We were an offshore island off the shore of an offshore continent, victims of a twofold alienation. Australia was chosen for settlement because it was so remote, and because it could scarcely sustain life. It served as a place of ultimate banishment and estrangement. Yet beneath its south-eastern tip was an even remoter version of itself, a site of internal exile. This was our little serrated triangle of rock: Van Diemen's Land, where a penal colony was founded in 1803 at Hobart. Australia is tempted nowadays to forget Tasmania, just as I had wanted in 1968 to walk away from the small past I had accumulated. At school we were given plastic maps to trace, with dotted lines standing for those invisible fences drawn across scrub and desert to divide the states. Tasmania, disconnected by Bass Strait, was an embarrassment to this cut-out continent; it was therefore simply left off. We passed the time outlining the contours of a country we didn't belong to.

Nor did Tasmania look like that burnished, seething, ancient mass above us which we knew as the mainland; the main land, to which we were an appendix, an afterthought. At my primary school – a conurbation of sheds across the highway from our house in the northern suburbs of Hobart – the only art-work on the premises hung in a corridor: a print of Ayers Rock as painted by Albert Namatjira. He had prettified it, rubbing it down to a violet, velvety mound and surrounding it with white, wriggling eucalypts; still, if this was Australia – an omphalos of burning stone which sacredly marked a centre in the unmapped sand – then where were we? Out the school window, contradicting that hot, planetary clump on the wall, was our local monolith, Mount Wellington. It was blue, not red; above it were bundled sleety storm clouds, not the metallic scorching sky of the Northern Territory; instead of reddening in the sun, it wore for half the year a toupee of snow. It was a source of chilblains, of frozen toes on the way to school, and of those mists of condensed white life you exhaled on the bitterest mornings with every breath. The Australian landscape had omitted us. Instead of an overcooked desert, we lived in a cool dripping jungle. On the mountain's foothills were groves of man-ferns, secret trickling crevasses choked with brown fronds. Beyond the mountain, the battlement which forbiddingly stopped Hobart just as it started, other mountains rippled indefinitely like hardened rearing waves until the southern ocean overwhelmed them, and the world itself set about ending.

Hobart figured in history as a last exit, the place of no return for its convicts, later a stopping point for whalers or Antarctic explorers on the way to the axis of ice beneath us. With our anchorage to the mainland flooded, dangling there tugged at by gravity, were we in danger of falling off the earth? On summer days the shadows things cast preceded them, elongated forever as if being dragged further

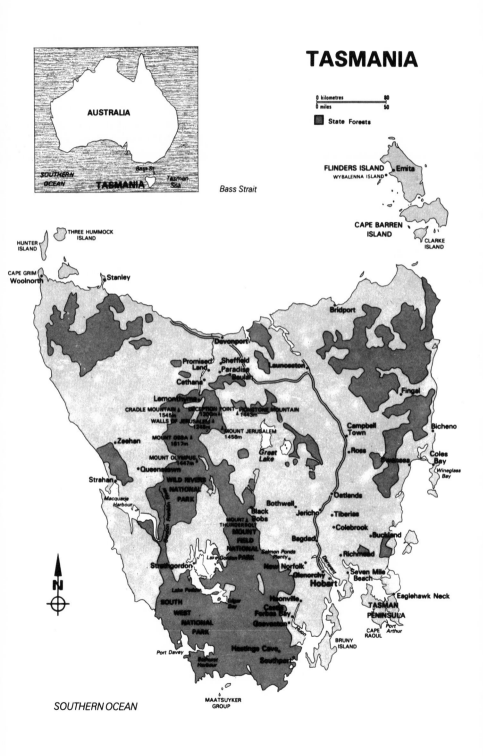

TASMANIA

0 kilometres 80
0 miles 50

State Forests

AUSTRALIA

SOUTHERN OCEAN
Bass St.
TASMANIA
Tasman Sea

Bass Strait

FLINDERS ISLAND Emita
WYBALENNA ISLAND

CAPE BARREN
ISLAND

CLARKE
ISLAND

THREE HUMMOCK
ISLAND

HUNTER
ISLAND

CAPE GRIM
Woolnorth
Stanley

Bridport

Devonport

Promised
Land
Sheffield
Paradise
Cethana
Beulah

Launceston

Fingal

Lemonthyme

CRADLE MOUNTAIN
1545m
WALLS OF JERUSALEM
1245m
DECEPTION POINT
1300m
IRONSTONE MOUNTAIN
1443m

Campbell
Town

Bicheno

MOUNT OSSA
1617m
MOUNT JERUSALEM
1458m

Zeehan

Ross
Coles
Bay

MOUNT OLYMPUS
1447m

Great
Lake

Swansea
Wineglass
Bay

Strahan

Queenstown

WILD RIVERS

Macquarie
Harbour

NATIONAL
PARK

Oatlands

Bothwell

MOUNT
THUNDERBOLT
Black
Bobs
Jericho

Tiberias

MOUNT
FIELD
NATIONAL
PARK

Colebrook

Buckland

Bagdad
Salmon Ponds
Plenty

Richmond

Strathgordon
Lake Gordon
New Norfolk
Glenorchy
Seven Mile
Beach

Lake Pedder

Hobart

Scotts Peak
Dam

SOUTH
WEST

Moonville
Castle
Forbes Bay
Geeveston

Eaglehawk Neck

TASMAN
PENINSULA

NATIONAL

Huon

CAPE
RAOUL
Port
Arthur

PARK

Port Davey
Bathurst
Harbour

Hastings Cave
Southport

BRUNY
ISLAND

MAATSUYKER
GROUP

SOUTHERN OCEAN

N

south. The mountain, the houses, your own insignificant body as you walked along the road were beckoned magnetically down that track into darkness. If you kept walking, would you come to the edge? The world resembled the humming, whirling top I had as a toy; we were its base, which tumbled over once the energy was used up. My head spun like the top to think of it. On the northern coast of Tasmania, there would at least have been the fancied mainland to imagine across the water. But Hobart was tucked into one of the bays which corrode the southern end of the state, so its view – over the harbour, down the channel, out into the sea – was towards oblivion.

We apparently had been disowned by Australia, when the land-bridge foundered. Who then could we belong to? A mother country was at once invoked. In dropping off Australia, we had tumbled south to begin a long northward climb beneath the pole towards our replica and source in the other hemisphere, England. At school, Tasmania was explained to us as a small lost England. Such was the blithe received wisdom of the time. 'Just a warmer England', a local traveller had written of the island while walking round it in the early 1950s. Didn't we grow apples, which were shipped in cold storage from the Hobart docks to be eaten in London? On our map were a cliffless Dover, a beachless Brighton, an unindustrial Sheffield; the suburb I lived in was Glenorchy, allegedly the facsimile of some-where in Scotland. But British analogies didn't account for the harsh, wild extremity of Tasmania: its saga of penal sadism, the prompt annihilation of its aboriginal race by the early settlers, the sightings of marsupial tigers in the bush. When I got to England, I found that people had only the vaguest notion of their country's duplicate down-under. They fancied that Tasmania had something to do with New Zealand, or believed it to be independent, outside the Australian federation. In America, I was sometimes assumed to be a native of Tanzania.

Growing up, I took heart when I learned that Merle Oberon was born in Tasmania. (Any reference to the place in print acted as an existential confirmation.) From this particular datum I concluded that (a) Tasmania must exist, and (b) there must be a way out of it into the world. Luckily I didn't know at the time that Merle Oberon had never set foot on our turf. The birthplace had been allocated to her by Hollywood publicists, who wanted to cover up her Eurasian parentage; Tasmania was a convenient nowhere, and since it was probably non-existent, the bluff would never be called. Errol Flynn's manifest destiny was clearer. He actually deigned to be born in Tasmania, but secured his early release by getting himself expelled from my high school for a minor prank. Where am I? is the first demand the wailing infant makes of the world he arrives in. Calmed and comforted, you stop asking after a while, and are soon so adjusted to reality (an adult invention) that you forget the question. I continued, inconveniently and unappeasably, to ask it in Tasmania. I remember a Sunday afternoon when I must have been four or five years old. My parents had taken me to a gymkhana at the agricultural showground near our house. From up there, on the dusty raised race-track, you could see the closed circle of our world: Mount Wellington to one side, to the other – behind the loops of bitumen and the bright weatherboard cartons of our suburb, set down on a hill only a few months before – glum, hunched Mount Direction; the choppy waters of our bay with its rank mud-flats, the frayed grass of the rifle range, the smoking skyline which was the zinc works. A northerly wind whipped up small tornadoes of grit. The sky, overcast and opaque, stifled the scene as if beneath glass. There were cheers from the track: someone or other had won a race. Wandering through the sparse crowd holding my father's hand, I began suddenly, inexplicably to cry. I remember the heat of the tears, and my gasping for breath in order to wail some more. My parents were mystified, embarrassed, finally annoyed. What was the reason? they asked. I was too busy bellowing to say. They were with another couple, who also had an only son. He too looked on, aghast at the exhibition. 'Graeme isn't crying,' they pointed out. Well, no, of course he's not, I suppose I thought; how could he be? The tantrum was my own exclusive means of self-expression. My parents had no choice but to bundle me home, their day ruined; and I think they were a little suspicious of me ever after, afraid of the inordinate demands I'd make on life, and of the dissatisfaction and frustration dramatised by my outburst on the showground.

My silly fit of misery in the grey afternoon repeated that first cry of the displaced infant. Where *am* I? it insisted on knowing. The mountains told me that I was in Tasmania, which only made things worse. This was not the life I wanted; somehow I'd been given the wrong one. My tears raged at the injustice – or incompetence – of it.

What continued to terrify me was the rawness, the shivering vulnerability of the place. A settlement had happened here by chance, in a landscape which didn't recognise it. Our suburb was knocked into shape yesterday. The families allotted to the wooden boxes eyed each other warily over their back fences, while their children threw pebbles and abuse in the street. The yards were quagmires; all the trees which grew here had been flattened, and replaced by saplings. It would take a long while for the world to acquire upholstery, the soothing sense that it has been made ready for us to inhabit. Rain played the iron roof like a kit of drums at night; mornings began with visits to a shed in the backyard, and once a week the night-cart toiled round the streets and a dunny man – as we sat inside pretending not to notice – lumbered up the path with our can of soil on his shoulder. Only much later were pipes laid in the yard, and we got a potted cataract inside the house. Our country cousins made a point of trying it out when they visited, giggling as the cascade gushed.

In the thirty years since those early days, centuries have passed. The place has lived down its provisional look, its unaccommodated feel. My parents, remaining in the house, have achieved a humble miracle of colonisation. The churned waste is now a flower garden. Their pride in it, and their hard-working devotion to it, make it their thing of beauty, created to mark the spot where rude nature gives way to nurture. In every letter they report on what they have planted, or what's in bloom. They make sacrifices for its sake, and won't have a dog because it would dig up the beds. The house has changed as well. Its weatherboards suggested temporariness; onto them has been grafted a second skin of craggy artificial brick. Once more, the early history of the land is reprised here: the house's new carapace repeats the colony's advance from wattle and daub to buildings of stone. What used to be the chicken coop also has a covering of left-over Quickbrick, and inside it a standard lamp with an art deco bowl like an overgrown ashtray – unfashionable, discarded – occupies the dirt floor where the chooks used to roost. Indoors, everything is clad, cushioned, supplied with a buffer against reality. The lounge-chairs have antimacassars, the video-recorder wears a leather coverlet at night like the cloth you drape on a cage so the bird inside will go to sleep; in the toilet, a spare roll on the cistern hides up the fluffy crinoline of a doll, who cheerily waves her plastic mitt. The world has been upholstered with a vengeance. The letter box propped on the front fence is a cottagey miniature of the house itself, carpentered by my father: an aedicule for the fantasy to curl up in.

There is no need any longer to be afraid, to feel exposed. Still, just outside this haven lurks the sense of destitution – of having been abandoned here – which started me crying at the showground. Across the highway, I walked through the grounds of the primary school, which opened the year I began there. Though the blinds were drawn and the buildings closed for the summer holidays, it was all as I remembered – loud-speakers on the roof-tops to bark commands; the flagpole, a snarled wire snapping from it, where we had to line up in paramilitary rows; on the blistered tarmac, the ruled insignia of team-playing: boxes for hopscotch, goals for football. On a window, someone had scrawled 'Fuck my bum' in excrement. Down a grassy slope, beside the special school for retardees, two dozen car tyres painted white have been planted up to their middles in earth and organised into dwarfish avenues and turning circles – an imaginary roadway, where the unbalanced children could be taught to ride bicycles. The past waited here to take me prisoner. This – the asphalt playground with its compulsory squares, the rubbery buried road going nowhere – was what I had run away from. Seen from school, the street on which our house stood ran to the steep top of a hill and then, its gravel glaring, dived like a ski-jump into nothing; after it there was the barrier of Mount Direction, in its olive drab camouflage. I refused to believe that the world stopped here so prematurely.

Through my bedroom window I could see a cabin behind the house next door. A hanger-on of the family has occupied it for years, tolerated in the unkempt rubbly yard but not allowed in the house. Since I left home, he has had two strokes and a heart attack; he passes the time by drinking, and allegedly killed off some berries my parents were growing by his habit of peeing through the paling fence. In summer he wears a white singlet, in winter a cardigan red as his face, with always a pair of emerald-green bell-bottoms. Every day when I was back I'd see him through the open door of his hut, sitting bent forward and cradling his head in his hands, beneath a row of kitchen utensils hooked on the fibre-board wall. The cricket score drawled from the radio, or sitcom laughter cackled at him from his television set in a corner. A few yards off, out my window and over the fence, quiet desperation squatted in its box. Moving only when he lit himself another cigarette or refilled his glass or tottered to the fence for a pee, he was an image of resignation to the awaited end. My protest was against such a terminus.

Busy imagining the beyond, lying awake at night and dreaming of the lighted world which hung around the curve of the globe above us, I paid less and less attention to Tasmania itself. Since I never saw the rest of the state, except for a day-trip to Launceston at the top of the island when I was twelve, I could easily deny it, or behave as if it didn't impinge on me – as if I were merely serving a term here, doing time like the convicts, in the hope that good behaviour might ensure parole. Mentally I left very early, though the body had to wait much longer before it could follow. Once I began to read, I discovered somewhere else to live: the Noddyland or Neverland or wonderland or secret garden of English books. Art even at its most naive could colonise the hostile world; it freed you from facts by inventing alternatives. Thus I became unassuageably homesick for a place I had never seen, which existed only in writing. That fantasy was my home.

Near us there was a house exactly like ours – the government department which built these suburbs had only a limited set of prototypes – except that its front porch displayed a plank of polished Huon pine with an inscription branded in by pokerwork. The board said EMOHRUO. It puzzled me for a long time when I was a child. An aboriginal incantation? The family name of some clan of what we called new Australians – Greek perhaps? I decoded it eventually, and as I grew up it became a curio of suburban kitsch for me, along with black swans preening in wrought iron and bulbous plastic tomatoes whose stalks squirted ketchup. Now it has turned back into a puzzle. Why, if you're bent on announcing to passers-by that this is your home, would you choose to do so backwards? Was the title reversed out of shyness? Did the sense of belonging fear to declare itself directly, in dread of rejection? Was there a superstitious obscurantism to the name, as if the spirits of place spoke a dialect which isn't ours? Or maybe it uttered an exotic yearning. The sign uprooted the house which it should have fixed on that lawn of concrete; it gestured towards some Polynesian island.

Today when I walk past, the back-to-front babble resounds with all the first pushy improbability of homesteading in this country. It's the act of bravado which requisitions space and stakes a personal claim; it spells out in morale-boosting plural the collective need to imagine a home, and thereby reminds me of what I can never have.

But by its nonsensicality – no more or less absurd than calling these streets Glenorchy, or nicknaming this funny forgotten realm Taswegia, as we used to do at school – it concedes defeat in advance. Our home garbles its own name, renders itself unreadable and unattainable. Could Tasmania after all tell me where it was, or where I am?

II

JOURNEYS

On the Road

Before confronting the unknown, I rehearsed the familiar: the main road from my parents' house into Hobart, on which I'd long ago set out on my journey through the world. This was the one thin strip of Tasmania I knew by heart, having trudged it into my memory over a decade of repetitions. Beyond it lay mountains, farms, beaches, Tasmania seen from above and from below. But the main road was my urban landscape, whose dreary length as I shuttled back and forth along it had become a narrative, a march-past of totems and friendly fetishes and sacred places, a story of eternal returns. The main road was the outer limit of my world, and therefore the first reality on which my imagination went to work. The better I knew it, the stranger I longed for it to be: denied experience, we have to invent it.

We lived beside the new highway, near a roundabout which when I was growing up was notorious for its perils. Saturday nights would be cheered by the squeal of tyres and often the cymbal clash of metal; on Sunday mornings there would be wreckage to inspect, and sometimes juicy stains on the bitumen. But the highway, driven across farms when the suburbs were settled after the war, wasn't the so-called main road. That straggled through the shops and houses on the other side of the railway line, half a mile further on. It began its career on the wharf in Hobart, strode up a hill past the Post Office, bent and slouched through five miles of petrol bowsers and used car lots and timber yards to get to us in Glenorchy, and from there hiked on over the midlands to bisect the state, arriving hours later in Launceston. It was our main road, and Tasmania's; it divided the terrain and ruled it. Everyone lived just off that road. It was the encyclopaedia which indexed all possible knowledge: my father, teasing one of his brothers who professed to be an old friend of every person in Tasmania and could retail all their genealogies on demand, said 'Jimmy reckons he knows everyone from Southport to Bridport – both sides of the road. And he knows their ages.' If you strayed too far from the road, you arrived at nowhere – the sodden jungles and

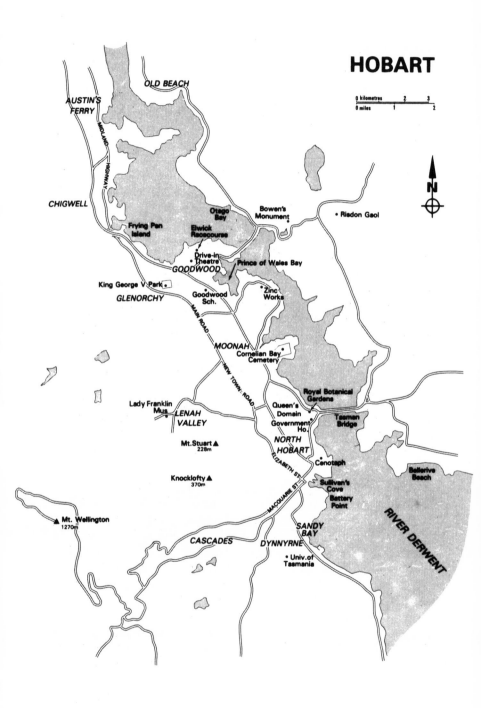

HOBART

OLD BEACH

AUSTIN'S
FERRY

MIDLAND HIGHWAY

CHIGWELL

Otago Bay

Bowen's Monument

• Risdon Gaol

Frying Pan Island

Elwick Racecourse

Drive-in Theatre

GOODWOOD

Prince of Wales Bay

King George V Park •

Goodwood Sch.

GLENORCHY

• Zinc Works

MAIN ROAD

MOONAH

Cornelian Bay Cemetery

NEW TOWN ROAD

Royal Botanical Gardens

Lady Franklin Mus.

LENAH VALLEY

Queen's Domain

Government Ho.

Tasman Bridge

Mt. Stuart ▲ 228m

NORTH HOBART

ELIZABETH ST.

Knocklofty ▲ 370m

Cenotaph •

Bellerive Beach

▲ Mt. Wellington 1270m

MACQUARIE ST.

Sullivan's Cove

Battery Point

SANDY BAY

RIVER DERWENT

CASCADES

DYNNYRNE

• Univ. of Tasmania

0 kilometres   2   3
0 miles   1   2

N

soiled mountains of the west coast, the incest-ridden, fable-haunted backblocks of the east. It was the geometer's first notional organising of the wild. Beyond its thin, safe line were dragons, or at least devils. Our domesticated, bedraggled stretch of it had always tugged at me. This was the rolling pavement I wanted to be aboard, and every school holiday I would start out to explore it by walking the built-up, boring, congested miles into town. My parents nodded sadly over these expeditions. What was the point? They had a car, and there were buses; instead I preferred to tramp that dusty ribbon of pavement in order, once I'd got to the centre of the city, to reverse and go home again. This nomadism seemed to them an insane eccentricity. To make it worse, the trek was so ritualised that I used to love impeding and protracting it – to dawdle or divert, competing with myself to see how long I could make it last. I was trying to turn the dull concrete and black tarmac into elastic: to elongate the road and thus expand my world, like a dog on one of those coiled leashes which seem able, if the animal insists enough, to stretch as far as the horizon. Yet try as I did to rubberise it, the track contracted. Every time I made the trip, it seemed shorter, the end closer, no triumphal avenue into the future but a constricting circle which sent me back to where I started. Eventually the road wasn't enough, and its place was taken, on my few trips as a student to Melbourne and Sydney, by random, rambling tours on trams and buses, spending hours to get to the end of the line. I loved the featurelessness of the scene we crawled through, the painful slowness of our advance, the sense of never achieving the goal: it was all a promise of infinitude, proof that the world wasn't small, as the main road, when it shrank as I grew up and outgrew it, had been.

Much later, the very predictability of the main road – which made me realise that I was only walking round the boundary fence of my prison – returned to me with a different meaning. It became the landscape of my nights in England. To sedate myself when I couldn't sleep, I'd order myself along it, forced to picture every house or shop or factory in their proper order, not letting myself proceed until the image had come clear (and on both sides of the road). The rote was so calming that I'd be unconscious before I got to Moonah, the next suburb along from ours; I assume I went the rest of the way in my sleep. Now, rather than the perimeter of frustration which I couldn't get beyond, the road was a zone of recovered tranquillity: not an inadequate rehearsal for the future but a tunnel into the past. When that happened, I knew it was time to go back; and when I got there, I set out on the road again. It was to be a journey of recollection, replaying childhood, yet as well an exercise in social accountancy, recording what had changed since the jaunts along it I remembered, and calculating how much I had lost.

Between the highway and the main road there's a short spur where the country and the suburb still haven't resolved their conflict. A farm has shrunk to an overgrown backyard, with a goat grazing on weeds and chickens excavating the grass under a rotary hoist; over the fence are fuming chimneys and triangular roofs of corrugated iron – the wartime munitions works, now a silk and textiles plant where in the 1960s I used to scavenge squares of florid psychedelia and get my mother to sew me gruesome home-made ties and floppy pocket handkerchiefs. Further on, beside a warehouse of doors panelled with stained glass – enabling you to cathedralise your cottage – there's a garage full of damaged garden gnomes, their noses chipped, their bobbled caps toppled, their bellies dented; next to that, a flotilla of plastic bath-tubs put out to pasture. On the other side of the road is one of the fenced-off fantasy realms of my childhood: the agricultural showground, site of my existential tantrum, where for a few days each year (having squeezed through that fence) I could prowl among tractors and sheep- dips and fishing-tackle and collect bags of brochures printed on squeaky paper. The imagination makes do with whatever poor reality is to hand, and for me the showground with its manured trails and flimsy sheds was a magic kingdom. Later, obligingly, it became exactly that, when the draughty interior of one of those pavilions was turned into a studio, and at the age of fourteen I acted in a film there. Now the showground hosts the trots and the dog races. Behind the fence, cranky horses kick and stamp inside their stalls and greyhounds have hysterics. The hunting bugles and the revved-up patter of the commentators, drifting over the highway, used to taunt me on inert summer evenings: there was excitement a few hundred yards away; but only the excitement of watching animals run in circles.

To get to the main road, you have to cross the railway line. Another of my treats – part of my hopeful quest for new angles on this familiarity, from which it would look strange – was to travel into town by train, seeing the main road from behind and looking in over the unguarded back fences of the houses whose fronts were as well known as members of the family. That view is no longer available; trains don't use the line now. Growing up here today, I'd have one less visual option.

Arrival at the main road is marked by a shop which used to be our butcher's. The place was run by two beefy brothers called Ralph and Ronnie Grubb: allegories of their trade, like emblems of a medieval guild. They worked in a den of chilly, sweetly rancid death, wearing morticians' aprons and beaming as they hewed and sawed and chopped at bluish carcasses. The counters were marble, the floor a turf of sawdust, and when they heaved open the door of their refrigerated back room they disclosed an Auschwitz of flayed cattle, hooked whole to the ceiling. Now came the first of many deconsecrations: the butcher's was a video lending library. A sign painted on the wall recalls the heroic bluster of the Grubbs with their chubby forearms, their cleavers and their good cheer as they waded through gore:

Movies from

DOLLAR

it says, with the numeral flattened into the semblance of a beer glass. The base is hoppy brown, and at the top the tilting lip represents the overflow of white froth. This, we're to understand, is a movie pub. Or so it was, for it's already defunct – empty, with only a flattened cardboard super-hero and an axe murderer stranded in the window, pausing from their cosmic combat among gathering dust and circling flies.

Here I turn towards town, and start my progress through a wonderland of ingenious mythology. England and America, Australia's twin and schizoid self-images, abut on the road: a bear-skinned sentry painted into his box stands to attention at the London Deli; opposite him the white-suited Kentucky colonel revolves on a plastic sign over tubs of frying chicken. The Carlyle Hotel advertises levitation, a vertical take-off which even I, so anxious for new points of vantage, hadn't imagined. It has, the notice says, 'the only rising

glass stage floor in the southern hemisphere'. Behind it is its Liquor
Barn: the bottle-shop disguised as a rural granary. Superwheels, the
used car lot, has a mural of affluent Porsches, sleek Trans-Ams and
volatile Thunderbirds on a ground of blue brick. Before these
archetypes are the cheap actualities, hosed down to look fresher,
bonnets agape like slaves in the market-place showing their teeth.
The health food company Sanitarium portrays its ethic in sanitary art
deco: stainless steel lettering, and streamlined curves like efficient
intestines. It's a temple of moral hygiene, founded by Seventh Day
Adventists to manufacture fibrous wafers like miniature door-mats
called Weetbix. The Goliath cement works, raising against the sky a
bulbous grey pipe whose bulges are swollen muscles, prides itself on
the gigantism of heavy industry. On a strip of lawn beside the
pavement, the Hydro-Electric Commission puts the armaments of
engineering out to pasture. Here it has parked an eight-ton turbine
which at the Tarraleah power station from 1938 to 1959 revolved
4,000,000,000 times; consumed 600,000,000,000 gallons of water
weighing 2,678,570,000 tons; and produced 1,760,000,000 units of
electricity. Who was counting? The rows of noughts dramatise the
dynamo as an epic labourer. Now, however, there are cobwebs
between his bolts, and his water-shunting cups are rusted.

The most deceptive of roadside myths is that of self-renovation.
The Trim Shop invites you to come in and consult its style books:
since identity depends on hair, new selves are on sale within. A mile
or so further on, Lyke-Nu dry cleaners renovate the language at the
same time as laundering your clothes. For my parents, the idyllic
offer of the suburbs was newness. They always sniffed at old things,
and were dismayed when I came home from the Salamanca market
this year with a pair of smeared and tattered army pants which had
cost me three dollars; my father objects in principle to watching black
and white films on television, and says they're out-of-date. Yet for
me, in this newly-made world – colonising the cleared bush in a
house built weeks before, re-enacting that first venture of settlement
in a place without a history – the immediate necessity was to unearth
a past. In our house, what past there was had been unregretfully
packed away: a mahogany box of old photographs on the mantelpiece, a trunk in my parents' bedroom with souvenirs of the war.
When starting out along the road, I was travelling in search of
ownable pasts. That's how I came upon English literature, in musty

cartons of Victoriana discarded in the Salvation Army shop at Moonah. The chapels I pause at now on the road are sacred to the second-hand: a bookshop which dangles threadbare ballet shoes, bowler hats and ratty fox-furs from the shelves; an emporium of junk, with a sofa of floral foam, a plastic Smirnoff bucket and a concussed crash helmet in the window; in North Hobart, a store which euphemises its wares as 'pre-owned furniture'. The shop calls itself Boomerang, which hints at the reincarnatory mystery of the second-hand: are you buying back the impedimenta of an earlier life?

By now, novelty has worn off the suburbs, and even the new has a mortuary air of age. Soundy's clothes shop in North Hobart exhibits a ghost story in its window. The dummies stand frozen in ancient poses, like crazed native dancers. The female has eczema on the lacquer round her neck, and wears a fanatically chaste flannel nightie with a mauve plastic mac over it. Her male companion is impeccable in a thinly striped business suit, but has forgotten his wig and flaunts sockless, shoeless feet. The window is their airless padded cell and their transparent crypt.

My first trips on the road were in search of a past I could rummage for and carry home to read and to re-enliven. Now I find myself looking everywhere along the road at a past debarred to me, dead and irretrievable. Half the distance into Hobart, there's a way-station which always symbolised the adjacency of the past, the closeness of the fourth dimension. It's a green door in a red-brick wall. A Victorian eccentric had made a folly for himself on a corner of the main road, its carious turret consumed by ivy. That secretive door, if I could open it, would grant me admission to everything I'd dreamed about – tangled gardens, tumbledown towers, a house as labyrinthine as the brain. Needless to say, I've never been in. And I see now that the place is used as a Multifunctional Centre for the Handicapped, administered by the Down's Syndrome Association. It has the toy town I imagined, but while my fantasy was of childhood recovered at will, it's actually given over to those who suffer arrest in a childhood prolonged by accident.

A mile away, I left the road on an impulse and discovered another enchanted spot: a mansion where an uncle and aunt had once had a flat, before they moved to their semi-detached crate further out. I groped up the hill as if in a dream. Through a stone gate, round a flowery drive, in a garden of willows and magnolias, there it waited, unoccupied. Cane chairs on the verandah, gleaming brass bells and separate entries for House and Stable, sitting rooms with books piled on polished tables. The shock was to find the past restored so immaculately. I remembered the house as dark and shabby, arbitrarily partitioned. My uncle and aunt had a corner of it, with their kitchen in a hall behind a curtain. A clock was always clucking its tongue dolefully there, and when it chimed it tolled a knell. To me the gloom inside was intoxicating. Most of it was off-limits, and the corridors extended into mysteries; it probably even had a staircase, which for me, who'd never been in a house containing one, would come to symbolise complication, concealment, and the dizziness of mental ascent, enabling you to look back down on a level world you'd left. That house was a cavern of holy terror and insidious intricacy – my Otranto or Udolpho, a lair of phantoms in hiding from the severe Australian sun. Since then, the place had been reclaimed, repainted, made elegant as it never was in my experience; I later found it had been listed by the National Trust. It was this elegance which reminded me I was trespassing, as you're able to do with impunity only in dreams. I fled.

Along the road were other vents through which as a boy I could gain admission to the past, or at least to elsewhere. Moonah had a disgraced cinema resigned to reruns, where I saw my first film: the costume drama documenting the Coronation, its soundtrack oiled by the voice of Olivier. To stumble out of the musty darkness of that theatre and out of the celluloid spectrum of the abbey onto a street of brawling pubs and betting shops was one of my first disorienting shocks. Already art was making me dissatisfied with life. The next film I saw there was *Mrs Miniver*. Would my mother, I wondered, qualify as Greer Garson? But she grew blowsy chrysanthemums, not clenched eugenic roses. The place where all these visions were conjured doesn't exist now. Nor does the other rickety hall, further down the road in Glenorchy, in which I had my first remote sight of America. On Saturday afternoons I'd be sent to crowd the benches with the fighting, giggling kids who'd been incubated, like me, in the suburb. One day we watched a western called *Escape from Fort Bravo*, and I saw at once that there was another world available for escape into – as well as the feudally ornate and ceremonious England ruled by matriarchs like Elizabeth II or Greer Garson, there existed this male America, an empty space under the dominion of violence.

Thus the two termini of my imaginative life were marked out, a mile apart on the main road. Yet neither could be connected with the facts of my condition. In contrast with the buttressed stateliness of that cinematic England, all orbs and sceptres and deference, we lived in a raw and unmade America; yet in contrast with the singed plains and skyscraping buttes of the American west, our island was a green and weepy fragment of England. The fictions quarrelled, in long bouts of shadow-boxing.

The Queen quite soon came to Tasmania, but stayed for only about five minutes – not long enough to explain the place to me. I remember thinking, a week or so before the visit, that everything would have to change once it had happened. I was walking on the main road at the time of course, looking at the sordid gutters and blowing papers. All this, I thought, would be cleared away; they couldn't show her this. Maybe they could dress those corrugated roofs in wigs of thatch. In the event, nothing changed. She didn't travel on the main road, and therefore had no chance to redeem it. But the main road was the place where America belatedly arrived in Tasmania, at a point half way between those two degraded picture palaces. Here, in 1960, the American 1950s crash-landed. A bowling alley opened in Moonah, announced by an elephantine ten-pin planted on the kerb like a Neanderthal's club. Television began the same year. We didn't have a set, so I made excursions over the back fence. Our neighbours had won a set in a raffle a few years before, and although no programmes were being transmitted, the box sat in a corner of their lounge to be stared at like a murky crystal ball. Try as we might, we couldn't will it to give forth images. When at last it did, they were all of a faraway and anyway obsolete American decade: the domestic bliss of *Leave it to Beaver*, the domestic mayhem of *I Love Lucy*. This contradictory world, with its pious family councils and its exploding mod cons, its gravely genial suppers and its maniacal kitchens, didn't resemble the households I knew about. Here no one was wholesome like Beaver's family, and when there were rages they weren't funny like Lucy's. Art mocked us with its perfection, and its harmlessness.

England and America still alternate along the road. In New Town, there's an ancient cottage of crumbling stone, its steps fenced with pot plants, called 'Harvest Holme'; behind it is a wrecking yard of gutted autos, ripped-off doors and torn upholstery. Rustic England supplies the false front, but the moving parts which make it work belong to America. Elsewhere, the road has been gaudily Europeanised. In Moonah the Delishus Konditorei sells continental bread and cakes in the shape of glazed, candied poodles; the Mediterranean Lighting Store displays curlicued chandeliers which for all their bulk look weightless as feathers, and porcelain lamp bases where budgies bill and coo. Nearer to town, the proprietor of Fat Albert's Lebanese Fish and Chips maligns himself on his outside wall as a leering golliwog. Asia too has its solitary ambassador on the road: Peter Nguyen practises acupuncture and massage.

Above Hobart, the Victorian nineteenth century resumes. Here, on its last downward slope to the harbour, the road is flanked by abrupt hills, the pinnacles commanded by churches. Religion supervises the low huddled city. To the west, where the streets are steepest and most penitential to toil up, rear the Catholic schools, sinister under their peaked roofs. My cousins on my father's side of the family went there, and those buildings always had a grisly fascination for me: inside them I imagined priests in black practising a ritual mumbo-jumbo. To the east, behind the chimney of a deserted mill, the Anglican church keeps an eye on a row of dourly stuccoed Victorian villas – Mentone, Craiglie, Wendur, Hillbro – and a graveyard of pitted tombs on pedestals, corroded by factory smoke. The solemnly spirey church hall, its bricks the badge of a grim and deadly earnestness, has tried to lighten its mood by re-opening as a dance academy; a corner of the cemetery is now an adventure playground, where yellow slides and pink tunnels choreograph the crises of entry into and exit from life, depositing you at last in a sand pit. Further down is the citadel of the Congregationalists, affrighting the night sky with a neon cross. Outside, a glassed-in tablet broadcasts uplifting texts. Its frame announces that it's the James Marsh Memorial, and underneath it classifies its moral lessons as James Marsh's posthumous utterances: 'He being dead, yet speaketh.' What he speaketh from out the tomb today is an anti-Papist diatribe, advising that 'Obedience without the consent of conscience can never be a virtue.' On the opposite corner, deaf to Marsh's ghoulish sermons, a cousin of mine who set up shop as a chemist has turned his pharmacy into a headquarters for home-brewing supplies.

A lane nearby leads off the main road into another alley of

memory. Here, now replaced by a warehouse of office kit, there used to be a fruit and vegetable market at the weekend. Once on a Saturday morning my parents took me there, and bought a pineapple. 'Imported', they said, by which they meant that it had come from the distant, exotic mainland; from the tropical north of a country whose frosty wind-swept south we were. It was an object of wonder to me: a hedgehog of spikes which when carved open disclosed a yellow wood of foreign sweetness – a taste from beyond, like the effervescing caramel of Coca-Cola, said by those who had tried it to be lethal with Aspro (I never dared). Ours was the island of white-blooded Coxes and Granny Smiths, the most Anglo-Saxon fruit imaginable. This thorned coffer of acid juice seemed to have fallen out of the sky. Mangoes, I'm told, are still banned in Tasmania. Everything had to travel so far to get to us that the most ordinary items – that supernatural fruit; English magazines, three months out-of-date when they arrived – had an aura because of the distances they had crossed.

My traversal of the road was an experiment in flexing distance. When you're small, the world is so amazingly, bafflingly enormous. I can still hear myself telling the grocer one Christmas Eve that we were going to the Huon Valley the next day. An uncle was coming to fetch us in his car, 'and it's *forty miles* away!' If only forty miles still meant as much. Instead space puckers, and I find now that the epic walk can be done in a morning. The road itself, having reached the centre of town, has nowhere else to go. It passes the Commonwealth Bank with its grey stone mural of Hobart's history: whalers tussling with a leviathan and bullock trains hauling cargo, troops of matchstick men building the world. It passes the Post Office, with its unfunctional arches, chimneys and cupolas, so keen to put on a show and to signify something. It passes the square where Sir John Franklin, an early Governor, stands frozen in metal among the trees, dead on his quest for the North-West Passage while a fountain jests at his ice-bound end. It passes the Hydro-Electric Commission, whose walls at night are a luminous flare, celebrating the state's official cult of water power. And then, extended for a while along a wharf beside empty sheds from which the apple boats used to be loaded, the road drowns itself in the harbour. The last thing I saw on this journey, standing on the edge of the pier two blocks from the centre of town, was a jelly-fish dilating its parachute and agitating its fronds just under the sleek surface.

The road dissolves; the city it has led me to occupies a speck in space, between the stern mountain and the gaping bay. Hobart has the institutional compression of a village. The Post Office and the newspaper stand side by side, with the Town Hall and the museum across the street. Parliament is on the water's edge, next to the park where colonial worthies have their graves. It faces a row of warehouses, shipping outfitters, and a pub which when I was a boy was still a sailors' bawdy-house, run by a grizzled cussing madam called Ma Dwyer. Fishing boats dock outside the factories.

Behind the wharf, the gas works is being demolished. A grimy red-brick chimney holds out, and walls of grey pebbly stone with nothing to support; still there's the sweet smell of gas in the dusty air, though I can't summon up again the sickly reek of sugared fruit which used to breathe from the IXL jam factory, also long gone. The ruins of industry have been reclaimed by art. The sail-makers and tallow-chandlers are supplanted by galleries showing prints of departed vessels. Use is converted to otiose beauty. One of the factories near the gas works and the charred railway roundhouse has been declared a 'lifestyle centre'; it offers hydrossage and boasts a solarium. On Saturdays, Salamanca Place exhibits a collective nostalgia like mine, and grants the past a second coming. The market brings yesterday out of hiding: choirs wearing sun suits sing madrigals and a pipe band drums and whines through a Scottish version of 'Waltzing Matilda', while stalls display the fatigues of dead diggers and yellowing lengths of frayed lace among pots of basil, bars of herbal soap and bottles of home-made ginger beer. Some of these merchants have unearthed time's left-overs in urban attics or gutters. Others, reversing history, have gone to ground in the grubbed-out orchards of the Huon Valley, where they live as sophisticated peasants tending plots of simples. Among the crowd you're the member of a congregation: everyone who comes to the market is fossicking, like me, for a past they can inhabit, even consume; the trophies we find are salvage from our wrecked childhoods.

Beyond what used to be the gas works and the railway station, on the bushy hump of the Domain, are icons of another remembrance, less comforting to me because shared by everyone who was in the world before me. The Domain is devoted to mourning: its motto, on the grey obelisk which closes off an avenue of funereal lamps, is LEST

WE FORGET. The cenotaph, mythologising war, has multiplied it. As well as WWs I and II, Korea and Vietnam, it promotes skirmishes or showdowns into wars by tallying THE MALAYSIAN EMERGENCY and THE INDONESIAN CONFRONTATION. The elegiac history goes even further back. Across the road a verdigris gunner stands on a tumulus of sandstone inside a wrought-iron fence. His pouches are slung over his shoulder, and he lowers binoculars through which he was peering – before he was transfixed – in the vague direction of Antarctica. He too keeps watch there IN MEMORIAM, specifically for '32 Tasmanian soldiers who died in the South African War 1899–1902'. The park is a lawn cemetery, every cypress tree dedicated to a fallen soldier by the plaque which tags it. I recollect the dawn vigils here on Anzac Day, and having to listen on the radio to the expiring trumpet cadences of the last post. A photograph hung all my childhood on the wall above my bed: the ghostly uncle, a flier shot down in the Mediterranean, after whom I had been named; the first dead person I knew. Yet the crowded plural in 'Lest We Forget' excluded me. How could I forget what I couldn't even remember? I inherited as a boy my father's army hat, its curly brim still stained and stiffened by the sweat of New Guinea. It stank as pleasantly as old boots, and I liked the tinny badge with its bristling sunrise, but it didn't fit my head.

I don't associate the Domain with the bereaved marchers of Anzac Day. For me those lawns, empty now, remain the site of the fun-fair which used to sprawl across it during the Hobart regatta. Our clan had its own gum tree, under which we'd gather on rugs between excursions to the side-shows and share out banana sandwiches, with butter and a grating crust of sugar sprinkled on; then came the treat of fairy floss, a pink beehive hairdo on a stick (which when you got to it would probably splinter your tongue). The carnival was an innocent saturnalia to me then. It made danger hilarious: the lurching of your stomach as the ferris wheel jolted you through the air on a suspended bench, the giggling terror of the haunted house where once a bored spook, with too few customers to frighten, stepped out of his niche in the wall and grabbed me in a suffocating hug. Inside a steaming lavatory under the cenotaph I used to spend what seemed to be hours studying the lewd limericks and ballads of sexual bravado someone had inscribed on the cubicle wall. That tiny improvised timber room was a library of filth, and every regatta more of it would acquire a meaning for me. Somehow memory saddens the happiest or most ribald experiences. I used to love trying to choke the gullets of those clowns who revolved their heads and tried not to swallow the balls you aimed at their mouths. Now, with their whitened faces and their dunces' caps, they seem tragic. Unhinged necks distribute a silent scream across 180 degrees; their intestines are exposed in a glass case. The rotating alimentary pipe lobs a cannonade of plastic golf balls into their tummies; they jostle there like dancing ulcers. How could I have been amused by their tawdry anguish? These days the fair is louder and less villagey. When I went back to find the tree which was our family's meeting-place, the spot my grandmother used to occupy had been usurped by a camel, awaiting its entry into a circus tent. One more past was closed to visitors.

East from the centre of town, the way led across the shaggy Domain to the English pastoral of the Botanical Gardens and the baronial folly of Government House. No guards manned the gate, which was always open. The barrier, however, was impassable. Here, where superannuated grandees sent out from London represented (and once a decade entertained) the Queen, our vernacular reality stopped.

My world was able to extend in another direction. I lengthened the main road by cutting a trail of my own to the south, where none of my family had ever ventured before. This led past the wharves and through the Georgian cottages of Battery Point, jumbled on a hill like a midget impromptu Bath, to Sandy Bay, the university, and our local unkempt Bohemia. Its headquarters was a coffee bar called the Brazil, with a nicotine-smirched photo-mural of Rio de Janeiro, over which Christ on the mountain-top stretched out his arms in unheeded benediction. Five miles to the north, my parents were a continent away. The streets around the campus had escaped from the domesticity of the suburbs: a warren of ravaged houses sliced into flats, dingy rooms with mattresses on the floor. In this arena of anarchy you could lose your virginity, and all other regular habits.

Even so, I caught the bus out along the main road every Sunday, and took my dirty clothes home to be washed. All journeys end up circular. I liked to think of the road as a straight line going on forever, revising horizons. The circle sounded depressing: a manacling ring of steel. I was always downcast when, reaching home after a Sunday drive, my father announced as he pulled into the garage 'Now we've done the round trip.' This couldn't be travel, because you were condemned to return to the place you set out from. I no longer expect anything else. The main road is the loop inside which all stations of my life are gathered. The journey bends backward into a circle because life does too.

On the Mountain

My childhood was overshadowed by a brutal, bad-tempered eminence: a mountain. Hobart belongs to Mount Wellington. It looms suddenly above the city and grimaces from a height of four thousand feet; it squeezes the settlement, denying it toehold. The streets run out of town sheer up its sides, the houses forced into clefts between the foothills. It terminates every view, and invigilates every backyard. When you stepped through our kitchen door onto the porch, it was the first sight of the day. My parents would sometimes anxiously peer through the window before venturing out, 'to see what the mountain was doing'. It dictated our blustery, lachrymose weather, and in turn determined our moods. Writing to me, they still report on its caprices as they might on the behaviour of some domineering, unanswerable feudal overlord: now it's snowy, or else it's mockingly bright up there while it rains beneath; in winter it has the habit of vanishing for days behind a wad of cloud, and everyone waits nervously for its reappearance, wondering if it will have changed its contours while away. It lies along the sky like a crouched lion, its head rearing directly above Hobart. Across the river, behind our house, is its lower, echoing colleague Mount Direction, the hump of another talismanic beast whose body has subsided beneath the earth. I grew up between those animals of obtuse rock, always expecting them to pounce.

Wellington is a tribal elder among the geological beasts which crenellate and fret the surface of the state – sulphurous Mount Lyell, the jaunty bonnet of Frenchman's Cap, Cradle Mountain with its nestling hollow, Mount Picton which by a mere gust of draughty energy almost knocked down the propeller plane I was travelling in, the Sleeping Beauty which lies beside Wellington as its consort; a numberless clan of authoritarian presences. Tasmania is, it likes to say, the most mountainous island in the world. Not for it the flat sizzling coppery distances of the Australian mainland, or those waveless oceanic skies. Every horizon in Tasmania is crinkled, a blockade of dolerite; and the irregular crust begets morose clouds, which look like angry thoughts.

Though intimidated, we accepted the jurisdiction of those peaks. Driving back to Hobart from the north, where the Derwent Valley is foreshortened and Mount Wellington, instead of the familiar leonine profile, compresses to an unrecognisable jumble of rocks, my mother always asks hopefully 'Is that our mountain?' Yet it's not ours; we are its. People are owned by their landscape, which outlasts them. The mountain ignores the incursion of its human users: the scar of road which crawls round ledges to the summit, the television towers which have been screwed into its adamantine head. The bushfire scorched it in 1967, but twenty years later its sides are still pronged with tall dead gum trees, their limbs twisted like silently screaming mandrakes. It is the land's skeleton, indifferent to organic fates or elemental distresses. Climbing out of Hobart on the green avenue of Davey Street, all honeycombed Georgian stone and oak trees, you turn the corner and suddenly come upon the reality beyond this English verdure and veneer: a craggy monolith, bristling with spars of burned wood.

Under the mountain, we were all students of it, like Cézanne with that cubist outcrop of Mont Saint-Victoire which he painted so relentlessly. You had to check on the mountain every few hours (or minutes), because of its volatility. Or did it remain stubbornly fixed, while only our fickle impressions of it altered? It had a career in the course of the day – blue or purple in the direct light of morning, abstracted by the afternoon when diagonal bands of glaring white arrowed across the sky from the high clouds and the mass of rock desolidified behind them. That scene always reminded me, in alarm, of Victorian illustrations in a bulky family Bible. The avenging heavens, ensconced on those pompous charioteering clouds, might have opened just above Mount Wellington. In rain, the grey showers streak and liquefy it. The stolid thing seems to be washed away; but it always reassembles itself. Sometimes a rainbow stays on the lower slopes, a spectrum of fuzzy neon from violet to orange spanning the drenched city. I watched it one afternoon last January from the centre of Hobart while the weather quarrelled above it in the sky. To begin with, in an electric flash of sun, its contours came up sharp, chiselled, steely; then the storm swallowed it, leaving only the faint profile of the peak blurred by rain, and it receded into the sky; minutes later it had struggled free of the thick smothering air and draped the storm clouds across its face like the wispy beard of some sinister Father Christmas. The mountain was a practical joker, a master of disguise, taunting us with its transformations.

Emotions about mountains have a complicated history. Superstition has always viewed them as deformations of earth, Gothic horrors. In the late eighteenth century, that changed. High mountains, according to the romantic poets, were 'a feeling', serener in their silence than the hubbub of cities. The change in taste happened just as Australia was being settled, and the country's landscape followed it. At first the terrain looked eerie, ghastly, all palsied trees and agonised squawking birds: a Gothic mystery. Then, in the course of the nineteenth century, it was romanticised. Instead of locating topographical spots on a map of mental terror – Mount Despair, Mount Warning, Cape Grim, Hell's Gates, Devil's Kitchen – imagination began to see Australia sunnily, a blazing noon of optimistic waratah. But the ancestral identity of the country, as a place to be feared not loved, wasn't forgotten. Mount Wellington can still commute between these meanings. One day it's as alarming as Mussorgsky's bald mountain, or the shaggy, witchy peaks where Mephistopheles leads Faust; the next it's benign, draping itself along the haze of the horizon like a dozing sun-bather.

I had both experiences of it when I was back. Within the same week, I went to the summit twice. I'd only ever been there once before, on a school excursion. Though we spent our days looking up at it, and during the summer could see the glint of cars toiling round the bends to the peak, no one thought of looking down from it. Like a cathedral spire, it observed you from its lofty height; you weren't supposed to use it as your own eyrie. So, returning, it was one of my first ambitions to see Hobart from up there. For days I kept watch, waiting for the clouds to clear from the mountain's head. Then one morning, though batteries of grey vapour were still pushing the sunlight across the sky, I decided to risk it.

The result was an hour in a Gothic climate. By the time I got there, a cloud had muffled the top of the mountain; inside it, a blizzard hung suspended above the summery city. From the road to the top, the sky looked like boiling broth. Wind scourged the creaking trees, and the boulders on the slopes could have been strewn by landslips that morning.

The mountain's face is an Aeolian orchestra: the sharp-edged columns which slide down from the top are locally known as the organ pipes. To name them is to tame them. The metaphor pacifies the geological hazard, and romantically pretends that nature is sounding a solemn diapason. Driving beneath the cliff of stone pipes, you can watch the image go in and out of focus. Close up, the simile is seen to be a deceit: this is just a chaos of cracked facets and broken ledges. It's the same with the Sleeping Beauty, on the other side of the range. Seen from the south in the Huon Valley, she is a drowsy anthropomorph, the giantess who bars the hero's advance with that body which she stretches along an entire horizon. The foothills are her unbound hair, and thanks to two hillocks she can cross her hands on her chest. But see her from another angle, further towards Hobart, and the gentle metaphor crumbles. The profile doesn't hold together; it furrows, turns knobbly, erupts in warts. The princess has aged unflatteringly in her paralysed sleep. The mountains, under that thick turbulent sky, change their expressions as you advance through them. The face that first day scowled, wrinkled in hostility. Mount Wellington is a goblin of rock; the organ pipes actually house a population of leering gnomes, robbed from suburban gardens and planted there for a prank by climbers from the university. Their bright complexions weathered and eroded, they now look as if they have grown from the shelves where they are set. Climbers tell gruesomely funny stories about them: the wind keening, the city beneath you, you fumble for support, pull yourself up a precipice, and let out an involuntary screech as a plaster dwarf stares you in the eye. Van Diemen's Land retains its demons.

The summit that day was an arrival at extinction. Erased by the frozen air, the city had ceased to exist. A map at the lookout directed attention to the absent places beneath; the view was of nothingness. This alp, swallowed by the sky, had become a site for death first by heat, then by cold. The wood of the bent shrubs beside the road was burned black, then lit with a bleak white halation of ice, as if solarised. Where the gale caught branches, it stiffened them in quills of ice as prickly as razor blades. Snow doesn't soften the world, swathing things in cotton wool; it is cutting, crystalline, and here it exposed the eldritch forkings of the battered trees. The television towers disappeared inside their fence of mesh which the ice had barbed. When the wind struck at them, frigid planks clattered down from the girders to crash as brittly as glass on the road. I had always wondered what was happening inside those clouds which drifted round the mountain. Now I knew: they were capsules of nuclear winter, in transit above us.

On my next trip, the mountain had banished its phantoms. Now it was tropically dry, the peak a desert of blue crags with lizards like flicking shadows between the roots. A currawong, coal-black except for a yellow eye and a white fan of feathers in its tail, flapped across the road, wheeling in a cavern of air to settle on a young gum. Perched there, it twisted its neck in a circle to study the view. All the world lay beneath it, bared in the lucid air. Before Hobart had been wiped away by cloud; today it was lost in the landscape. After the thin strips of settlement along the harbour and the river, it ran out so soon. Here was Australia in little: a society gobbled up by an allocation of earth too large for it, clinging in trepidation to the shore. The perimeters of my life could be clearly made out from up here, a patterned algebra – the straight line of the highway, the oval of the race-course, the concentric circles of our suburb – but none of them mattered. They were scratches on an old, forgetful surface, too callous to feel them. And inches beyond what was supposed to be our street, that surface began to buckle and fold, wandering off in tangled valleys and amorphous hills. At this southern extremity, land itself was running out. The bottom of Tasmania trails fronds and fringes along the ocean. Water invades everywhere, wearing down those crooked arms and peninsulas, leaving only threads like Eaglehawk Neck to connect one mass with another. The island, here at its terminus, looks from above as if it's fraying into an archipelago of stranded islets. The mountain on which you stand marches across the skyline towards the south and west, merging with others into ranges which fade in a silhouette of crested waves. The view extends not only as far as the eye can see, but as far as the earth can travel. The world is about to end.

Above too there is a glossy emptiness. The pylons in the Telecom compound, blotted by the snow before, listen to the sibillations of the sky. On top of one tower is an elongated barrel with a blunt pencil protruding from it – a missile? A satellite dish, a sparking red bolt of electricity painted across it, takes dictation from the air; another tower wears a brass band of surveillance instruments, their music as silent as that of the organ pipes beneath – a grey kettledrum, and a pair of cymbals. Though there's a shed, no one's about. The hibernating gadgets have their own lives up here. Dwayne has carved on a boulder his love for Elaine, but even though their names rhyme, this hard, arid place has little tolerance for human affections. The mountain like the desert is a location for the ascetic. I see now why those who live under Mount Wellington don't come up it: its lesson is disillusionment, the reduction of individual existences to specks and our brave little social camp to a brief sprinkling of dust.

Though the summit is austere, fit only for hermits, the lower slopes make room for romantic fantasies. The road descends to Fern Tree, where through the thickets you can see the forking rivers far below as they quit the remnants of Tasmania and decant into the sea. Fern Tree is a humid plantation of glades and bowers. Though hanging on a ledge of the mountain, it's like being underground. A furry jungle of creepers shuts out the light, or filters it so the beams are amber, sealing insects and floating spores; everywhere there's the throaty gurgle of water rushing from the springs high above. Death here is organic and fruitful. Further up, the trees are stricken, detained for decades in their last white protesting attitudes; here they subside to the soft floor and are fed on by the moss. Wood melts into the chocolatey bog: a fallen swamp gum is now a funnel of compost for ferns, its concave insides moistened to pulp. The corpse quivers with bright sickly life: seeds, damp spiders' webs, the squashy glands of mushrooms. The ground squelches. In this fertile crypt the air is green as mould; here is the festivity of nature, nurtured on decay.

Wading through this fungous growth, I found one of the places where the past is stored, silted in a warm sopping tunnel under the ferns. The mind began an association game, startling me with the images it exhumed. On a corner of the track an air-force of blowflies homed in, droning, on some putrid morsel. The sound made me think at once of Christmas dinner: sweltering roasts eaten on a verandah south of here in the Huon Valley, with the buzzing horde of blowies dive-bombing the screen door while the Queen's frosty voice exhorted us from some dim northern winter on the wireless in the next room. Here I could let the memory operate automatically. There was another gully on another slope of the mountain, behind the sober stony penal façade of the Cascade Brewery, which I'd discovered on a school outing and had gone back to repeatedly. It was a secret garden of rampant dream, like the one I'd imagined behind the door on the main road: a long steep labyrinth of gold light, green shadow and soaking warmth. The ruthless sun and blistered ground which are mainland Australia were excluded by this kind cavity; you could be embowered or enwombed here. Nature consented to seem maternal.

Then my cul-de-sac of contemplation was invaded. From higher up came the thud of feet and the yelp of children's voices. As the sound approached, I turned away from it, annoyed at having to share the place where this waking sleep had overtaken me. The feet beat harder and the voices shrilled right behind me. I thought perhaps if I didn't look they would dematerialise; still they pressed on my heels, and then streaked past. Amazed, I saw that they weren't the infant bruisers I expected but a pair of anachronistic wood nymphs: girls with ringleted goldilocks, in filmy white party dresses and long white socks, pink ribbons in their hair, giggling as they raced on towards the spring. Were they escapees from some enchantment on the mountain? At once, hard behind them to jolt me from the reverie, came two brawny female hikers, alligators on their chests, packs on their backs, one of whom demanded, 'Do you know where we are?' The accent was American.

I told them they were on the way to Fern Tree, without being sure that I could answer their question. Where were we? On a mountain which could produce a litter of dryads from nowhere, and follow that with these twin laboratory specimens of tanned Californian health. What other mutants were wandering here, seeking the overgrown path leading out of the fantasy? I was right to have been mystified all those years by Mount Wellington. It's a reserve of magic, populated by gnomes and currawongs, spectral children from a fairy-tale and satellite towers from science fiction. Deep within it, a volcano bides its time. Its unstable temper means that you can never know it, or even feel confident that you are seeing it properly. Supervising Hobart, it set a limit to our world. Below it skulked our reality, ruled into streets and planted with weatherboard cartons; behind it was a wild actuality of forests and torrents and ravines, which I hadn't wanted to see and tried not to think about. The mountain had always served as a convenient bulwark, keeping Tasmania out. Now it was a wall I must try to look over, if I were ever to understand where I came from.

On the Farm

It was possible to bypass the mountain, sneaking round its base on the road which twisted past Fern Tree and emerged, when the bends levelled and the spindly naves of gum trees cleared, in what for me was the happy valley: the Huon. My mother grew up on an orchard there, and met my father when he and one of his brothers were picking apples during the Depression. My father's brother married a girl from a neighbouring farm; two of my mother's sisters married onto orchards nearby; two more stayed at home to look after her two brothers, while they looked after the apple trees. For me the whole valley was a prolific crop of uncles, aunts and cousins. Barricaded off by the mountain, they never intruded on my suburban life, and this isolation was what made them precious. They offered an alternative world, available if you could negotiate that tortuous road under Mount Wellington. We spent every Christmas holiday on the farm where my mother was born.

She always referred to going back there as a trip 'down home'. The phrase has resonated the length of my life, though it means to me something she may never have intended. She was taking note of the vertical scares of the journey along the Huon road, crawling above crevasses on the mountain and then sliding over the last hill onto the plain. But she was also looking down on this abandoned home: she had escaped from agricultural serfdom, picking and packing apples, to a life of modest consumerism in the suburbs; she didn't fancy the idea of going back. For me, the phrase she used had more of yearning in it than of dread. It spoke of the past as a treasure to be dug for at the bottom of a garden; it imagined time travel as a descent through layered, impacted emotions. The place it arrived at was the paradise you couldn't even remember losing, because you were ejected from it in being born.

The farm to me was a wonderland: acres of space to get lost in; tumbledown barns like toy-chests of quirky gadgetry; forests of fruit trees with a long unkempt uphill paddock where plovers nested; the bed of a sunken creek, choked with ferns disputing its trickle of

water, whose course could be tracked across the valley; bridges of
shaky planks, stiles to be clambered over. I found, when I was home,
a photograph I'd taken when I was about ten. The snap sums up my
hopeful picture of the place. It's of the back gate. There was a front
entrance, which we never used: a lawn with one path leading to the
formal door glazed with an art nouveau tulip, and another to the
kitchen at the side of the farm house; but Australians dislike the
swank of frontal assault, and I don't remember the main door ever
being opened. We always came in the back way, past the barn, the
garage, and the kennels for the hounds with their drooping jowls
and bloodshot eyes. This was the gate I photographed with my box
Brownie, which taught me how to alter life in the act of reproducing
it. The snap is obsessively composed: an out-of-focus apple bough
hanging overhead in shadow, and in the centre, blindingly sunny,
the gate of filigree wire standing open in invitation. Geraniums
sprawl over the fence, vines scramble down the side of the house.
The path, roofed by ferns whose green is over-exposed as white,
wanders on until it reaches a dark porch. Here is the route to the
paradise garden.

Of course, romantically, I was doing away with the place's drab
reality. Now I see that the photograph in its ruthless candour
contains all the evidence to disprove my pictorial fancy about the
farm. Above that open gate is the sagging rubber tendril of a drain
pipe; the path is bordered by the iron tank which stores the house's
water; and that dark cloister where the trail expires is the outside
lavatory and newspaper reading-room. The disillusioning of the
view brings remorse along with it. How my enjoyment insulted the
hard-worked truth of the farm! Everything I observed as a marvel
was a back-breaking chore to those who had to perform it every day.
The gum-booted trek through mud and green pancakes peppered
with gnats to the milking shed where the cow had to be bossed and
shoved into position: Phyllis, the aunt who milked, did it morning
and evening, and suffered occasional kicks from the beast whose teat
she was tweaking. The churning of butter, which thickened and
sweated in the wooden mixer: when I tried that, my arm went numb
with the dulling pain of it. I used to beg to be allowed to visit in the
autumn, when the apples were being picked. I loved the nights at
the grader, which sorted the apples into sizes and rolled them
down chutes where they were twirled in tissue and crated up for

consumption in England. I busied myself weeding out the crabby specimens, or the ones the crows had pecked or the hail had pitted, but mostly I delighted in the engine's clatter and the varnishing of the barn by the oil lamps. How could I not have realised that this was a primitive factory, with my relatives as servants of the machine? This, I imagined, was a genteel life on the land; only much later, too late, did I see that in fact it was hereditary peasant farming.

I can recall the moment when the recognition occurred to shame me. A few years after I'd left, Tasmanian apples were ousted from the market stalls in England by piddling French brands. The orchards in the Huon failed, and my uncles called in bulldozers to grub out the trees. Hearing about it, I thought of Goldengrove unleaving, and was as wistful as Hopkins's Margaret – though like her it was myself I mourned for. When I returned to Tasmania for the first time, I saw the photographs my aunts had taken from the verandah as the trees were felled. 'It must have broken your heart to see that,' I said. Dorothy, my Auntie Dot, looked back blankly. The sentiment meant nothing to her, though she alone had any right to it. 'No,' she said, 'it didn't, I was *that* pleased. We slaved over those trees all our lives. Even when we were kids we'd come home from school and have to go out to work in the orchard. It was day in day out, all the year round. Now we've got rid of the blessed things, we're going to take it easy a bit.' The felling of the trees meant the overthrow of a hated taskmaster.

The farm, to me a playland, was to those who lived on it an onerous dead-end. The family had been procreated to supply it with cheap labour: my grandmother unluckily produced five daughters in a row; my grandfather insisted annually until she came up with two sons, after which, exhausted, she died at the age of forty-seven when my mother was still a girl. No one knew what she died of. She'd had ulcers, the disease of frustration and despair; I suppose it was cancer. I have never had the gumption to ask any further. My grandfather survived for another thirty-five years, a grumpy patriarch. My mother, after her escape, had taken up the urban habit of smoking. He disapproved, and when we were there on holiday she had to sidle behind the woodshed for a surreptitious puff. I last remember him, after he'd been jerked askew mentally by a stroke, chasing me through the orchard with a stick because he thought I was an intruder. Or at least that is what I thought he was thinking. Maybe he just disliked me.

I wasn't entirely to blame for my romancing of the farm. Our indoctrination at school, in the neo-Elizabethan 1950s, gave us to understand that Tasmania was an expatriated England, with the hop fields up the Derwent and the orchards beside the Huon constituting its Kent. Only someone who'd seen the original – as none of our teachers had – could know how ill-fitting was the facsimile. Looking down the Huon Valley from Bullock Hill, you notice the inexactness of the metaphor. There's a narrow stretch of cultivated ground, and the foothills are shaved up to their crowns; then the glowering bush resumes. Down in the valley, you hear a perpetual muffled roar above: the tall gums on the heights, which sigh and crack and thrash in the wind like the rigging of a ship at sea. The Huon River glowers too. The seepage of acids from the roots of plants has blackened it; it looks lethal, Lethe-like, and its impromptu islands of rushes clog the stream.

When the trees were grubbed out, the villages perished too. The settlement in the curve of the river where my mother's family lived is derelict now. My grandparents stretch out in a brass-railed terracotta double bed, between an unfenced remnant of orchard overrun by bracken and the old apple-packing sheds. Medievally, they and the other clans are planted in their work-place like the trees. The church where they were married and buried was sold and trucked away to supply some livelier community with a hall. They were Methodists; across the road, next to a boarded-up shop and a petrol pump gone dry, the Catholic church still stands. But its windows have lost their glass, and from every slat and crevice of the weatherboards fume plagues of bees. Inferno has been established inside: a black humming hive has taken over the erstwhile altar.

My uncles put their farm out to pasture. A few cows graze around the imprint of the absent trees. The other side of the valley used to be foreign, inaccessible, invisible; in this denudation it advances, and stands only yards away. Everything dwindles: the dam, which I was so afraid of slipping into, is a pond; even the dangers have been diminished. A friend in England years ago told me of a story she'd heard about a valley in Tasmania where the apple trees, deserted, went to seed. They intertwined their boughs and wrapped their trunks round each other like limber legs, feather-bedding the earth with a humus of brown rotten fruit; the rioting orchard became a cocoon of gnarled bark, clustering leaves and gently decaying pulp: a wood of error for some pre-Raphaelite crusader to crawl through in a Burne-Jones illustration. The reality, however, is cleared land, not this over-ripe fancy. The outposts of my illimitable little realm – the milking shed, the vegetable garden with its scaffolds of climbing beans, the wattle grove where the cattle came to slap their tongues over a paving stone of salt strung to one of the trees – have to be imagined on humps of bare grass. Now the only topographical division is the thin threads of electric fence to shock the cows into discipline. When I came back to the house after my first exploratory prowl, one of my uncles asked with a snide curl of the lip, 'See any apple trees?' They are still amused by my selfish sentimentality.

Yet they seemed to have come round at last to my sense of the farm as a playground for imagination. Once the orchard lost its economic function, running the place turned into a hobby. My uncles and aunts had worked since they were children; now, among the wreckage of their labour, they were engaged in elderly games like my childish ones, rearranging the useless left-overs into fantasias of bric-à-brac. Behind the house, the surviving pear trees wear drying rabbit skins on their branches. The crook of one withered tree serves as a shelf for stacking green timber; a bough sports bangles of barbed wire. A eucalypt's tumour, nut-shaped and as big as a clenched fist, has been amputated and plugged with a young sapling: together they make a waddy, the club for some aboriginal warrior, here strung peacefully from a clothes line. The chopping block – a scored trunk, as lined as a human palm, where every slice-mark is the memento of a chicken's death – has a kitchen mincer screwed to the side of it, suggesting recondite post-mortem tortures. Into another stump, an old spade with no handle has been driven, just for the look of it: the combination makes a sculpture. A bird cage is stuffed with plastic bags, used for the feed of the long-gone residents. Every object memorialises a loss. Mechanical parts come together in polymorphous marriages, skewering each other with their prosthetic limbs; machinery copulates, despite its arthritic rust. A hail rocket, a relic from the 1950s like a home-made sputnik with a pound of TNT in its head and a cartridge to fire its load of gunpowder, now impales a deflated tyre on the sawdusted floor of the barn. Chandeliers of chains clank from the beams of the ceiling, and suspend coffee tins of pedantically sorted nails, bolts and screws which will never be needed again. The rubble feels cosy, because it has been reshaped into dens and shelters. A ventilator salvaged from some hydro-electric works, its chimney fitted with a plastic porthole, is carpeted with hay and commissioned as a kennel (or motel cabin) for the hunting dogs. The geese live under the severed bonnet of an old car, which serves as their thatch-shaped roof; the peacock and his hen occupy an oil drum with a door of mesh.

The ragged garden is a nest for battered ornaments, or toys made from the vivisected bits of other objects. A rubber pelican, weighted with sand and crumbling brick in its squeezy hollow middle, hides among the blades of a cactus, raised on an honorific plinth which used to be a water spout. The bird began as a lolly bottle; could be converted into a money box; has become instead a garden god. Pot plants have been sown with chipped china birds, which bring their white sprigs of artificial foliage to these new homes of real dirt. In one hanging planter, a plastic coat-hanger broken in half has been stuck upright: seen in profile, the curly mauve hook which gripped the bar inside the wardrobe is a crested bird.

This is the bricoleur's art, making matches between unlike things, encouraging form to belie function, and it translates the farm into a funhouse of talismanic resemblances. The crazy triumph of this method I found above a barn door. Uncle Arthur had nailed there a steer's skull, aristocratically long and lean, the bone bleached to papery fragility by the sun. It was his tribute to the horned heads which crown the entrance gates to Texas ranches. But by his additions he had changed the totem into a diabolical bauble. Two white plastic bottles were rammed into its sockets for bulging eyes, with the manufacturers' labels glued to the flat base where the pupils ought to be. Horns of whittled wood were drilled into the head, carved from the fretwork of the old Methodist church before it was sold and sent away. To confound symmetry, a third tusk of green timber was forced into the cracked snout, making the beast a mutant; and, to cap the uncoffined ghoul with a mortician's dapper gentility, on top of its head was stretched a sun-dried rabbit skin for a toupee. I didn't know whether to laugh in delight or run away in horror.

My uncle gave a sly smile when I asked him about it. He had no need of introspection, and it hadn't occurred to him to inspect his motives in piecing together this devil of detritus. He turned away and put the cattle through their paces for me, cursing the dogs as they forced the protesting bullocks to leap across a creek and hurling a mallet at the flank of a reluctant calf: 'Go on, you red-headed bastard!' A black bull snorted and kicked one of the frantic dogs. 'Marvellous what a bashing they can take,' he grinned when the dog rebounded. Even this was a circus routine, as balletic as a wrestling bout.

Feeling somehow unhoused in Tasmania, exposed to a life too harsh and hard, I imagined an alternative and recoiled into it. Through the lens of my camera, the farm could be made to look uterine; life could be refracted and revised inside that mystical chamber. For me, art originated when you shut your eyes against the world to enjoy a private darkness. But there was also an art carpentered and cobbled from the substance of that world, which it didn't need to deny: the fabrication of shelter, a stouter defence than my squinting reverie. Ned Kelly's armour is the primary exhibit. He fashioned his iron helmet from the mould boards of ploughs, and cushioned it inside with blue quilting. Now the head was impregnable. Inside this cranial sentry-post, he could conduct surveillance of a world which was out to get him, peering at it through that slit like a letter-box. He had rudely engineered Hamlet's dream into truth: to be bounded in a nutshell, while counting yourself a king of infinite space.

Battering and padding that protection for himself, Kelly was the first of our bricoleurs; and my uncle – more gently, disarmed, with no grudge at all against reality – was among his inheritors, devising companionable fetishes from the rubbish and randomness of life. In the cellar, strung from a rafter, I'd found a plastic eaglehawk, brown with black flappable wing-tips, once used for scaring off birds which preyed on the cherry trees. Its tail feathers were weighted with streamers of coloured twine, and in its beak it gripped a dog-eared calendar, distributed by a milk bar and grill room in Geeveston (further down the river) for use in 1975. Speckled now with greasy dust, the calendar's bright illustration irrelevantly showed off Big Ben, Parliament Square, and a bed of flowers in bloom. The two had been joined together under the house for a purpose: volatile time was stalled, agitated only by the occasional gust of wind through the planks of the door; the immobile bird and the defunct year both belonged in a museum of memory.

At Huonville, a packing shed has been reopened to commemorate the apple industry. It's an infirmary for the past, exhibiting a tree scaled with bark disease, and the hessian bandages used for treating it; the elderly lady who is the curator says: 'This used to be called the Garden of Eden down here – now three-quarters of the orchards have been bulldozed out' (and on those which remain, as my uncle snarled, 'hippies grow drugs'). The dispersed community here has a ghostly reunion. By the door is pinned a portrait of some antique newlyweds, with a sign attached: 'These old photographs were found in a house at Dover. Can anyone tell us who these people are?' Identification would retrieve two more existences from the callous forgetfulness of time. The typed query has a tone of urgency, trusting in memory as extreme unction and as a recipe for raising the dead.

The machines still know how to do their tricks: the grader which relegated apples to bins containing those of similar size; the spindly robot which picked up planks, clapped its hands together and fastened them into the form of a crate. I even found in the museum some mementos of my own chore on the production-line. My job was to paste labels on the side of the boxes when they were packed, and to stencil destinations on the end. The museum has a display of the labels I used to slap onto the glued, viscous pine. They all pandered of course to my dream of apple-growing as an Arcadian pastime. One of the paper panels has the brand-name Beaucaire, embodied as a dandy with frilly cuffs, white wig and satin pants; the Page brand employs a dapper Buttons, posing in the course of some courtly errand in his red uniform. W. D. Peacock's vainglorious bird unfurls the title across the fan of its tail on top of a red apple, and Beautiful Isle (Fancy Grade I) compresses Tasmania into a synoptic landscape – Mount Wellington slopes into an orchard which in turn is bordered by a yachting beach of lemon sand. More tantalisingly still, my next task was to flick a brush of black ink across the stencils to mark the case's destination. The old plates are nailed to the barn wall, calling the roll of outlandish places where, thanks to my addressing of the boxes, the fruit would be eaten: MADRAS, OSLO, SING(apore), EIRE, ZANZIBAR. I really believe I envied those apples their journeys.

Nowadays, they stay at home, wizen, and when they're inedible are sold as souvenirs. Among the icons of contemporary Tasmania are the vinegary race of Applefolk: shrunken heads mounted on pine plinths inside plastic casques, like the morbid trophies of Amazonian savages. The browning rind is peeled from the apple for their skin; their eyes are pips, and the gouged-out cores supply their carbuncular noses. They bear a family resemblance to Mrs Bates, fruitily decomposing in the cellar in *Psycho*. If you wish, you can buy them in striped convict uniforms, which give them the look of shrivelled cadavers mouldering on a gibbet. A guarantee on the packet assures you that they will get even rustier and more desiccated with age.

I had the feeling every moment that this was my belated first chance to see Tasmania properly, and also perhaps my last chance to see it at all. So it proved, at least with the farm. My Uncle Arthur had a heart attack soon after I left; a month later he died. My mother wrote, after his will had been read, reporting that he had left me and my four country cousins equal shares in his 'personal affects'. Her spelling mistake was inspired. The things I had found on the farm were to me the effects of affection. Inheriting a percentage of them, I was to have a title at least to that portion of my past.

On the Water

In Tasmania you are always watching land end. It does so in different moods on the different coasts of the eroded, abraded island. To the west, it gives up sullenly and sulkingly, bludgeoned by surf which, wrinkling across an empty globe all the way from South Africa, concusses the beach like falling masonry. To the east, it resigns in a dazed, blissful sleep: down this coast the beaches relax into a calmer, brighter ocean. To the south, the last stand of earth before the pole throws up a fractured seismic architecture of leaning pillars and shattered buttresses, as if the encroaching ocean had rolled up over the continents to swamp Piranesi's Roman forum. The precipices are diving-boards into oblivion. Marcus Clarke in *For the Term of His Natural Life* set two despairing convict boys atop one at Point Puer on the Tasman Peninsula and then, shedding crocodile tears, gave them a push. He was encouraging them to obey the behest of the landscape. Earth here appears to hurl itself underwater, in a fury of uprooted boulders. The north-western tip of the state, at Cape Grim, has an inlet called Suicide Bay, remembering an aboriginal tribe driven to self-destruction by attacks from posses of former convicts. George Augustus Robinson, making peace with the natives in the 1830s, said he found blood on the cliffs and bones in the caves beneath them. The scene, however, is land's suicide. The crags are carved by wind and guzzled by water. How can earth, you wonder as you totter upright in the gale and control your dizziness as you look down, hold out against this assault from the other elements? Being aboard Tasmania is a lot like being on a lifeboat, and a leaky one at that.

Mainland Australia, like southern California, has the desert's love-affair with water. Its national icon is the surfer: amphibian man. Off Manly in Sydney Harbour, boys skid over the bay on their boards, swooping as the sails they hold aloft catch the breeze, dodging the wakes of the ferries, dancing on water. Green, saturated Tasmania isn't parched like the rest of the country. It is battered by water, rather than irrigated by it. Sometimes the island resembles a subsiding Atlantis. The Nut, the volcanic knob at Stanley on the north-west coast, is a mountain which has abruptly dived into the sea, leaving only its flattened, furrowed summit showing. Tasmania was separated from the mainland when the land-bridge over Bass Strait caved in; ever since that prehistoric calamity, the island has been working to complete the process by submerging itself. Its hydro-electric schemes answer a deep-down wish to drown the land. Lake Pedder, once an alpine pool among the central highlands, is now a grey gluttonous tank which has swallowed the entire range. Tasmania has its own pocket-sized Niagara at Russell Falls, where the water, gushing down a terraced cliff in the middle of a swampy forest, launches itself exuberantly over each ledge it encounters and is dashed to a spume of rainbows on the rocks below.

The west coast is Tasmania at its starkest. Land ends here, at Ocean Beach outside Strahan, in bleak exhaustion, without the protesting geological upheavals of the Tasman Peninsula. Burned black scrub and white sands leech earth of colour; when it gives up, the grey waves go on for eight thousand uninterrupted miles until the next continent. Macquarie Harbour, however, exerts itself to keep out this percussive, lashing ocean. It's larger than Sydney Harbour, yet the aperture leading in is only two hundred feet wide. Frustrated waves unable to shove their way through leap up at the heads, as if to vault across; the sea bed is corroded with wrecked ships. In its passage through the heads, the current becomes a cataract. It is a landscape adapted to despair, and the entry to the harbour is called Hell's Gates. Inside, the very emptiness of space qualified it as a place of incarceration. There was a convict settlement on Sarah Island in the harbour, specialising in second offenders who committed fresh crimes after arrival in the penal colony. Escape was debarred to one side by the choked rain forest and tiered mountains, to the other by the ocean. Off Sarah Island is another clump of rock, Grummet Island, where the worst recidivists were sent. Weather constituted their prison. They worked a twelve-hour day in the lime-kilns, timber-mill or shipyard, then would have to wade back to their open cell to sleep in wet clothes, drenched all night by spray.

The harbour bottles up the most insidious water I've ever seen – black near the fickle spit of sand at the narrows, further in the colour of stewed billy tea, dyed by the tannin in the roots of the button grass. The surface is striped with bands of scum and ruffled always by spiky waves like rising hackles. Under a jetty behind the bluffs, rheumatic tree trunks whip a spongy broth of suds from the ripples. The King River, draining into the harbour, is a sewer for the mines at Mount Lyell. At the far end is the wild, twisting Gordon River which, joined by the Franklin, twines through the chilly jungles of the south-west. Cruise boats ferry you down the Gordon to see the reflections: here nature calmly admires itself, the cliffs of matted myrtle staring at their image inverted on the stream. After the sublime frights of the harbour – a lake of pitch for Milton's Satan to founder in, patrolled by black scavenging birds and bordered by chemically poisoned mountains – the river settles down into being beautiful. Yet its mirroring is a deceit, an illusion to make the world easier for us. At rest, the water heaves sluggishly; in motion it churns and swills in dyspeptic violence. Cascades on the banks gush red, as if the soil is bleeding through them. Beyond these picturesque, navigable bends, the river's career is unimaginable, as it flails into rapids and writhes through its channel of gorges. Like Mount Wellington retiring behind the clouds, it disappears into a mystery.

The map of Tasmania is Janus-faced. The west coast is its tragic face: a maximum-security prison built by nature, and a rational hell devised by men. The land has been brutalised – timber felled by the convicts, ore gouged out by the miners at Queenstown. But the east coast smiles. The miles of sand behind Coles Bay are known as the Friendly Beaches. Waves curl in and slump on them lazily, suddenly furling from green into white. Emptiness here is Adam's pleasure not Satan's penance. The world belongs to sunlight and to me. Here you can feel you're the first man on earth, greeting it in wonder; on the west coast, you're the last of your race, chained to your rock in solitary confinement. Explorers called the three peaks above the fishing port at Coles Bay the Hazards, but their rosy granite blushes gently to deny any threat. This is the land's happy, human, comic face. The stones at the water's edge are freckled yellow. A track leads through grey sandhills and along orange ledges across the Hazards. Close up they're cake-like, edible layers of seemingly soft rock; the tumbled boulders might be immense eggs. The gum trees here look delicate not skeletal. Where bark has peeled from the slim boles, they expose a skin of striped, sappy lemon. Their roots twine across the path like sunning snakes. From a lookout between the Hazards – a pink crag crusted with pale green lichen – you can see to a cove called

Wineglass Bay. It too deserves its name: a crescent of cream sand holding emerald liquor, good enough to drink. Homer, describing his seas as wine-dark, must have imagined something like this. The metaphor intended to befriend nature, subduing it to human purposes; and the same verbal charm operates here.

As I slithered back down the pebbly slope, I passed two campers on the way up, a portable kitchen of pots and pans clattering on their backs. 'How much further to the top?' one of them asked, pausing to let the sweat dribble off him.

The rocks exhaled heat, and cicadas in the trees buzzed like electric wires. Sun made the bush sing. About ten minutes, I told him.

'Beauty,' was all he said – the most laconic Australian expression and the most eloquent, voicing a shy admiration for the landscape: a love that doesn't usually speak its name.

The view was worth it, I assured him.

'It'd wanner be!' he grinned, and struggled on with his clanking hardware. The grudging note said it all. We dare Australia to be worth our affection, and the effort we expend on exploring it; in our stoical way, we pretend to be surprised when it is. The English dote on their country and, gardening, tend it with an adoring patience. Americans expect America to impress them: at Yellowstone, the tourists gather to watch Old Faithful spout as if he were one of Liberace's fluorescent fountains; when the sun sinks through the crimson smog of New Jersey on summer evenings and disappears in a glare of toxins, the Greenwich Villagers on the banks of the Hudson are likely to give it a round of applause. Australians are neither so shamelessly fond of their land nor so naively awed by it. They remember that it was allotted to them as a punishment, and that it remains a deadly place. The compliments they pay it are the more heartfelt for being so rare, and so tersely expressed.

Tasmania doesn't often tolerate the geniality you feel at Coles Bay. The south-east tip of the state, the Tasman Peninsula, rebuffs such emotion. Attached to the rest of the island by the sandy ligament of Eaglehawk Neck, where a cordon of hungry dogs made sure that the convicts couldn't cross back to freedom, it's a preserve of topographical terrors: a demonic theme park where nature imitates perdition. It begins with the map of a drowned world. At the Neck itself, there's a tessellated pavement. The tiled formation of rocks has been cracked into shape by erosion and, with waves sucking and swirling across it, it experiments with Tasmania's fate of immersion. Treading along it, you seem to be walking on a subaqueous city. The fissures are highways or railway lines, the stagnating squares of seaweed its gardens.

Further down, whirlpools disclose the populations of the doomed: colonies of kelp, whose thick green rubbery tongues slap and babble in the tides. Octopoid shapes attach tubes to the rock, and flourish there like cankers; whole forests of rubbery stunted trees shudder under the surface, their arms clutching the water. Geological faults begin to invent traumas – the blowhole for instance, a vortex created by an eroded tunnel. The kelp languidly flexes and slurps, while a sudden vertical jet of water spits at the sky. A canyon in a cleft of bent pines with the vexed sea swilling pebbles at its base is known as the Devil's Kitchen. You automatically attribute the landscape to him, and wonder what he's cooking up down there – human souls? platters of polyps?

The people who live here cheerily ignore the demonism of the place. Beside this ancient catastrophe of broken stone and battering water, they have built a settlement of fibre-board huts on concrete stilts, painted pink and lemon with bright blue hat-bands round the roofs. Their little suburb is called Doo Town, and the shacks have chiming name-tags burned onto wooden boards in Gothic script or spelled out in rococo twiddles of wrought iron: Love Me Doo, Doo Us, Doo Us Too, Doo Nothing, Make Doo, Rum Doo, Didgeri Doo, Doodle Doo, Much Adoo. . . . There's comfort in kitsch. Its masonic private joke holds the conclave together; the brash colours outface the aged, blackened stone and the grey water. Doo Town retains a sense of what it was like to colonise Australia: pitching camp in the bush above a stormy sea on a site whose only history is of cruelty and despair, you keep your courage up by painting your shed as gaudily as you can to fend off the darkness. This world needs all the defensive good humour you can muster. But those talismanic names betray themselves by the very abjectness of their appeal. 'Love Me Doo' begs this inimical place 'Let Me Live'; 'Doo Us' and 'Doo Us Too' know that despite such pleas it probably won't. 'Make Doo' is Crusoe's uncomplaining creed when the bushfire comes to purge your intrusion. Australia is a tragic country. Its valour and virtue is its refusal to see itself that way. On the contrary, it's always congratulating itself on its good fortune, and planting more hydrangeas in its nature strips.

Past Port Arthur and its penal ruins, near where Cape Raoul with its spindly chimney-stacks of splintered rock tumbles into the breakers, you can see Tasmania from under water. Clamber down a ramp through thick scrub to the bottom of a chasm, stand on a steep shelf of boulders, and you are at Remarkable Cave. Above is a funnel of ochre cliffs twittering with insects and dangling shaggy grasses from every crevice; ahead – in a shaft carved out beneath the arching stone – is the cave. The long perspective frames the triangular shape of Tasmania at its opening. The nibbled, crumbling map contains an ocean which you look at from beneath, watching as it curves upwards to the horizon in layers of white froth, green algae and remoter, unruffled blue. The water pointlessly, angrily circulates in the passage, nagging at its walls and withdrawing in a rumble of swirled stones. The outlined Tasmania at its outlet is an orifice eaten in the foundation, swallowed and blotted out as the tide floods in. Stay long enough, and the state is erased by water.

Beaches sift earth into water, resolving matter into meditation. Seven Mile Beach, though just outside Hobart, is seven miles of mostly deserted sand, no arena for the bronzed body but an open-air hermitage where the mind, unleashed from that querulous flesh, hesitates on the edge of landed reality. The low arms of the dunes curl to encircle a sky which is indistinguishable from the sea. In England the sky is the ceiling of a room; here you look through the roof, and into an upside-down evaporated ocean. Earth has dwindled to an observatory for light. I lay there one evening watching events above: streaky rain at one end of the domed brain, ladders of fuzzy golden sun let down from a gash in the clouds at the other; a green and yellow glaze to the south, enamelled blue to the north; wet grey dirigibles tethered in the west around Mount Wellington. We look up from our pit, and wonder what stories the sky is telling.

The beach reminds you that you're travelling on a flimsy floating platform between infinities. At Clifton, also a few miles south of the city, spirits crowd in. The tree branches creak with possums, bandicoots rustle in the bush. A kookaburra wheezes mockingly, and the yellow-faced parrots screech. Their hoarse rasping cry is said to be the lament of dead aboriginal children. During the day, nets trailed just beyond the breaking waves trawl the secrets of the deep. Once we hauled in an elephant shark, a miniature monster with skin like slick gun-metal and flopping ears above its gills, which spilt its brilliant bilious green innards on the sand when hacked open. Porpoises pirouette and lollop past. There used to be whales further out. Perhaps Tasmania, like the leviathan in Milton's poem, is the slippery torso of some sea-going beast, which we only imagine to be solid and anchored. And when night falls, the beach at Clifton becomes a landing-stage for birds which spend their day in the air or on the water.

The hills above the beach are mined by a rookery of mutton birds – meaty, greasy gulls called moon birds by the aboriginals, which fly each year from Tasmania up the Pacific basin to Russia and back; they fish on the horizon until sunset, then drop out of the sky into their burrows. My friends at the beach took me once to wait for them. We lay on the grass, staring up. The darkness above was a battlefield of rocketing bodies and thrashing wings. The wheeling birds, descending in dozens, turned the air into a smothering mesh. Then suddenly they had tumbled from it and waddled past or over us to their holes on the clifftop. When they were gone, the sky they had thickened began to glow, with avalanches of stars pouring down it. Its sheer size was exhilarating, and so was our own insignificance. Afterwards we groped down the cliff to wait for the penguins to come ashore. They reconnoitred among the thudding breakers, called to each other to check on numbers, then shambled beside us up to the dunes. We held our breaths, willing ourselves to be invisible, aware we were spying on a nocturnal rite as the sky and sea gave up their cargo of creatures which use the earth – so prized by us – as a mere dormitory, a place good only to be unconscious on.

In fierce sun next morning, the land loses bulk and weight again, just as last night it was rubbed out by darkness. The assault of light flattens it: the cliffs are depthless planes of cut-out paper, the rim of the sea an imagined line, improbably straight; the scene is as illusory as a cyclorama. At times – crouched yesterday among the tussocks of the rookery or huddled in bunkers of sand; floating now, in this bath of heat, on air as on water, all will and energy sucked out by the blaze – there's a pleasure in feeling that you don't exist.

T. S. Eliot set the world's end on a beach. When Nevil Shute localised the extinction in Australia, Tasmania became the ultimate, fragile toe-hold of sand left to men. The characters of *On the Beach* wait for the radiation to waft down to them in Melbourne, the most southerly big city in the world. Yet even when the sickness gets this far, Tasmania remains in mind as an epilogue to life on earth: 'New Zealand may last a little longer, and of course, Tasmania. A fortnight or three weeks, perhaps.' Dwight the submarine commander asks Moira's father whether he'll evacuate, and proposes Tasmania. The old man won't consider it, even to prolong his life.

Shute's novel depressed me all through my adolescence, because it stranded us on that final littoral, which Eliot's poem hadn't specified. On the beach now, I don't feel that way. The place is an exercise in understanding and enjoying the buoyant lightness of your own being. Here where earth is ground to fine white dust and absorbed by water, there's a truth to be learned about Tasmania: this far south, the human race runs out just before the land ejects a trail of full stops into the ocean; it is a world which never needed us, where we never belonged – and that is its beauty.

In the Air

One afternoon I finally saw what lay beyond the rampart of our mountain, and beyond the bucolic fiction I had cultivated for myself in the Huon. I flew to the end of the world (and hastened back). The destination was Port Davey, a gash in the coast opening onto the wildness of the south-west. This area is now a national park, and occupies about a quarter of the state – but it's not a national park like those in the United States, where you drive through in an air-conditioned cocoon, pause at the designated photo-lookouts, and plug your trailer into the electricity mains at the end of the day so you can watch sitcoms. The Tasmanian south-west is a drenched, wind-lashed nowhere of boggy plains and jagged peaks. The road runs from Hobart along the Huon, follows the coast to Catamaran, and then resigns. From here you can only walk in to Port Davey; it takes a week.

Or you can fly down in a propeller plane, which shuttles you within an hour from the companionable suburbs to this landscape fit only for anchorites in oil-skins. You're made aware of the journey's drama because it depends on omens and the interpretation of the intemperate Tasmanian sky. For a week before I made the trip, I telephoned the airfield daily, only to be told that Big Chief Thunder Cloud had advised against take-off. Mostly there were black fronts of rain bruising the sky, driven by the winds which lash Tasmania in the summer and pluck the occasional roof off a house; once there was bushfire weather, a blue tingling haze with sparks singeing the air and the mountains smouldering yellow. The sky that day was a big dipper of thermal bumps and sudden plummeting slopes. Again the trip was postponed.

Finally the weather cleared, and we were allowed to leave. The grizzled gum-chewing pilot led me to his metallic insect, sat me in its nose-cone between the buzzing wings, rode it along a diving-board of tarmac and coaxed it, shuddering, into the unsteady air. We swooped over parched hills, across the crinkled harbour, and then lost the city. The zone of familiarity inside which I'd lived was a momentary incident only. Now the landscape began to reorganise itself as an abstract. Australia seen from the air is the map of another planet: I remembered looking down on the Nullarbor Plain – riveted squares the colour of corroding metal, ponds of sulphur and purple ridges, a bleached desert snapped off into the ocean; across it, incredibly testifying to a human presence, the single unkinked line of a road. Tasmania is never dry enough to appear so lurid, or so extra-terrestrial. The view from the air here is not of an uninhabitable world but of one where habitation pushes against the wet, seething entanglement of nature and the cranky irregularities of terrain. Avenues have been razored through the bush for power lines or as fire breaks. Off Bruny Island the water is fenced for a salmon farm, as if a town had sunk under. Settlement soon wears threadbare. Opossum Bay extends a furry prehensile arm; the twin islands of Bruny are held together by a fraying cord of isthmus. After that, there are only clouds to imitate land, imprinted like submerged plateaux on the clear water. Whereas on Nullarbor earth is estranged because it blotches and reddens in the heat, here earth is engulfed, saturated, dematerialised by moisture. The air turns to dewy drops on the window; the sky condenses in a film of showers.

The route leads south, towards the cape where Tasmania breaks off. Even before the land surrenders, there are glimpses of its death by drowning: the milky whorls and serpentine green curls of Southport Lagoon, as somnolent as the moon; a fringe of rusted offshore reefs. Though the vertical distance stills everything, smoothing and patterning the scene into pictures, you understand from this height the combats and collisions which have given shape to Tasmania. To the north, the sea gobbled up the mountains and severed it from the mainland; here in the south, spars of basalt crumble into another sea. The Southern Ocean continues to undermine and whittle the rock. Water like time is an inexorable sculptor, hollowing caves and incising channels, deforming the land and weakening its supports until it capsizes. The catastrophe happened eternities ago, yet seen from above it might have been minutes before, because the splintered excrescences are still there. Earth had not expected to go under so abruptly. The capes dig fingers into the swells, feeling for a grip. Maatsuyker Island, protruding between the south-east and south-west tips, was just now set adrift. Its ledges, tipped at sick angles, remain green – excerpts from the forested bluffs; they annoy the ocean by resisting it, and it pummels them with mallets of solid white water. Here the plane, having glanced over the edge of our flat, broken earth, turns back inland. At Cox Bight there's a meeting of waters: blue waves, jerked in spasms towards the beach by indentations on the surface, are stained by the brown streams pouring from the hills; frosty transparent ocean against those rivulets which are the blood of earth, discoloured by its secretions. The acids sweated from rocks and roots are soon flushed away in the purging of surf. The Ironbound Range has been carved down its spine by the disagreement of weathers. Towards the ocean, the wind strips it bare; on the other side, sheltered, the rain forest dankly clings to it. Where no mountains fend off the gales, the scrub we fly over has been bent level. Trees grow only in fugitive gullies, and behind Cox Bight even the low pelt of paperbarks has been picked loose, rubbed away by wind until the ashen bone beneath the soil shows through.

To my amazement, we can land here. The terror of the journey is its demonstration, once again, that earth is an interruption in this waste of water. Yet we jolt down on a strip of beach, managing to halt just before the sand does. Outside, a windsock slaps and billows; a gyrating vane records the force of the current. There are some huts, the scars of a tin mine, but no people. Those of us who crawl from the plane feel embarrassed by the emptiness, and the howling silence between this marsh and the mountains. Some hikers who have travelled down with us leave here to spend a week walking back. They're solemnly farewelled – 'Got some salt for the leeches?' asks the pilot – and trudge away through the tussocks. One of them, a Frenchman, had costumed himself in a beret, handlebar moustache, cut-off jeans and woolly leggings; his knapsack was leather. Off he swaggered, gallantly dandified. Within minutes, he was a dwarf, then a dot which no longer moved ahead but wavered against the bleak distant wall of dolerite.

In a shed beside the landing strip, along with picks, shovels, lanterns and tins of emergency food, are the belongings of the long-distance walkers, deposited here as hostages to their reappearance. Someone has left a balaclava, which instantly suggests Antarctic exploration a little further south and the stroll outdoors taken by Captain Oates; a label pinned to a plastic bag of belongings jauntily announces that 'John Rees and Anne Kiely are here too!! S.W. Cape on 30 Jan'. A circular quizzes the dispersed campers about their rite of passage through the bush, and begs them to be truthful since replies are anonymous. What did they do with their rubbish? – burn, bash or bury it? How did they dispose of faecal waste? – dig a shallow grave for it, make an eiderdown of leaves and twigs, or pile rocks on the turds? Did they gouge drainage channels round their tent, and scavenge local vegetation for bedding? When washing, did they use normal or biodegradable soap and swill the dirty suds in a creek, or did they scour themselves with sand away from the water? And did they suffer from gastroenteritis? – stomach upsets, vomiting and diarrhoea are specified. They are then asked to provide details of educational level attained.

The questionnaire supplies the scenario for an experience I'll never have. It is no romantic connoisseurship of landscape but a test of your capacity to survive, and its moral nicety is that you must do so without imposing yourself in any way on nature, or seeking help from it. The National Parks and Wildlife Service promotes 'minimal impact' or 'no trace' bushwalking. Those seven days on the track to Catamaran must be spent in pondering your own irrelevance to this realm which has, as the Parks propaganda reminds you, been '50 million years evolving': you are in transit; it persists. The rage of our lives is to leave some mark on the world, which is why we enjoy defacing it. Here you're forbidden to meddle. You must glide through spectrally, recognising that the scene exists without you. The Parks Department actually distributes in schools a kit about a 'phantom walker': ghosts can be relied on to leave no trace. The perfect hiker might decompose en route. I found myself wondering whether the Frenchman's beret and his tanned knapsack would biodegrade.

The Tasmanian south-west forbids any sense of romantic kinship. Romanticism is the fair-weather creed of milder climates and a domesticated nature. Keats encountered the nightingale in a Hampstead backyard; the impressionist paintings which used to mesmerise me in art books when I was a boy all depict picnic sites. Down here, nature and human affection are incommensurate. The skyline is the allegorical graph of our dreads: behind Huonville, on the edge of the south-western no man's land, looms Mount Misery.

For the fly which was buzzing, trapped, in the walkers' hut, it was all too much. When I opened the door, it crossed to the plane, circled in and travelled back with us to Hobart. We took off towards the north, over the black foam-striped water of Bathurst Harbour, past the tusks of the Arthur Range. To the right, a fist of rock poked up inside the clouds; in an instant, I rose from my seat without uncrossing my nervously clamped knees, banged my head on the ceiling of the plane and slumped back down. My internal organs followed some way behind. The pilot, wrestling with the wheel, smirked, 'That was Mount Picton. He always does that to us. We ought to take the road-grader to the bastard.' It was a tone I was often to hear in Tasmania – humorously vindictive, coping with the aggression of nature (in this case a mountain which idly exhaled energy and knocked passing planes a few dozen feet down the sky) by mobilising machines, amused by the challenge to battle; it was the tone of my uncle inquiring if I had seen any apple trees on the farm. This is what takes the place of romantic empathy in Tasmania: a sporting sense of the landscape as adversary, to be conquered by the axe or by engineering. The ethic of minimal impact may prevail in this part of the state, but elsewhere impact is maximised, because men have only been able to live here by ravaging the land. Half of Tasmania is a savage Eden, pristine because impenetrable; the rest is a factory with its own manufactured scenery – the mines with their alps of yellow slag, the power stations with their dammed involuntary lakes. At the northern border of the national park is the featureless inland sea of Lake Pedder, flooded by force until it drank the mountains.

On this margin, near the Lake Pedder airfield, Tasmania reveals its fatal flaw: a dotted line where the earth's crust has been ripped. The suture is the Edgar Fault, and it's the seam along which Tasmania, in some millennial future, will probably split apart. The fault is a tectonic rift. The mountains here are a symptom of convulsions beneath, and of the implacable drift of continents which tug these soldered masses apart. Tasmania lost some of itself when its glaciers melted; the drowned underside pulls from the depths of the south-western sea at what remains above water. The island is a delinquent appendix of land, vexed between the mainland with which its connection has been cut and this kingdom on the ocean floor whose periscope it is. The quarrelling forces have inscribed that crack among the button-grass. Flying over it is like anatomising the schisms of a body laid prostrate on an operating table. The earth's agitations, invisible because we don't last long enough on it to notice them, somehow become apparent here. In human terms, the south-west has no history. Its time is that of geology. It could serve as the warp where the monsters of Conan Doyle's lost world prowl; from above, you can see by what ruptures and eruptions it was made, and can spot exactly where fatigue will one day unmake it. I can hear the rending sound, and see the open mouth of that ultimate advancing wave.

After this preview of apocalypse, the plane veered towards Hobart – or, as I was now scared into considering it, home. We crossed the Huon, and within minutes personal landmarks appeared: the family farm, its barns, the huddle of wattle trees, everything where it was. My aunt, when I told her a few days later that I'd passed over, said, 'You should have given a wave. I was probably out the back hanging up the washing.' Yet the shadow of where I had been extended this far. The vertical view marked how promptly the patch of cultivation gave up. At the top of the valley, half a mile above the house, that bulwark of tall gums moaned in the wind. I'd never been behind it, because there was no road. Now I saw what lay just outside my imagined garden: the forest of the Hartz Mountain, its dead timber a convocation of upright twitching corpses.

Round the forehead of Mount Wellington, we lurched over water and bounced back to land. The company which flies the planes offers you, when it's all over, a stomach-settling cup of tea and a biscuit, as if you had given blood. That indeed is what it felt like. I was light-headed, never more glad to be on the ground and never more sceptical about how little security it guaranteed. I could still feel it moving beneath me: those sliding, clashing rafts of rock we call continents; the buffeting road of air, and the cavity suddenly opened in it by Mount Picton's side-swipe. The afternoon was exhilarating and dismaying, as visions of the truth are said to be. I had seen at last what kind of country our tent was pitched on.

While I was down at the world's end, the Hobart Cup had been run on the race-track behind my parents' house. The Governor of the state drove up the course with a police escort, and a racing Mass blessed the nags. One of the entrants had been bought by his trainer for $80 when earmarked for dog meat; the winning horse flew in from Melbourne that morning and left for the airport within an hour of the race. The event is the local Ascot, and wits attend in fancy dress. As I got back, two adolescent ancients in togas wreathed with plastic laurel were looking for their car. Around the corner, I came on Scarlett O'Hara in a purple crinoline, escorted by an epauletted colonel under a spiked helmet. (The Neanderthal bikers who roared past yelling abuse were real, I think.)

Somehow it seemed logical – the tatterdemalion pageant following so hard upon those aerial perspectives of punished rock and furious water, scrub crippled by wind and gums hollowed by fire, razored escarpments and bituminous lakes under pelting boulders of cloud. Behind Mount Wellington pre-history hid; here in the streets, history was summarised as a jumbled absurd charade by preposterous Romans and fake Ruritanians. Society had turned its back on inhospitable nature, assembled its glad rags and improvised a ritual to cheer itself up.

Under Ground

From the air, Tasmania is alien, intractable. That day on the plane I felt amazed and ashamed that I'd lived on the edge of this wild immensity and had known nothing about it. But if I had known, how could I have coped with the knowledge? That lost world won't ever be conquered; the rest of Tasmania is habitable only under duress, in narrow valleys between the mountains. Living there, you resolve not to notice, or else you'd be demoralised forever. My tendency too, after that aerial survey, was to burrow. Up above, it may look desolate. Down below, crushed and compressed under ground, there is a weird, subliminal beauty – a surreal Tasmania guarded in the darkness.

The miners who hacked into the mountains of the west coast struggled back to the surface carrying wonders. They had turned the earth inside out, and discovered a crystallised light trapped far beneath. The Memorial Museum of the pioneers at Zeehan displays the instruments of their research – an antique blasting box, gelignite cartridges which look like fat cigars, yellow braids of detonator – and mocks up a facsimile of their underground laboratory: toiling dummies shove carts of rubble along railway tracks under a roof of wire mesh and papier-mâché glistening with gems. Their excavated treasures are on show in glass cases, and they expose the fires in rock concocted by the heaving and slippage of the crust. The violence deep down has created beauty, like the oyster ulcerating itself to make a pearl. On the shelves there are inadvertent ornaments which, beneath the earth, have shaped themselves into replicas of contradictory objects above it – a clump of lead chromate like a bird's nest dyed red, and some copper sulphate so blindingly blue it might have been chipped from a ceramic Australian sky, a specimen of crocoite or pyromorphite cooked into a bank of blade-hard moss, a green boulder of stichtite with an interior of streaky violet, aragonite from Wilmot like an arm of soapy seaweed. Sometimes the rock mimics fragility. Cerrusite passes itself off as a brush of silver hairs. It's also expert at pretending to be edible. The chrome-cerrusite has a pie-crust covering what looks like a thriving colony of edible grubs. Dolomite makes a bowl of sugar cubes, barite from Rosebery a glued confection of candied fruits. One opalised branch from Gretna looks like a chocolate log, another like a side of cured ham.

Above ground, the miners constructed temporary palaces of artifice for themselves inside the Gaiety Theatre, festooning it with floral wreaths for a highland ball or dangling ropes of ersatz icicles from the ceiling for their snow carnival. Their special pleasure was singers, who decanted the most precious metal of all in liquid form from their throats. There's a local legend that Caruso came to Zeehan to perform for them; one of the diggings outside town was named, in honour of such a visitor, Melba Flats.

At Hastings, in the far south, is another subterranean grotto of likenesses: the Newdegate Cave, discovered by timber-cutters in 1916. The path leads to it through a forest of spindly gums, beaten by wind until they sound like hissing surf. You seem to be on the bed of an evergreen ocean, with the waves far overhead. Lyre birds metallically chirp and chuckle out of sight. A barred gate clanks open onto a spiral staircase. Down you fumble on damp steps past a suppurating wall into this dark cleft of impersonations, irrigated far beneath by Mystery Creek, whose source has never been traced. The cave is a garden of rock as soft and spongy as algae – moist knobs like mushrooms, tufts of mineral broccoli, calcium cones of spun sugar, all nurtured in this den of wet fertility where you watch the stealthy growth of stone, as drips gather on the nozzles of the stalactites and crust there before they can fall. An icy fountain of dolomite spills and billows: it's known as the frozen waterfall. These thin moist accretions, growing towards each other from the roof and the floor but never meeting, act out architectural fantasies. In one cave there's a teetering pagoda; in another some wreathing shawls with the leathery consistency of bats' wings surround a stage of igloos, white banyan trees and frothy cliffs. Resemblances are painstakingly pointed out: with the aid of light, an inclined rock like a horizontal cactus becomes a dragon, its slimy wings rusted by iron impurities; in Titania's palace, sunrise glares from an artificial lantern, and the shadowy pimples on the pavement are said to be people hastening to leave the ball. The wall has the feel of congealing mucus; inside the earth, it's like travelling through a sleek humid human body.

The metaphors are inescapable. How else can something so subterranean yet so outlandish ever be comprehended? Metaphor is a carrier, and its burden is to transport significance from known things to those unknown: to make correspondences between familiarity above ground level and these lapidary oddments below ground; to discern in the upside-down southern hemisphere the translated replicas of northern meanings. From the first, the only way Australia could be conceived was as a metaphor. Marcus Clarke thought the gum trees had been carved with hieroglyphs, signifying a horror he couldn't decipher. James McAuley defined the 'mythical Australia' of the explorer Quiros as 'your land of similes'. Randolph Stow has declared that 'what . . . I see in Australia . . . is an enormous symbol.'

But a simile or symbol of what? The semblances are always illusory. Language tags and captions the blunt inimical contents of the world, and doing so colonises them. Tasmanians can still play at being Adam in Eden. Because their world is so new, they can saunter through it distributing names. My host on Flinders Island took me to see a rock he believes looks like a sea lion and another with the gaping jaw of a shark; on the Darling Range he pointed out a peak in the image of a short-stoppered gin bottle, and next to it the profile of an old English perambulator. Yet the metaphor, turning mountains into bottles or crystals into desserts, confides its own inadequacy. 'What thou art we know not,' Shelley says of the skylark, acknowledging ignorance. In compensation, he can only ask 'What is most like thee?' All attempts to define Australia evade the issue, because they liken it to things elsewhere which it doesn't resemble. Even so, the game must be played: the alternative is that idiotic world Macbeth feared, signifying nothing.

At school we were told that Tasmania had the same shape as a human heart, or saw it drawn as one of its own apples, with a leaf protruding from the estuary of the Tamar. Marcus Clarke, however, thought that the coast in the south-east was 'a biscuit at which rats have been nibbling'. The practice is as imprecise as reading tea-leaves or the creases in the palm of your hand, and as self-revealing. For me, Tasmania symbolised the state of insulation, the solitary confinement of those cells where the convicts went mad within a year. Every man is an island. The name of the place might be Tasmanoia.

It was a troglodytic world. The aborigines, dosed with strychnine-laced oatmeal by the white settlers, retreated to a cave beneath the cliffs at Cape Grim. The convicts in the coal mines on the Saltwater River were locked in a network of underground brick cells. The miners at Queenstown became prisoners in Nibelheim when in 1912 a fire in the pump-house seven hundred feet below filled the tunnels with poison gas. Forty-six of them died; after four days trapped with his gang near a vent of compressed air a thousand feet down, a shift boss sent a message to the foreman in charge of the rescue – 'Will you try and send down some soft food next time. Some of the men are not able to swallow the hard food their throats are sore from the gas and on no account allow any more cigarettes to come down.' Tasmanian experience is an anthology of such notes from underground, handed up a shaft from the bottom of the world.

Underneath those inauspicious mountains I saw from the air is the secretive, concave Tasmania of my fern gully or that fantasy of the overgrown orchard with its boughs as closely stitched as a tapestry. Plato thought human beings were incorrigible cave-dwellers. They crouch, in his allegory, in the depth of their dim cavern, preferring the fitful radiance of the fire they have built there to the daylight behind them at the mouth: their moral folly is the choice of fancies and fables rather than the severe sunny truth. I am happy to be called guilty. I always squinted in the sun; I needed dark glasses to occlude the view; and I found my protective Platonic cave in a shed on the showground just over the highway from my parents' house.

At the time I didn't know it was Plato's, or that it belonged in an allegory concerning the mental recusancy of art. It had been imagined by Nan Chauncy, who in 1948 wrote a children's book called *They Found a Cave*. It's about four English evacuee children in Tasmania during the war who, accompanied by their indigenous friend Tas, run away when they're maltreated and camp in a cave in the bush. Tasmania, being a desert island without a desert, suits such exercises in self-sufficiency: the book was our local *Robinson Crusoe* or *Swiss Family Robinson*. Nan Chauncy was a tweedy lady who lived in a house without electricity on a nature preserve where a few dejected marsupials sought refuge, near Bagdad in the midlands. To my parents with their electrical appliances she seemed slightly loony, unplugged from the modern world, and my father referred to her as Nancy Chancy; to me, she was the sole available model of literary activity, scribbling beside an oil-lamp in a dilapidated cabin. When I was thirteen, a Tasmanian company made a film of her book. After school one day I presented myself for a screen test, and thanks to my proficiency at screaming in mortal terror and laughing hysterically on camera – indulging emotions I hadn't so far had much use for in daily life – I got one of the parts. Since there was no studio, the cave was constructed in a disused pavilion on the showground. Every morning, having been excused from school for three months, I'd leave home, dodge the traffic on the highway, find the loose paling thanks to which each September I gained free entry to the agricultural show, saunter past horse boxes, cattle pens and the grandstand with its flaking paint, pull open a sliding metal door and leave the day for an oblivious artificial night.

There on the concrete floor was the cave we were due to find (and some disjoined rooms of the house we'd run away from). The cave had a frame of chicken wire, to which a porridge of plaster was applied. It was painted yellow, with licks of black to indicate dents and dimples in the rock. Bags of sand were strewn inside it, though no one could explain how a cave in the mountains came to be carpeted like a beach. Around the entry they arranged a garland of saplings, stiffly standing in for the bush. Inside, it had only one wall; the others had been omitted so the camera could poke its way in. That single face of crumbly rock got battered by our romping, and by the end of the film you can see the white bruises where the plaster shows through. It was a ragged, jerry-built illusion. But then so was Prospero's, on his magic island.

Seeing the film again in Tasmania, I noticed the gulf dividing the real outdoors from that unreal interior, which the technicians hadn't the skill to conceal. One moment the children are forcing their way through thorny brush, scrambling up cliffs and dislodging showers of dirt, blinking in the summer sun; the next, they have crossed into fantasy, and tread on that ballroom floor of sand through screens of posed branches towards the florid shell which is the cave. The first thing any of them says when inside it is, 'What a queer light!' It was indeed: a sunset of orange and purple phosphorescence. Tas explains at once that it comes from a chimney in the rock. But the cave had no roof, and the false fires which danced inside it were produced by plastic filters over the arc lamps above. Plato could have conceived no apter image for deluding art. The cave, however, was the Tasmanian landscape where I felt most at home – that is, until it was hammered into dust at the end of the filming. Ever since, I have been trying to reconstruct it.

III

AN ARCHAEOLOGICAL DIG

Electropolis

Tasmania, despite its short life, is a palimpsest of different, antagonistic cultures. It was owned at first by the aborigines, who understood it and indexed it. They assigned a spirit to every mountain, stream and cave, deriving their ancestry from the land. They were dispossessed when the place became a penal outpost of England. A terrain their legends had placated turned ugly overnight. The topography of Van Diemen's Land was an illustration of hell, a catalogue of moral alarms – the dentated chasms of the Tasman Peninsula, the black gulf of Macquarie Harbour, the unnutritious forests which made escaped convicts into cannibals. When transportation ended, the state changed its name and (so it hoped) its identity. Now it was to be a genteel community of graziers, who settled the midlands in mansions of what might be honeycombed Cotswold stone. Since then, overlaid on their pastoral regime, industry has arrived to torment the land, rather than patiently tending it like the good shepherd: the mines of the west coast, the reservoirs and power stations of the highlands.

I began my digging on the uppermost level, and worked down through the stacks and storeys of the Tasmanian past. To start, I needed only to look out the front window of my parents' house. There, steaming indefatigably on the scruffy hills of Lutana, lit in a green shimmering haze all night long, was the zinc works. The scalloped section of river bank on which it stood was a long meandering necropolis, a suburb sacred to death: next to the zinc works were the low sheds of the abattoir, behind it the cemetery of Cornelian Bay; between the pens of slaughtered cattle and the crematorium to which all hearses sleekly hastened, a torture-chamber had been built for roasting metal, and steel tanks stored poison clouds of ammonia or seas of sulphuric acid.

To the right and left of our house, Mount Wellington and Mount Direction always worried me. They were the blunt giants who poised their clubs above the valley, and forbade escape. To the front, the zinc works sent up different signals in the drifts of dazzling white and purply smoke from its evaporating towers: it was a seething, thronging, frenetic city. It corresponded to the other man-made region of dreams out the back of the house where, in the middle of the race-course, a drive-in movie screen had been propped up. After dark I'd climb into one of the pine trees outside the race-track fence and lip-read the babbling of those monochrome beauties who swanned across the night a quarter of a mile away, while the zinc works blazed behind me. When the sun went down and those invigilating mountains sank into their trenches, the sky became a theatre of tinted gas and celluloid phantoms.

On the wall next to the view of the zinc works, ruled into stripes by the venetian blinds, hung a painting found in some family cellar, its varnish curdled to a tobacco colour and defaced by scars. It showed a ruined abbey with autumnal trees (or was it the sick varnish which had killed the leaves?), wading cows, and a meditative angler. The painting might have mocked the view, but it didn't. I found them both romantic, though in different ways. They were magic casements opening onto alternative fairylands: ancient England and futuristic America, where the streets breathed steam and arc lamps ignited the air. Coming down the ramp past Hoboken and looking across the river at Manhattan, that great furnace of electrolytic excitements, I'm still reminded of the zinc works. It was the first luminous horizon of my life. I populated its sooty roads – bridged by planks and bordered by gutters of effluent – with dramas too metropolitan for Hobart to afford: exchanges of gunfire from the clumps of residue; chases through the corroded sheds, their rippling iron gnarled by diseases; attitudinising deaths in the pits of manganese mud or the quaking vats and bubbling green ponds of the leaching plant.

Though it lay only a mile off, its nimbus of dangerous splendour made it inaccessible. It took me half a lifetime to get inside. When I did, I made the mistake – elated as I was by the thrill of ammonia and the sappy stink of phosphate, the pink fizzing jacuzzis of gypsum and the red coagulated ovens of cobalt batter – of commenting on the atmosphere. My guide, a hard-hatted employee, thought I was hinting at pollution, and at once got defensive. The river used to boil with discharged acid, and the Derwent oysters, guzzling heavy metal, had toughened into a zinc concentrate. Now the water is purified before it's released into the river, and barges dump poisoned earth in the rough seas off Tasman Island, over the edge of the continental shelf. I wasn't disapproving, of course. But the insistence on clean disposal depressed me. I wanted the zinc works to be dirty: the fur growing on the floor boards, the woolly scum on the tubs of thickener in the leaching plant, the coral reef of orange crystals on a pipe outside the computer room, the dust of acrid pellets everywhere – these were what it was about for me. Like a painter's studio, it was a place of licensed messes.

I think I warmed to it because it taunted nature. It parodies the humped mountains, blue as bruises, at both ends of the valley: out the back the zinc works has its own neat array of multi-coloured pinnacles – cratered piles of baked sandy rock from Nauru Island, the khaki stone of Christmas Island, yellow cakes of sulphur and grey tumuli of lime. Inside, the mad poetry of metallurgy outdoes organic growth. Cadmium germinates on horizontal trees whose boughs are rotating cathodes of aluminium. After seeding and sprouting for three days, it's peeled off and reformed into rods, ingots and anodes for electroplating. The zinc works prides itself on the universe of utensils it makes possible: carburettors and radiators, grilles, galvanised fences and boat trailer winches. For me, its proper business is the manufacture of useless, extravagant art. The liquid slabs which travel from the smelter to the casting machine are skimmed by hand as they pass on a conveyor; the metal froth hardens at once to jewellery in the air.

Nature, abused and assassinated, putrefies with an obscene beauty. At Queenstown on the west coast, the hills have been soured by the wastes which puff and leak from the Mount Lyell copper mine; nothing will grow here now. The road to the town has been carved through Tasmania's cool soaked jungle of myrtles and celery pines. Sudden glaciated chasms open beside it, splitting quartzite from dolerite. Mist unwreathes from the damp ranges. Abruptly, just before Queenstown, this dripping vegetation ceases. At first the stone is a chafed, irritable red, like skin with a rash; then it flushes scarlet and queasy bilious green. Around Gormanston, the peaks seem to be pyramids of cigarette ash, with some crags baked crimson. Terraces of mauve, rose and fawn rock conduct the road into Queenstown through a petrified sunset. Where the soil has slid away, tangles of roots still tread the air above parched gulleys down which the boulders have tumbled. Some of the scabby mounds have been levelled on top, so that streets can be built there: suburbs seem to perch on pustules. It is a scene of geological lunacy. The earth has been surreally flayed, and the rocks beneath it blush.

Queenstown is a mirage of the same misleading colours which flicker in the cliffs above it. My father, as we walked down one of its shabby streets past the decrepit hotels where the miners drank when it was a boom town, remembered coming here fifty years before to look for work. After two weeks, one of his brothers, who had a job in the smelter at Mount Lyell, gave him thirty shillings to pay his hotel bill and bought him a bus ticket back south – 'otherwise I'd of still been walking'. Later, at home, he took down that mahogany box on the mantelpiece which contains the remnants of our past, and produced a snapshot of himself with two friends prospecting in the mountains above Queenstown. They squat beside a sluice with shovel and pan while water pours down the slope; grinning, they make a joke of their desperation in sifting the water for precious dust. Of course they found none. The only gold, ironically, has grown with age on the emulsion of the photograph: a yellow jaundice of the surface which has eaten into the image, attacking my father's foot and the blade of his shovel. The borders are blackened by inky thumb prints and grease, as if the picture itself had been dug out of the retentive earth; and in a sense, as one more buried treasure, it was.

Where the open cut cross-sections Mount Lyell, the hills have melted in avalanches of orange dirt. The mine is a graveyard of machinery. A brick chimney propped on a mustard pile might be incinerating the earth. The slag heap smothers the pioneer settlement of Penghana, which was burned out by a bush-fire; the pipes protruding everywhere from the gravel suggest an interred city under the sludge, gasping for breath. The miners are unrepentant about the devastation. The timber was cut, they point out, to build the town and fuel the boilers; and they grudgingly admire the resilience of the massacred trees. A retired shift boss indicates one indomitable battler: a stump of blackwood, officially dead for eighty or ninety years, with new shoots growing from it. 'You wouldn't think the bugger would still have any life in him,' he says. Personifying the tree compliments it as a comrade. Tasmanians matily ingratiate with the things they kill. The trees dare them to combat, and the challenge can't be shirked. But the axeman's victory is temporary only, because this wilderness, indestructible in the end, will grow back the moment he's gone. Hence the reverence accorded the blackwood as a wounded, carbonised old soldier, a better man than whoever long ago chopped or poisoned or set fire to him.

Queenstown surveys its defoliation with something very like smugness. As for the muddying of the King River by mineral filth, the shift boss with his mottled face and bleary eyes smirks, 'It's lovely to swim in now – you can just walk across the top.' In the centre of town, a set of sculptural reliefs narrating the history of the mine concludes with a scene on the Gordon River in 1983, where protesters gathered to prevent work on a new hydro-electric reservoir. It shows 'the Salvation Army serving hot hot drinks to police at dam blockade'. The tautology is cast in bronze on the plaque; the over-heated double adjective expresses warmth of approval for the police, rather than measuring the temperature of the tea. Once more, tender feelings for landscape are discounted by those who have to live in and wrest a living from it.

Driving into the highlands above Ouse, you see nature supplanted by technology, trees transformed into girders of metal. Dead gums, their trunks hollowed by fire into little charred habitable chapels, claw the air with white branches. Once they give up, the pylons take over. These iron abstracted conifers bestride the valleys, transferring power from the generators among the mountains down to the city in a relay race of cables. Legs spread, they deal out flex from their layered sets of multiple arms. Nearing Tarraleah, the electrode robots assemble on every summit. Their heads buzz with coiled nerves; around their gaunt midriffs they wear placards announcing DANGER. The forests have been felled to accommodate them, and they occupy fenced-in plantations of their own. In these lethal parks, silver similes of trees hum and whine behind signs denying the romantic notion that nature is good for the soul:

HIGH VOLTAGE

the lettering says in a blitz of red lightning bolts,

NEAR APPROACH
WILL CAUSE INSTANT DEATH.

Maelstroms crackle above inside the wires. Floodgates of levered concrete slabs discipline slack, sullen-looking lagoons, or hustle water along a canal of racing waves towards the pipes which will hurl it down the hillside into the rotating turbine's plates. At Tarraleah, you can stand on a gantry above the swollen tubes which suddenly internalise the torrent, hurry it into two thick chimneys, then thrust it over the precipice. The pipes ray out down a steep wedge of shattered timbers; far beneath in the gorge, the power station churns a swill of green water into the river, and pylons climb the opposite hill on the long march with their shunted electrons. The storms of transformation happen out of sight, the only visible evidence that sink of used, spewed water. But the whole valley electrically vibrates, played on like some magnetised harp.

Anywhere in the highlands, one of these necropolitan marvels is liable to appear. On the way to Cradle Mountain, you cross a valley sliced from the rock where the Cethana dam has dropped an abrupt impervious curtain. A triangle of yellow and red pebbles, hand-placed and patterned like streaky bacon, slants three hundred feet down the walls of mountain. The angular base it rests on is a cage of rockfill, spiked to the middle of the dam to strengthen it against floods. On the other side, unseen, is the heaving reluctant lake. A hatch drilled into the cliff leads to the power station, locked an unimaginable distance underground. The wayward rivers of the plateau have been joined by canals and tunnels or stilled by dams; the trapped water is shoved along flumes, down vertical shafts or inside penstocks over ledges of the escarpment to be whirled in electrostatic fury by the turbines and excreted through the tailrace to begin the long cycle of circulation and atomised destruction all over again. The landscape is compelled into submission with an Egyptian arrogance. At the zinc works nature is cooked and boiled in the ovens. The mines envenom nature with their toxic smoke. The power stations rule it by reorganising it to suit themselves. On the Tasmanian heights the mind of Prometheus, who first stole that galvanic secret, casually tramples mass into energy.

Six hundred feet beneath the Gordon dam I visited a dynamo, the stainless steel genie which now performs the combustible work of Prometheus. A lift plummets in ninety seconds from the snaggled, scything mountains in their whirlpools of mist and the bottled ocean of the new Lake Pedder to a technocratic cathedral hewn from rock.

Plated bolts anchor faults in the walls of stone; the mountain is then clad with concrete, spray-painted a moony silver to prevent seepage, finally bricked over. Domesticated, the underworld is a home for self-sufficient machines. Like the trees at Queenstown, these are respectfully personified by human intruders in their realm. A red light on top of a filing cabinet is addressed as the Annunciator: not the dove which hovers above the Virgin but the guardian who announces faults. A blue drum is the Exciter, stimulating the rotor and turning it into a electromagnet. In charge of all these anthropomorphs is the turbine's Governor, a gadget whose lair is a door reinforced with four locks. Who is he? My guide explains the all-seeing demiurge. 'He senses everything,' I'm told; 'when there's a problem he picks it up.' He's a god who knows if everyone in Hobart, a hundred miles away, has plugged in their toasters simultaneously for breakfast. If so, he opens up the guide vanes to keep the turbine revolving at the same speed. The Governor stores his cerebellum separately, in a grey flue on a yellow pillar. This is the Actuator: 'he moves up and down, and controls the little valve sensors.' Further down, lying on its side, is a self-excited AC generator, another autonomous agent which calmly takes over in case of a power loss. The turbine, though creating heat, is cloistered behind a green door with its own air-conditioning. Industrialism began as a hell of volcanic cauldrons and engines powered by steam. At the zinc works, it remains true to its old gospels of fire and dirt. But here in the power station, the chilled machines perform with clinical serenity.

They also disdain the element they exploit. The hungry boilers of Queenstown demanded whole forests as their food: machines whose life is fire have hearty appetites. In the power station the turbines consume nothing. They take in water, then spit it out again. The Hydro-Electric Commission is synonymous with water, and everyone in Tasmania refers to it as the Hydro rather than mentioning the electricity it produces. Water is its credo. One of its brochures even quotes the romantic biology of Goethe, who believed that 'All is born of water. All is sustained by water.' It's a faith germane to sea-beset, rainy Tasmania, whose west coast is the wettest part of Australia. Yet the only water visible inside the Gordon machine hall is in what's called the dewatering pit, a brown cistern forty feet beneath the gallery, with spots of light wobbling on its surface. Here leakage is pumped out through a submarine gate. The contents of the pit suck and swirl: 'When it gets agitated,' a technician shrugs, glancing down at the dewatered water, 'it foams a bit.'

Above is the supine lake, into which the mountains have capsized. You can look across it from a path along the concrete shell with which the dam obstructs the valley. That sickle-shaped membrane holds in a dull trough of heavy water, swelling through the downpour to fill up the landscape. Thrusting up from within it are improvised islands, actually the peaks of the submerged range; shaggy timber grows beneath the water-line. The dam wall intercedes between a tank large enough to drown the valley, flooded to its rim of scorched hills, and a ravine empty except for a torrent far, far below. On one side, that weight of grey captive water rises to the top of the world; on the other, nature resumes, in the green crevice with the leaping stream along its floor. Here too the rods, cables and angular zig-zagging metal stairs of the dam wall and the perfect girdling line of the concrete contradict the wrinkled irregular rock, the gouged-out angles of the gorge and the unruly thrashing rivulet: nature cannot aspire to such straight lines, or to such elegant curves.

Standing on the rim, it's impossible to balance an equation between the two views, between the lake's engineered calm, and the savagery of the thin, torn gulf. But the imbalance sums up Tasmania. This wilderness couldn't be colonised. Instead it was killed, so its life could be transfused into all those toasters and deep freezes and television sets in the city, to which the battalions of pylons advance with their deadly wires; and thirty years ago, it enabled the zinc works to fume and snort all night, made those electric chimeras dance across the sky beyond the pine trees, and lit up the crackling valves of the bakelite bedside radio which brought me news from elsewhere.

Ghost Story

Before the engineers thought of diverting rivers and shearing hills, transforming a plateau into a pond and crushing boulders into roads, all civilisation could do in Tasmania was stay indoors and look through its windows at an arboreal screen representing England. To protect their fiction of rural gentility, the colonists transplanted the landscape they had left. Along the Derwent, banks of willows attempted a facsimile of the Thames. The peeling, bedraggled local trees suffered social exclusion: there's a field outside Ouse in which haughty poplars join ranks on three sides against a single unkempt, stringy eucalypt. Oaks were honoured as imperial ambassadors, leafy flagpoles for a remote home. At Lilydale Falls, acorns despatched from Windsor were ceremoniously planted on Coronation Day in 1936. Tasmania still quotes from this distant, indistinct prototype. In the midlands, Georgian country houses shimmer through incongruous dusty heat, and little girls with riding hats and jodhpurs trot their ponies past the red-whiskered mountain men who are mending the road.

But once the view from the landowner's window stops, the truth of the country reasserts itself – dry and windy plains like a desert of spiky grasses, hilltops turned into dunes by the glare; and to confound the oaks with their umbrellas of shade, the presences which dominate everywhere are dead gums, twisted in arthritic agonies but unbowed. Travelling round Tasmania, I came to remember individual specimens as vividly as if they were human casualties I had met. At Jericho in the midlands one of these wooden stoics shared a paddock with a grazing superannuated horse. The tree's head had been sawn off, but its writhing withered limbs were flung wide to mime pain; fire had seared its trunk. Behind it, other dead trees displayed their splintery twigs in outline, like an overloaded nervous system laid bare and registering distress in every ganglion. Close by, a living gum grew so crookedly that it seemed to be kneeling, or to be crippled by some rheumatic ailment. Outside Buckland, on the way to the east coast, I passed another maimed gum which returned to haunt me. It had been tortured into asymmetry: one black arm was lopped off before the crook, and held out its wound as aggressively as a mendicant; the other flailed the air. The bark, scrofulous, dangled from its skeleton in strips. Past Mount Arrowsmith in the west, summits of burned celery pine twisted and twirled above the green myrtles like gaunt paraplegic ballerinas. What pain could those figures be semaphoring? They are ghouls explicable only by a religion prolific in prowling spirits; and the settlers hastened to replace them with more sociable English species, which spread through space as if graciously creating rooms beneath their branches.

The stark, gesticulating trees stand in for vanished populations – the settlers with their failed pastoral dreams and their decorous wistful head-stones, the convicts in their anonymous dumping-ground on the Isle of the Dead off Port Arthur, the aborigines with their drifting diffused ashes. Tasmania is funereal. There are so few people to go around that you're left with the sense of an abiding emptiness, an open space marked only by wracked trees. Thomas Wood, passing through in the early 1930s, applied the customary British metaphor but noticed how Tasmania had hollowed the original by depopulating it – 'the island is as big as Scotland: all the people in it are fewer than those in Aberdeenshire.' Everywhere in Tasmania, with cicadas drilling the bright air and wind punishing the joints of bony timber, I found myself looking for the human beings who had unaccountably quit the scene.

It is a countryside of ghost towns and graveyards. In the west are the remnants of its infant El Dorados – Adamsfield, once an osmiridium mine, whose collapsing shacks are wallpapered with the yellowing news of 1925; Linda, across Cemetery Creek outside Queenstown, where all that's left is the Royal Hotel, a roofless box of grey dust; or Zeehan, with a rusted cannon parked in a field of daisies outside the cream and blue-trimmed hut of the Returned Servicemen's League, its metal drooping with fatigue and rot. The chimneys of the Magistrates' Court here serve as flower pots for weeds, and the Gaiety Theatre has outlived its name: in its front window a hairdresser advertises the fluffed-up glamour of a generation ago, and a craft shop sells knitted kangaroos. A row of crimson bucket chairs is positioned in the art gallery for observation of some local landscapes, but no one sits there. Campbell Town in the midlands is bisected by my main road, on its way from Hobart to Launceston. On one side is a homestead general store with a display of bristly brooms, on the other the white, extraneously Aztec pile of the town hall. No one ventures across. It's as if the town had been split down the middle and its twin halves parted by a crevasse. Even Hobart can seem suddenly drained, bereft. Long before sundown in the summer, its streets tip to the water in dreary, downcast solitude. All the cheerful commodities in the shop windows have gussied themselves up in vain, since no passer-by comes to covet them. When there's nobody to share the world with you, you begin to doubt whether it exists at all – or whether you do. Trudging those melancholy pavements, I often thought of myself as ectoplasm.

Perhaps I was tracking my own unreconciled, unquiet ghost, the spirit which had chosen to return here to do its dreaming and now dragged the body along behind it. Once you look back to inspect your own past, you see with a shock how much there is of it; the exercise is a study of your own mortality. Wandering through the state, I became a connoisseur of graveyards. They were the places, in this landscape without figures, where I felt closest to the people I would like to call my compatriots. I was moved always by their resignation in consenting to die here. Their monuments were so meagre, as circumscribed as their lives had been on this little island; their tombs lay there at the mercy of a nature they had trusted. The cemetery at Strahan, the only town on the west coast, is a chance get-together of fence-post crosses and marble urns. One or two mournful angels contemplate jam jars of stagnant water, or plastic posies looped with ribbon. Ferns and brambles twine over the rubbly beds. On its bluff, the burial plot hovers undecided between the abiding mountains and the amnesiac sea. At Richmond, on a knoll of dried grass behind the Catholic church, the dead are more restive. Have they got up to go on walkabout? Chipped, tilted stones are rolled away from the graves as if the rumbling and tossing beneath had made the hill quake. A tarpaulin held down by ancient bricks is an emergency shroud. Behind them in the porch of the church they have left an icon of local agony: a rough hand-carved crucifix warped like those pained trees in the paddocks. Christ's rib-cage has caved in, his stomach is slit, a nail has jarred through his feet; his mouth turns down bitterly at the corners. The carver was killed in the 1967 bushfire.

Other memorials summarise, too tersely, stories of desperate heroism. At Bicheno on the east coast there's the grave of an aboriginal woman, Wauba Debar. She died in 1882, aged forty; the tablet was erected, as it says in self-congratulation, 'by some of her white friends'. She drowned while rescuing two of the sealers who captured and enslaved her people. One was her *de facto* husband. Rewarded for her racial treason, she reposes in front of the frothing bay, where waves of molten lead lurch on stormy evenings. Further inland, in a ragged family plot, is an unsung victim from the other side of those battles: John Allen, an English settler, born in 1804, who died here in 1826, fighting off a tribe of aborigines single-handed. What remains of her is an abject, sacrificial love, which its objects could never have deserved. Was hers an act of forgiveness, or of pathetic demoralisation? What remains of him is a schoolboy's extravagant valour, powerless in this wild place. Where now there are holiday bungalows with barbecues in their concrete gardens, ordinary people behaved with self-denying charity like Wauba Debar or reckless courage like John Allen. But their martyrdoms didn't secure a society. Above the town, from a salmon and purple lookout rock greened with lichen, you can see how signless the land remains. The scrub is briefly scribbled on by sandy streets and parking lots for a population which hurries off once the sun goes in. Everyone who ever lived here bequeathed a death, like the aboriginal woman and the English boy, to tether the settlement in earth and raise a stockade against the bush; so far, there haven't been enough deaths.

In any case, this tough and taciturn landscape, inured, can absorb an endless succession of them. At Wybalenna on Flinders Island are the graves of a hundred aborigines, who sickened and pined here between 1833 and 1847. Rounded up on the Tasmanian mainland, they were brought to this marshy cove to be retrained as medieval peasants, catching and curing mutton birds and selling wallaby skins at a weekly market. Despite the routine of catechism and lessons in embroidery, they couldn't abridge the centuries. They made common cause with their warders' dogs, and defied Christianity with their body paint and their corroborees. Their compound of wattle and daub huts was soon an insanitary slum. Their most enduring legacy from the Europeans was the diseases the missionaries and convicts transmitted: catarrh, influenza, tuberculosis. When they died off, there was no thought of requiem. The chapel was commandeered as a shearing shed and re-roofed with corrugated iron. Restoring the site in the 1970s, archaeologists dug up a treasury of relics outside – networks of terraced floors, pots, shell ornaments and particles of beaded glass. A layer of hard quartz gravel was promptly spread across the uncovered area, reburying history. Now the walled white cairns are fenced off inside a paddock; cows manure the grave-sites and wallabies bounce across the grass. The land finds forgetfulness easy.

Another community is interred at Jericho, in dehydrated grass off the highway through the midlands. Two spires protrude in the yellow valley – the church and the village hall. Both are locked, and the keys might have been thrown away. Merry-makers had scratched their names from the inside on the painted glass of the hall windows; through the slits I could see a chandelier of crêpe paper streamers and a discoloured portrait of some municipal elder on the wall. The open porch was floored with blown pine needles and painted with bird droppings. Behind the hall a lavatory, its door ajar, had been occupied by cobwebs. They spanned its entire width in a cat's cradle of white sticky thread. A wet tangled toilet roll unravelled in the wind; the pan housed a colony of ants. From the inspection of an ancestral earth closet, I moved on to grave-robbery: any dirt is fertile for the grubbing memory. The graveyard was filled with pious Victorians called Uriah and Horace, Louisa or Jessie or Elvina or Christiana. The name of one of them, born in Shropshire to die in Hobart in 1874, was printed across her tomb in letters of grey alloy, plugged into the stone by little prongs. Over a century, the alloy had shrunk and softened, and the letters tumbled from the pin-holes where they were fixed. They lay about on the pebbly counterpane, a scrabbled alphabet to be re-assembled into words at the last judgement. The woman's middle name could still be deciphered from the outlined plugs, though only the initial letter remained in place: it silently mouthed the word

E

I gathered up a handful of the scattered capitals, and took them away with me. They were asking to be souvenired, for what they plaintively spelled out (in translation) was the request the dead make to the living: 'Remember my name'.

Among the weeds in a corner I found a more rhetorically morbid trophy. Two pieces of tin – guttering from a roof, their paint flaking and rusted – had been wired together and then nailed to make a cruciform marker. On the cross-bar, the word 'RESERVED' was legible still; underneath on the upright strip behind the twine of barbed wire was the terse supplement 'PAID'. Was it the receipt for a purchased rectangle here, or a portable allegory of the debt we owe and the promptness with which it comes due? I left it lying in the thistles, ready to remonstrate with the next quester to pass this way.

Jericho's citizens are its dead. In Hobart too, the dead don't disappear; they move aside, but continue to oversee the activities of the living. Small towns have long memories, and the place a person vacates isn't soon filled up. St David's Park in the middle of the city was the early colony's cemetery. The more officious tombs still flatter their tenants on pedestals among the flower beds, and shade the picnicking office workers at lunch time; headstones uprooted when the lawns were planted are cemented along walls at the side of the park: the past constructs a boundary fence. Since then, the dead have gone to live in clubbable retirement at Cornelian Bay, on a shingly headland above the river.

Cornelian Bay was one of the fabled vanishing points of my childhood world. The language of self-contained Hobart had geographical euphemisms for every excursion beyond its pale – Bermuda Triangles yawning just outside the boundary of the familiar and the conventional. 'To go to New Norfolk' was one of these. It meant, I knew, to go a bit funny; to lose your reason. The asylum was up the river in New Norfolk, behind an unscaleable wailing wall. On Sunday drives, the gentler loonies could be seen roaming the lanes – elderly women with ponderous floppy bows in their frizzled hair, young men dreamily babbling. My mother, exasperated, would tell me I'd soon have her in New Norfolk, 'what with all my worrying', or prophesy that I would end there myself if I went on reading books. Then there was an obscurer rite of passage, 'to go to Melbourne'. I later discovered that the purpose of this trip over the edge of the known world was abortion, not tourism; the local doctors either wouldn't oblige or couldn't be trusted.

About 'to go to Cornelian Bay' there was no secret. It meant to pass over, or rather to move house. When referring to a dead person, you'd say, 'Grandma's in Cornelian Bay.' Since as you got older everyone you knew transferred there, people came to think of it as a Hobart of the fourth dimension, even quieter and better tended than its above-ground model; and they visited it so often that they knew its ground plan by heart. I've more than once heard my parents establish a date by consulting their mental atlas of the place: Aunt Sadie must have gone to Cornelian Bay in 1957 not 1958, because it was definitely 1959 when Tommy Baxter followed; he's four blocks away from her, and it couldn't have taken less than two years to fill in the area between with bodies. The order of arrival in the earth is the most reliable chronology of all. People like the spatial coincidences Cornelian Bay arranges. One of my parents' friends, a widower, dwells contentedly on the fact that his spouse and one of his army mates are just round the corner from each other there. Though they didn't know each other when alive, it's as if he's generously encouraging them to get acquainted now. Its progressive urbanisation is a matter for civic pride. 'Cornelian Bay's full up now,' my mother remarked one day when I was back. Like a sold-out theatre, it was a pleasant thought to her. The dead had their convocation there, and would always be at home when you went to call.

These were, still, the sentiments of a pioneer. In communities which drive sticks into the resistant ground on the edge of nowhere, the graveyard is a guarantee of continuity, in which everyone has an investment. It vouches for history by assuring us that we have predecessors. This was the lesson of my cemetery-mongering, or my digressions in those defunct towns: Tasmania records the wishful abracadabra by which human beings establish themselves in the unknown, and draw a circle round their small citadels; but it acknowledges as well how momentary are the settlements they consecrate. Its shabby ruins are more distressing than immemorially mouldering castles, because they grieve over deaths which happened yesterday. And those shrieking trees remain to frighten off other foolhardy invaders.

My own childhood, I realised, had been emotionally that of a pioneer. At Narryna, the folk museum on Battery Point, among the wax Victorian spinsters at their arrested looms and the silver haloes of daguerrotyped faces fading on the glass, there's a hand bell used in the early colony at nightfall to call back children who might have wandered away to lose themselves in the bush. I could have done with one of those myself, to summon the troops of objects I secreted as hostages in our backyard every evening – a balding tennis ball and an eye hospital of bloodshot marbles, a motorcade of Dinky toys and a service station my father had carpentered from masonite for me, some plastic Anzacs who came inside cornflake packets and a dog (soon to die of distemper) which howled in a box next to the chicken coop. They were all placed at risk when dark overtook them. I invented extensions to the Lord's Prayer to seek protection for them, along with the blessings I'd been taught to request for my parents, though I always worried that I hadn't listed every item which needed a guardian angel. As I lay in bed listening to the rain on the roof, I wondered how many of them would still be there in the morning. My first routine of the day was to call the roll and check whether they had survived.

Outside were the atavistic terrors of the bush, even though the trees had been sliced down when our suburb was designed. The shaggy mountains maintained their barrage; on the vacant lots the earth split open in summer; the mud flats stalely sweated. There were tribal feuds over back fences between the families assigned to these weatherboard oblongs. The Fuchses threw stones on the Goldings' roof; Mrs McGuire (known on the block as Patsy Fart-Tail) hollered abuse at Mrs Atkins. When in the late 1950s teenagers were invented, gangs of them roamed the streets, war-whooping. Our games of cowboys and Indians didn't require all that much imagination: with its perilous open spaces – the racetrack and the showground, the rifle range and the paddock between my school and the factories – this was an undefended frontier. Once the lavatories moved inside, my friends next door annexed the outdoor privy, installed a seat ripped from a wrecked car, and called it The Fort. The loss of life during one siege was enormous. We even had our own ghost town across the street. Three times during my childhood I was hauled from bed to watch neighbouring houses burn down, while sparks showered over us and people screamed. The blackened rafters remained standing for years before the houses were rebuilt. Those stumps, with their searing persistent smell of timber grilled to carbon, were my first emblems of temporariness.

Wauba Debar, John Allen, the Eliza whose name I put in my

pocket at Jericho, the old woman in the house opposite ours killed when she tried to drag a grandchild from the fire – they all donated deaths so this tenuous epilogue to the world could seem real, could have a history. My ambition was the opposite one: to save my life by cancelling that reality; to replace the world with words describing it. The colonists retired behind a false front of elms and oaks. My family could afford no such protective avenue. But after a while I found the windbreak of English literature, and pieced together my own unassailable fort of paper.

The Van Demonians

My ignorance of Tasmania was itself a Tasmanian trait. What little history it had amassed by the middle of the nineteenth century, the colony made haste to forget. When transportation ended, the Van Demonians or Demons – as they were known on the mainland, where their turpitude was proverbial – legislated a new name for their tainted island. Port Arthur also adopted an alias: from now on, it wished to be known as Carnarvon, and officially posed as a replica of coastal Wales; a scene of Celtic fancy not Gothic misery. Cattle grazed where the barracks had been. Towards the end of the century, arson beautified it. A fire gutted the penitentiary, and left behind a husk of orange stone and yellow clayey brick among emerald lawns and avenues of oak and maple. The prison commandant's cottage became a hotel, and in the 1890s a guest who couldn't pay his bill painted the verandah and the outside walls with other elegiac architectural illusions – the Parthenon, the basilica at Constantinople, a purple Venetian column with a wreathed vegetative capital; in this company, Port Arthur qualified as a romantic ruin.

Since then, its history has been rearranged as a mildly spooky, salacious entertainment. At Copping, on the way to the Tasman Peninsula, there's a museum of convictry advertised by a sign which up-ends the ball and chain so it resembles a balloon taking off: the crippling, humbling weight which tugged the inmates to the ground is now inflatable and lighter than air. Outside the breeze-block shack which houses the museum, a dummy in a wiry wig and a convict's black and yellow uniform dangles from the jokey gallows of a gum tree and flaps in the wind. Tasmania lamely pays homage to Disneyland and its gleefully rapacious Pirates of the Caribbean. You can now take a tour of Port Arthur under the guidance – on audio cassette – of one of its inmates, Frank McNamara, known as Frank the Poet, a scurrilous balladeer transported from Kilkenny in 1832 for stealing a scarf. 'Experience the horror,' says the brochure invitingly; listen to the blarney Frank retails 'in his romantic Irish accent'; hear the dramatisation of a flogging, then rewind the tape at leisure and hear it again. Frank quit Van Diemen's Land with a curse, defining it as 'Prisoner's Hell! Land of Buggers!' Now he's back serving a repetitious sentence on those cassettes.

He is not the only convict posthumously maligned by the tourist industry. In the old gaol at Richmond, one of his colleagues in crime is incarcerated in a glass case wearing the regulation jacket of coarse felt. Yet to model his costume the designers of the exhibition have chosen a female shop-window mannequin from the 1930s, with a chiselled art deco nose, sensually narrowed blue eyes, a kissy rouged mouth and a pink pancaked complexion instead of the creased, pain-carved flesh you imagine. This male impersonator, playing at being a convict, wears the grey cap as nattily as if it were a chic bonnet. The comments in the visitors' book at the gaol compliment the triumphant fiction – 'interesting', 'different' and (best of all) 'unreal!' have been scrawled here, and someone who claims to come from the RRR ranch in Texas has boomingly inscribed his own gigantic adjective, 'great'.

The past palliated here was less a legal system than an institution-alised nightmare. To be a convict was to experience your own death. The most terrifying relics of the regime in Tasmania are the habitable coffins in which victims were locked for their journey outside life. In the museum at Hobart, there's a ducking-box which was suspended from the yard-arm of ships during the voyage out. Refractory prisoners, padlocked inside it, were submerged when the ship keeled. The crate is an upright watery grave, from within which the victims were expected to resurrect themselves. At the Saltwater River coal mines on the peninsula, the catacombed cells are sensory deprivation chambers: you stumble in, look back and see a glimmer in the tunnel but nothing in front of you; you have fallen into a pit, a blinded underworld. Outside, you can walk across the top of the tombs. The vault is carpeted with dried droppings. 'The possums must have been having a party,' a mother explains to her inquisitive child. At the Richmond gaol, buying your ticket of admission in the turnkey's den, you're directed, as if undergoing induction yourself, to 'stand in the men's solitary confinement cells to the left'. These measure seven feet by three, roughly the size of cramped lavatory cubicles. With all exterior light sealed off, they were rational, economical devices for obliterating the reason. Marcus Clarke calculated that in average cases they could reduce a sane man to dementia within twelve months.

Tasmania itself was just such a receptacle, a theatre where reality changed to an inescapable bad dream. The colony might have been designed according to the literary principles of the Gothic, which like the black boxes at Richmond transforms the world into a deranged fantasy. Five years before the first settlement at Risdon, Jane Austen wrote her Gothic novel *Northanger Abbey*. In it, Catherine tries to calm her excitable imagination by remembering that she is in the midland counties of England, where there can be no fiends or ogres. The Gothic is sent into exile, beyond the Alps and the Pyrenees; its abominations belong, Catherine believes, to Italy, Switzerland and the south of France. She couldn't have known that the Gothic monsters she had conjured up had been extradited to the antipodes.

Marcus Clarke understood Tasmania as a product of this imagination at its most freakish. *For the Term of His Natural Life* places it on Jane Austen's map of the Gothic, over the border of rationality: the palisaded fort of Sarah Island is 'set . . . at the very extreme of civilisation'. Shakespeare's John of Gaunt believes that England is a fortress built by nature for itself, protecting the precious Eden inside a moat. A more devious and malicious nature creates Tasmania as a geographical prison. Lieutenant Governor Arthur described the peninsula as 'a natural penitentiary' at the very moment – Port Arthur was settled in 1830 – when romanticism was allying nature with instinctual freedom; the station was evidence for a Manichee's world-view. Mr Pounce in Clarke's novel elaborates on the devil's providential foresight in Tasmania: 'This island seems specially adapted by Providence for a convict settlement; for with an admirable climate, it carries little indigenous vegetation which will support human life.' The only way convicts who fled overland from Macquarie Harbour could support human life was by eating each other. Clarke describes the infamies of drunken, profligate Hobart as the inventions of feverish imagination: 'all that the vilest and most bestial of human creatures could invent and practise, was in this unhappy country invented and practised without restraint and without shame.' For the heroine Sylvia, the southern hemisphere is a psychic basement where an upside-down consciousness participates in weird nocturnal revels: trying to recall her experiences at the convict's mercy outside Macquarie Harbour, she says 'it seems to me that I am double, that I have lived somewhere before, and have had another life – a dream-life . . . I dream such strange things . . . I am always falling down precipices and into cataracts, and being pushed into caverns in enormous rocks. Horrible dreams!' Those mental abysses are Tasmanian topography – the gaping orifices of the peninsula, or the blow-hole where Clarke places the climax of the novel. When Frere assures her that John Rex's narrative is a fiction, she says it *must* be true, like Dickens validating his own Gothic traumas by declaring in capitals that they are TRUE.

But the truths are the premonitory ones of dream, or the dangerously wishful ones of art. Clarke is himself a partner in the abuses he decries. The novelist runs his plot like a prison, manacling his characters to its coincidences; he creates people in order to confine and torment them. As he invents and practises it, the novel is a species of sadism perfectly adapted to the 'unhappy country' where it is set.

Clarke published his book in 1874; in 1927 it was made into a silent film, in which the Gothic depravities are the more alarming because they happen against the background of an actual, daylit Tasmania. John Rex makes his getaway through the craggy silhouetted Tasmania of Remarkable Cave. The convicts push logs through swamps of the Gordon River, swarming in its thick current like the uniformed leeches. 'This horrible thing must be a dream,' insists a title card as one of the escaped felons falls asleep and the cannibal Gabbett, on the edge of a cliff looking over into the valley of the shadow, advances to kill him – but it's not, because we're awake witnessing it. The vampirish transformation which overtakes the landscape occurs to Clarke's characters as well. Like Dr Jekyll, they regress to beasts as we watch. Sarah, with pursed mouth and flailing fists, turns rabid and vixenish, while Gabbett the slavering wolf-man grows sharpened fangs. With his 'devilish scheme', as another card calls it, to eat his fellows, he's almost kin to the snarling carnivore which is Tasmania's talismanic beast. The jerky motions of silent cinema afflict the actors with expressionistic fidgets. Dawes twitches epileptically on his bunk; the convicts troop on board the ship leaving Macquarie Harbour for Port Arthur with shuffling steps like the automated corpses who man Fritz Lang's metropolis. When the prisoners draw lots to kill each other, one of them asks Rufus if he thinks there's a heaven. 'I know there is a hell,' he replies. Clarke's inferno has been brought bizarrely up to date by the film's manic visual style: the cells at Port Arthur are here the cabinets of some imperially vindictive Dr Caligari.

The remnants of convictry look like props for a theatre of pain, appurtenances of an obscene, compulsive fantasy. At the Richmond gaol, chains and padlocks are still nailed into the timber walls, and trail along the floor as if for tying up dogs. Outside in a yard three poles are strapped together at the top like the struts of a tent: this was the flogging frame. There's a trough in a corner, and high walls all around; at the bottom of a well, you're mocked by the free sky. The system of graduated punishments repleted the entire space of society, and created a new iconography of entrapment. Richmond possesses an armoury of gadgets to furnish a sadist's back-room: gimlets, handcuffs, fire tongs, obsessively various arrays of locks and keys.

There are nightmares in which you're persecuted by a bombard-ment of outsize, inimical objects; in others, you are dragged down by some exhausting weight which crushes your volition. The technol-ogy of convictry made both these bad dreams true. The symbols of oppression, exuding authority, swell to super-real dimensions. In the museum at Hobart, there's a door lock with a brass knob from the Port Arthur penitentiary which is the size of a suitcase, and a key almost a foot long. A rusted pit saw on show at Richmond measures six feet in length, and has the profile of a laughing shark. In the same way, these torturing things, dead masses of stupid power, grow preposterously heavy and pendulous. A punishment fork with thick blunt teeth in the museum at Launceston weighs fifteen pounds. Punishment irons, used on board ship, are so strong they have dented and scratched the paint of the case they're displayed in. The world had been onerously, tediously ritualised. To be in prison is to serve time. At Port Arthur, the metaphor was taken literally. A tell-tale clock was designed which made both guards and convicts its slaves. The mechanism is worked by pegs next to the hour hand; warders had to pull a knob to keep it going every fifteen minutes. It guarded the guards, spying on their attentiveness over shifts of twelve hours and reporting on them if they nodded off. It also institutionalised the most wearisome and maddening aspect of those judicial terms: duration itself was the punishment.

Most designed environments are utopian. Architects like Le Corbusier imagined their clients occupying sun-drenched modules in radiant cities, bathing in pristine hygienic tanks, maintaining their stream-lined figures by eating modern meals off modern plates with lean modern cutlery. The convicts also inhabited a designed environment, but a dystopian one. Every item in it had been purposely conceived to cause them discomfort. Their pillows, for instance, were blocks of wood: you can see one in the museum at Hobart, worn down despite its hardness by the heads of the exhausted women who used it. The designer has imprinted his trade mark on everything: it is the government's arrow,

like the tread of a bird in wet sand. This is the most wounding aesthetic pedantry of all. The central ring of those punishment irons, the one which grips the chain, has been branded with the little signature, certifying that it's government property – just in case someone clamped into it had the notion of keeping it as a souvenir. The iron bit of a gag for violent prisoners, attached to the head by leather straps, has breathing holes which make it look like a black suffocating flute for screaming into, and the same bureaucratic, branding arrows.

Grisliest of these contraptions is an iron mask made from flimsy cloth, which hangs in the Hobart museum. It is a cowl worn by prisoners in solitary confinement when attending chapel at the Port Arthur model prison. The fabric is stained – with what? sweat? tears? Like a tea cosy, it has a toggle at the top where it's held when being dropped over the cancelled head. There are black dots to allow the eyes a peep-hole, and stitching down the centre of the temple and across the eyebrows; the cowl has been pulled out along these threaded lines, so in silhouette there does seem to be a stifled, flattened face behind. It resembles one of the proud, hieratic tribal masks of African folklore, except that there the wearer is ennobled, rendered impersonal and impervious, whereas here the person has been simply erased or – as the blanched white cloth suggests – relegated to membership of the dead.

The totalitarian prison had its start in a marshy inlet at Risdon, across the river from my parents' house. I always liked the view from over there: the barbered earth of the rifle range, and across the bay the zinc works dustily merging with its hill; under the grass, the rubble of that first settlement. Now the foundations have been dug up, and the huts reconstructed. A diorama represents Risdon in 1803 as a waste of papier-mâché streaked and dribbled with yellow, olive and khaki paint. Lumps of hardened foam are its spongy trees, impaled on pins. It is populated by toys – convicts like yellow stick insects, officers saluting, and a war party of aborigines gathering to attack. From the ridge, the view looks now towards what the locals know as the pink palace: a wedding cake iced in cochineal and decorated with electric pylons. This is Her Majesty's Prison. The colony which began as a gaol has thoughtfully situated its only prison here beside its birthplace.

The gaol at Risdon has the reputation of being the toughest in Australia. In proportion to population, there are more violent crimes in Tasmania than in any other state (and more fatal road accidents too). The state's one gaol is a maximum security prison: it contains, an officer at Risdon said to me, 'the worst collection of mongrels in the country'. The convicts were transported for petty offences, like Frank the Poet's theft of a scarf. Since then, Tasmania has bred more audaciously inventive criminals of its own: among the current internees are a man who fed his wife into the mincer, after perfecting his technique on a side of lamb; a doctor who asphyxiated his mistress while she fellated him, positioning his thumbs on her carotid arteries; a student, recently graduated from the university with a degree in Information Science, who became upset by his girlfriend's liaison with someone else and, depilating his face first, dressed himself up as a woman, adopted the name of Linda, called on his rival, vamped seductively about the room, and then – when the rival responded – defended his own feminine virtue by stabbing his attacker full of holes, only to tell the police when he was arrested that Linda did it.

In a small community, everyone owns the crime, because in some way or another each person is coincidentally implicated. The kinky doctor, for instance, had given some physiotherapy to an aunt of mine, most of whose maladies had to do with the sherry bottle. My uncle marvelled at the man's dexterity: 'he twisted her neck round so far she could see the seams in her stockings.' The night I arrived in Tasmania, someone was slashed to death with a Bowie knife in the centre of Hobart. The moment his name appeared in the paper – together with the information that he hailed from the Lachlan, an unregenerate valley behind New Norfolk – the hunt was on around our house to establish a connection. A sleuthing neighbour reported in frustration a few days later: 'I asked the barmaid up the local if she knew him. She's from the Lachlan, but she's never heard of him.' My father commented with his usual acuteness 'She might know his dog.'

Perhaps Tasmania, imprisoned on its island and depressed by a past which there is no room to outgrow, remains the Alcatraz intended by its founders. My time there wouldn't be complete, I thought, without the experience of incarceration, so one night I went to the beige pen at Risdon for a debate. The prisoners have a debating society which is allowed to be self-governing. It's called The Spartans, and its impedimenta are ferociously true to the phalanx of warriors. On its shield, naked gladiators strain in battle; its emblem is crossed swords, riveted together by a barbed swastika-like S. A pledge of obedience is solemnly intoned before the meetings begin, in which the members vow that 'we should not remain silent when we ought to speak.' The pious sentiment functions as an alibi. The purpose actually, as on the shield, is man-to-man combat. The prisoners join so they can learn to argue better on their own behalf in court, and they debate as if their lives depended on it, and as if they'll be satisfied only by the annihilation of their opponents. Their third speaker, shuffling his notes like cards in a poker game, suddenly rounded on our first and, to disprove some argument he'd advanced, aimed a finger and roared 'How would you feel if I stood here with a shot gun and blew your head off?' He almost managed to do so without the gun, by blasting ballistic eloquence. One of my team-mates leaned towards me and whispered 'That's what he's in for.' He was a messy, incautious hit-man who got drunk in the pub with some floosies after doing the job, and gave himself away by sounding off. There was another murderer on his team; the chairman, Rocky Devine, was described to me in advance as 'a medium-sized crim – burgs, nothing really nasty', and resembled Sylvester Stallone playing a Spartan: nipples like spikes under his gladiatorial T-shirt, biceps like Australian Rules footballs, and tattoos on every inch of belligerent flesh. I spent most of the time reading the notes scribbled during previous debates on the society's thinning white tablecloth. Unsurprisingly, the home team trounced us three weak-kneed civilians.

The debating chamber appears to be a room but is actually a cage, roofed with wire; onto this trellis, while we were being bludgeoned with words, a blue finch suddenly hopped and perched, looking down at the proceedings from a pipe. Sometimes life has no shame in its mimicry of art. Afterwards, there's a supper of tea in tin mugs and Spam sandwiches; a warder comes round and demands 'Anyone for medication?', with a tray of bromides on offer. I asked a shy cross-eyed ginger-haired youth – who turned out to be Linda's impersonator – how much longer he was in for. He told me the exact number of days: several thousand in all. Time remains the medium of punishment; you can hear the pendulum ponderously swinging through the air. As we left, before all the doors clanked shut behind us, one of the murderers, magnanimous in victory, thumped me on the back and said 'Come and see me next time you're in Tassie, Pete. I'll still be 'ere, I reckon.' Remember my name.

The problem indeed is our forgetfulness. Tasmania has unwritten its own history. Citizens who had made good vandalised the state archives to eliminate the record of their convict ancestry. A self-protective incuriosity about origins is an instinct bred into you: I knew nothing about my father's family or my mother's further back than the generation of my grandparents. In neither case was there a convict strain to conceal; it was simply a matter of agreeing not to remember things which were painful – the death of my mother's mother after stocking the farm with cheap labour, the drunken misery and death of my father's father who left his wife, in the backward Lachlan Valley, to bring up ten surviving children (one, who was found dead in bed as an infant, having been buried on the same day the next one was born). A convenient amnesia overtakes Sylvia in *For the Term of His Natural Life* after her ordeal in the wilderness: 'Nature', as a title card in the film puts it, 'maliciously withheld from her all memory of the past,' and at John Rex's trial, as Rufus testifies, 'Intuition of some great injustice struggled vainly to piece together the scattered memories of the past.' Nature was acting benignly not maliciously in blotting out her experience; but a past which isn't acknowledged can't be overcome. She was the first to suffer from this Tasmanian ailment, and she transmitted it in due course to me.

'Last of the Tasmanians'

Sylvia's merciful memory loss was extended in time to obliterate another cause of remorse: the aborigines, the first Tasmanians or, as they knew themselves, the Parlevars; a race isolated from all contact with other people for twelve thousand years after the flooding of the plain which is now Bass Strait. Hunted and harassed by soldiers and white settlers, they were at last rounded up by missionaries and sent to die of deracination at Wybalenna or at Oyster Cove on the D'Entrecasteaux Channel. At school, we were assured they were extinct.

The bones of Trucanini, alleged to be the last of them, were in the basement at the museum; I always confused her with the musty Ptolemaic mummy on show under the stairs. But the mummy's flesh had at least been preserved beneath those tight, swaddling cerements. Trucanini's corpse, on the contrary, was vandalised in 1876. The coffin meant to contain her processed through the streets with nothing inside it. Her body, meanwhile, was hastily stowed in a chapel at the gaol. Two years later, she was exhumed, flayed, and the bones boxed for consignment to the museum. The last male of her race, William Lanne or King Billy, was carved up in 1869 in a competition between the Tasmanian Royal Society and the Royal College of Surgeons in London. The scientists of the Royal Society coveted the skeleton as a curio; but before they could take possession, their rivals kidnapped the remains, skinned the skull and abducted it, placing someone else's head under the flap of scalp and pulling the face back over it as a mask. To spoil the College's coup, the vindictive local researchers sawed off King Billy's hands and feet, and kept these for themselves. Here was Tasmania at its most Gothic and ghoulish. That early romantic hero Victor Frankenstein disturbed graves and butchered their sleepers so he could usurp his creator and weld the bits into the semblance of new life. The learned doctors of the colony parodied his art. They vivisected the dead as a last triumphant demonstration that they had never considered these people living beings: they were at best an ethnographer's specimens, incapable of feeling pain. And the maimed rites issued a warning about the future. If history is the honouring of the dead, this mutilation of cadavers signified the denial of history. A race which had already been exterminated was now to be abolished a second time, extirpated from memory.

Like the convicts, the natives survived only in misrepresentations. Though Trucanini's bones were concealed downstairs, a skeleton in the state's closet, the museum had a corner for images which, whether satirically or sentimentally, obscured our understanding of the aborigines. Benjamin Duterrau painted the evangelist George Augustus Robinson reconciling them to entrapment at Wybalenna during the 1830s. With priestly stance, Robinson grips a grey convert with one hand while raising the other in tut-tutting injunction. The as yet unredeemed natives exchange sceptical grimaces, or go on with their business of whittling or biting sticks. A woman fingers her necklace of shells, wondering perhaps if this portly white gentleman with the kangaroo hound sniffing his crotch will want her to give her jewellery up when she becomes a Christian peasant. Duterrau's naive daubs betray his own misgivings about Robinson's redemptive project. His portraits make the aborigines look moronic or at least mongoloid, with their beady, receded eyes, idiotically grinning mouths and slate-coloured pudding basins of skull. The only thought of which they're capable is murder: they brandish their javelins or, like the east coast chieftain Mannalergenna in another of Duterrau's studies, whirl their firebrands. The face and character of Woureddy, the chief from Bruny who accompanied Robinson on his mission of recruitment, are elided by a russet mop of braided hair. The same Woureddy was sentimentally ennobled by Benjamin Law in 1836. His gaze sorrowfully averted, the man in his sculpture is as distant, dignified and uncomplaining as a negroid Christ; Law's Trucanini has the same downcast eyes, refusing to look back at you and guarding her grief. The coal-black paint on Law's plaster casts isn't skin colour only, but a mourning vestment.

Every image is elegiac. The aborigines in being represented are cancelled. Once the likeness is trapped, the physical presence can be dispensed with. John Glover, the most idyllic of Tasmania's colonial artists, painted the last muster of aborigines at Risdon. Three of them crouch in a bark tent beside a fire, grinning cheesily as if at Glover, who in witnessing them is farewelling them. For Robert Dowling, who lived at Launceston later in the century, the same Risdon landscape is sombre, murky. His 'Aborigines of Tasmania' are a frieze of posed bodies with neutrally smiling, non-committal faces; some lean sagely on their staffs, others squat with their catch of food. In every sense the picture is a museum piece: its subjects, arranged for this last pictorial testament, know that from now on they'll be tolerated only as exhibits; thanks to Dowling's stuffy academicism, they are dead already.

It was in this form that I got to know them as a boy, in a waxily morbid, bleakly lit diorama at the museum. The scene was a naked nuclear family, stalled in pre-history but occupying a landscape just adjacent to my own suburban one. A sandy beach of drift wood, charcoal and shells had been unloaded on the floor for them between grassy crumbling cliffs; a painted background showed the customary view of Mount Wellington, as seen from the rear of our house. There were three figures grouped around the hearth: the father with his red-tinted braids standing guard, the mother – her flesh beautified by scars – poking the fire, and a child staring into it with his sad ancient face. It had the appalling lifelikeness of the undertaker's art. Changing the colour of the skin, I could easily alter the identities of these doomed creatures suffering the curse of inertia behind their glass: my father armed with gladstone bag and tin lunch box not a spear, brilliantined rather than ochred, returning from work in the war-like company of his mates on the back of a lorry; my mother, who instead of the regulation choker of shells had a string of inauthentic pearls, jabbing a log with our copper fire tongs while currying a rabbit or braising a steak and boiling veggies to extinction for the labouring chieftain's tea; and of course the introverted only child, probably (if it was me) asking whoever he believed had created him why he had to be a Tasmanian aborigine . . . There we were, our protective mod. cons. and our wooden shelter taken from us, exposed again to the desolate, empty land, with Mount Wellington immemorially frowning. Under the sticks, the fire around which the models huddled was an electric bulb, flickering through tinted plastic – exactly the kind of imitation hearth which now pretends to burn in suburban grates.

The diorama worried me because its waxy reality was so plausible and yet so mad. These people had taken their clothes off on the sordid foreshore at Risdon; they had gone back to nature in a place

I knew to be littered with brown shards of beer bottles, soggy newspaper and twisted plastic cartons. It looked like a crazily ultimate act of alienation.

The truth, if I had known it, was even odder. Once they were near extermination, the remaining aborigines were honoured as eminent Victorians. Trucanini made her career as a white man's doxy, offering sexual favours to the sealers in exchange for provisions; yet later in life she turned regally respectable, and there's a photograph of her at Narryna in which she looks like a whiskery glowering Queen Victoria, dressed up in a frilled-out skirt and a flowered cap. Her symbolic role as the last of her race turned out to be hereditary. Her successor was a farmer's wife from the Huon Valley called Fanny Cochrane Smith, who in 1899 and 1903 recorded for the gramophone her claim to be at the end of the line. A staunchly Methodistical matron in black bombazine, she was photographed with the members of the Royal Society, staring with reverent dread at the contraption which will immortalise her and her extinct people. Speaking into the trumpet, she gave her name, her pedigree, her birthplace on Flinders Island and declared, 'I'm the last of the Tasmanians . . . I am the last of the race of Tasmanians.' To hear her records now is like listening in at a séance, as a spirit faintly wheezes from the beyond. Through the scratching and hissing of the cylinder, her sharp shrill breaking voice sounds in a register closer to bird song than to white speech: when she sings of the spring, her ululations keen like the wind. The ghost inside the machine stumbles over the earthly language it must use: 'I'm – I'm the daughter of Tanganitara, East Coast tribe,' she says. When she adds, 'I am just seventy years of age,' there's a hint of the spirit's fecklessness in that whimsically precise 'just'. Only children who aren't yet menaced by time and undying ancients who have outlived it can afford to be quite so finicky. Then the English words, which like the medium at the séance translate from one world to another, lose their way in this crackling ether. They're replaced by a runic babble of vowels: a song, accompanied by the clapping of bodiless hands.

Fanny Cochrane temporised between two cultures. On one of her recordings she sets out to chant a Methodist hymn. After ten measured, pious bars, another religion takes over. Like Tannhäuser at the Wartburg sliding back from Christian devotion to the pagan cult of Venus, she's led astray by the irrational impulse of song. The hymn is pulled apart by wild droning native scales; when she remembers, she tries to get back on course by illogically asserting 'Praise the Lord'. As well as keeping the Sabbath, Fanny preserved her aboriginal rites, throwing ashes into the air at the change of seasons. She even devised a merger of identities when dressing herself. For a church picnic, she augmented her sober Victorian gown with pelts of kangaroo fur and shell necklets; she designed her own amateurish tiaras from feathers, gauze, flowers and lace.

Despite Fanny Cochrane's eclecticism, the cultures couldn't be reconciled, or consent to live side by side. The aborigines had implanted meaning in every physical feature of the terrain they occupied. They made its rocks and rivers the scenery for a sacred drama acted out by their begetters. When the white usurpers took possession, they erased those meanings. Now instead of mythic genealogies, there were only approximate analogies to elsewhere, a cartography of misplaced metaphors. Glenorchy, the suburb where I grew up, got its name from Governor Macquarie, who fancied that it was reminiscent of somewhere in Argyll, Scotland – a glen of gums? The name had a nostalgic ancestral relevance only for him; to all the rest of us who entered the world there, it could mean nothing. I've never heard of any sacred drama transacted on Mount Direction, or any tribal rite performed near our mud flats. There were no stories about these places. They were simply ignored by those who lived beneath or beside them. I suppose that's why I was always fond of the main road. In burying the unloved, unimagined landscape, it at least threw up a skyline of mythic presences – the bulbous muscle of the Goliath bulk cement silo, the beaming Kentucky colonel, a video store which (let down by a mis-spelling) briefly renames the main road Hollywood Boulevarde. On a hill above North Hobart, J.R.'s Used Cars evokes the fabled swindler from Dallas, while on an opposite corner the Blue Gum Service Station erects its own totem-pole: instead of the tree, in its forecourt there's a conifer-shaped structure of blue and white plastic flags. At Mount Cameron West, the aborigines left a cosmic diagram of petroglyphs in the sandstone bluffs. These whorls in rock, according to anthropologists, 'perhaps . . . tell the story of totemic ancestors or creation myths'. Totemic ancestors and creation myths are exactly what white Australia lacks. The main road supplies those archetypal parents – Colonel Sanders, J.R., Fat Albert are its male potentates, and for a maternal symbol there's Mother Hubbard, who gives her name to a store selling second-hand furniture. And in the absence of creation myths, the white man makes do with the myth of laundered self-recreation: hence the Lyke-Nu dry-cleaning shop. But significances are attached to a source in other countries, which keeps us estranged from our reality. Macquarie's reference was to Scotland, the used-car salesman's is to Texas. We remain nomads, camping provisionally in a place we haven't made our own.

Our roadside mythologies, such as they are, provoke disorientation. Those of the aborigines rooted them in the land. They derived themselves from it: a star god had fallen to earth in the south-west and there fathered the kangaroo-tailed race of Parlevars; in time he solidified into a boulder at Cox Bight. I flew over that area on the way to Port Davey. With its convulsed mountains and boisterous seas, it's a proper place to locate the beginning of the world. The aborigines were able to incorporate geological accidents into their collective family history. Maybe the petrifying star god embodied their island, stranded when the land bridge sank after the ice age. The stone was their anchorage, and they constructed the world around it. The whirling discs incised on Mount Cameron West celebrate this victory of imagination: they propose the idea of a centre, a circle within which all experience has been gathered. For us, there could be no notion of centrality. Tasmania was the Isle of Wight in exile, twelve thousand miles from London.

To the bewildered European mind, Australia seemed a region of unruly inversions, where Christmas happened in midsummer, trees held onto their leaves and shed their bark instead, and the fauna had been created by ugly miscegenation. The birds didn't sing, it was reported; they jeered in mirthless hysteria. This continent of monstrosity had, however, been rendered intelligible by the aborigines. The Parlevars systematically classified their own natural setting. Men took their lineage from the sun, women from the moon. The mutton birds were known as moon birds, and because the moon directed the tides of the female body, women – even recently on Flinders Island – were prohibited from salting the birds which the men had caught if they were menstruating. Each tribe selected a particular tree as its totem, and guarded its identity by the imposition of taboos: the choice of food – male or female kangaroos and wallabies – was a continuation of their bloodlines.

Because they were the land, they wore it. The men modelled themselves on red-topped gum saplings, and for this reason dyed their hair with ochre; the women made necklaces of kelp and cats' teeth, strung on kangaroo sinew. The cicatrices they hewed in their skin were meant to recall the dotted mystic circles at Mount Cameron West: the body was vivified stone, and could serve as a scriptural tablet. They dug their implements from the ground, carving tools from opalised wood, amber chalcedony and rainbowed spongolite.

Their mental map of the territory had a metaphysical upper tier. With more acumen than Nevil Shute's characters, they went down to the beach when sick to discover if they were going to die. Low tide signified recuperation, high tide death; if the tide was turning when you consulted it, your fate was still in the balance. Death freed a spirit, who lived near the heart; when the body was burned, this soul transferred to the northern islands. It was believed to be white, the negation of their charcoaled flesh: the arrival of white men sailing down from the north must have seemed a second coming of spectres. So, in a way, it was. The occupying army of settlers cultivated the land, but at the same time desecrated it. It became the bush, that undifferentiated jungle where the streets end. Driving through it, my mother still notes, with a pioneer's shiver of apprehension, 'There's not many homes about here.' The settler's instinct is to control the land by defacing it, like my pilot jokily recommending the use of a road-grader to subdue Mount Picton.

Against this incursion, the aborigines were helpless. Since their sagas were of dreaming not fighting, they produced no bellicose Sitting Bulls or Geronimos; they resigned themselves to their own obsolescence. The diorama in the museum catches their mood. These aren't ferocious savages, cast up on their barren stretch of sand. They look preoccupied by worries within, and don't even consolidate into a group. Pensively detached, they are preparing to make themselves invisible. For this is what they did. They weren't extinct, as we had been told; we were simply unable to see them. Even as a child, I had my doubts about a family around the corner from us. Weren't they fuzzy-wuzzies, with their crinkled hair and burnished, almost violet complexions? But no, my parents insisted they were Eyetalians – which was almost as bad, since in the 1950s a new Australian was as invidious as an ur-Australian. I didn't realise until later that Fuchs (or the Fucksies as we called them) was unlikely to be an Italian name. Ignored, the aborigines lived on under camouflage. There were probably never more than five thousand of them, and today there are almost that many in Tasmania and on the Bass Strait islands.

At last, when I was back, I met one – Ida West, a matriarch known as Auntie Ida, who has written a memoir of her childhood on Flinders Island and who helped to scatter Trucanini's ashes when those abused bones were finally cremated in 1976. She lives in a retirement village by the river past my parents' house. Next door, outside a motel, is a beached metallic arch which was Glenorchy's triumphal offering to the Queen when she visited Tasmania in 1954. It has four bow legs which straddled the route on which the Queen travelled into Hobart; gripping those limbs are discs like atomic orbitals, and on top of them is planted a tiny crown. This swaggering pin-headed spider drills its calipers into the tarmac beside Auntie Ida's unit, where the decor consists of two gilded cherubs and two tea-towels pinned to the wall, illustrated with American presidents and Australian parrots. Ida West, bright-eyed and buttoned-up in a pink housecoat, is the politely aggrieved conscience of her race. Though she admits 'we're a bit mixed up in the blood', she offers herself as evidence that 'we're still 'ere – our brains are still functioning'.

I talked to her about snakes. I'd read her book, and it seemed to be infested with them. Tasmania is an Eden where reptiles thrive, and they're all poisonous. I was always frightened of them. Every twitching or slithering in the grass made me shudder. I was sure they were all around, and yet for all my panic I never saw a snake. Ida West, however, had grown up with them, and writes of those which crept into the dug-out toilets on Flinders Island almost with affection – tiger snakes with their diamantine markings, thin cheeky copper-heads, the death-adder with its rat's tail. What could better represent the difference between the black and white understandings of Tasmania? I was terrified of something I'd never seen; she was respectfully wary of something she saw every day. Her fear was rational because superstitious, trusting in omens and instincts. 'I *was* afraid,' she said; 'that's how I learned to believe in the Lord.' Once as a girl she was about to vault a fence, then somehow couldn't do it. She drew back and went through the gate instead. As she did, she saw, just in the spot where she'd have landed if she had jumped, a pregnant female snake. Another time she was walking to a friend's house with her mother after dark, on the way to hear a serial on the wireless. Suddenly she told her mother to hop aside: 'There's an extra gum root on the road.' When they shone the torch on it, the root was wriggling. Ida is blasé about her powers of divination: 'We kind of knew how many gum roots there were on the road.' Her father taught her to study snakes, and she tracked them over sand or watched them negotiating buffalo grass, which they disliked because they couldn't cling to the leaves. She has her lore for fending them off: you must run away in a wiggly line, since as they travel so fast it's essential to confuse them; you can lure them out of the house by putting down a saucer of milk; and if all else fails, you should hypnotise them into submission, staring them out – 'I've done it,' she assured me.

In an emergency, they can be killed. But it must be done correctly. She remembers with shame a childhood episode when another pregnant snake turned on her and some friends. They bludgeoned it with a stone, and the unborn rabble in its belly spilled out in a puddle of slime. Her father rebuked her for being so cruel. He and his colleagues, she says, 'were real hunters', but they always observed the deathly protocols: a wallaby's neck had to be broken, a crayfish must be dunked in boiling water; when there were kangaroos to be slaughtered, Ida's job was to pull the joeys out of the pouch and 'brain 'em on me boots'. There was a clement etiquette in these matters. 'That was our orders,' she says: 'sudden death.'

I thought, by way of contrast, about the rabbit-murdering sprees of an uncle of mine, who lives with his ferrets just across the river from Ida West. He had been a champion wood-chopper, slicing trees for sport; in later life, he shifted his motiveless rage to rabbits. Now he plots ingenious ways to massacre them. He paralyses dozens at a time in the beams of his car at night in the bush, then guns them down at leisure. He digs trenches and lays out poisoned feasts for them. He's expert at sneaking up from down wind, and once caught a pair copulating in his rifle sights. He picked them off with two shots, counting on their preoccupation. He hunts them to their burrows and inserts an evil twine of wire which he can twiddle underground until it catches on their fur; then he hauls them up like hooked fish. Outside in the backyard, the ferrets sniff in their cages: mustard-coloured pipe-length rats, like extensions of a gnawing snout. The aborigine kills a fellow-creature as a necessity; and because to do so is a religious transaction, he performs the execution sacrificially. The white man, with no such moral delicacy, kills to prosecute a war of wills against the country, whose recalcitrance goads him to this show of armed strength.

Ida West had none of the aboriginal trinkets and charms I expected. There were only the cherubs and the decorative tea-towels. But she conserved a tribal mind, an ancient way of seeing and categorising things; and I found myself relegated to an eco-logical niche in her universe. The next morning she telephoned the friend who had introduced me to her. 'That bloke you brought out to see me,' she said, 'I looked 'im up. 'E's a slippery eel, that one.' She added – since she was taught to be merciful – that she hoped I was 'a good'un'. I could only wonder at her taxonomic exactness. She dealt with me by assigning a spirit-animal to me, and she chose the right one. I was the worm of self-consciousness which spoiled an innocent, unreflective paradise, akin to those same snakes I'd always thought were stalking me. Marianne Moore, perhaps remembering Satan's disguise in Eden, said that poems were imaginary gardens with real toads in them. Imagination can invent an ideal haven, but must staff it with the threatening, unworthy inhabitants of our real world. In my anxiety to find a poem in Tasmania, I had reversed the proposition. I was the imaginary snake in Ida's real garden. The spectres from the north cancelled out her people by misrepresenting them; before I could do the same to her, she countered by defining me with an image of her own.

Tasmaniosaurus

New countries aren't supposed to have a history. But if anything, Tasmania possesses too much history: a succession of pasts, queuing up like unappeased revenants to accuse the ignorant present – the graziers with their pious, neglected graveyards, the convicts rattling their chains, the aborigines pressing their land claims. And before these human histories begin, Tasmania has another abysmal past, when it was a zoo of antediluvian monsters.

Because settlement has only scratched at the topsoil of this hard land, pre-history seems closer. At Old Beach, over the river from my parents' house, the rock dislodged to build a road gave up a cache of ancient vertebrate bones. A plaque now imagines the fossil site as it was all those uncountable thousands of years ago, crawling with indigenous nasties – the crocodile *Tasmaniosaurus* and the fish-eating reptile *Derwentia* sun-bathe on this same river bank and mangle their prey among a sci-fi vegetation of spiky pines, pronged cactus-like bushes and seed ferns with what the inscription calls 'a creeping habit'. The lost world resumes at the end of your garden.

The museum has its own collection of bogeys, reconstructed from fossils: Pleistocene megafauna, which had the state to themselves between two million and ten thousand years ago. Along with the Egyptian mummy, the bones of Trucanini and the amphibious coffin of the convicts' ducking-box, they made me think of the place as a haunted house, Tasmania's Gothic compendium of horrors. The dimly-lit room where the elephantine fossils are kept still has the power to alarm me. Like the beasts at Old Beach, they occupy exactly the space we thought we had colonised and made safe: a rocky habitat of dry grass against the inevitable diorama of an arctic Mount Wellington.

The *Zygmaturus trilobus*, dug from a peat bog at Smithton in 1920, appears in duplicate, as a skeleton and in plastery-fleshed reconstruction. The skeleton, with iron struts to prop it up, is the evil idea of the creature, like Blake's ghost of a flea. Its eyes are missing, but the teeth still grind; with its creaking joints and its pointed tail, it's the blue-print for a murderous machine. Next to it is the reified thing itself: an overgrown wombat, lumbering and snub-snouted. The *Zaglossus robusta*, a swollen echidna, wears a jacket of bristly needles. *Simosthenurus occidentalis* is a kangaroo with a single taloned toe; it spends its time in the museum scratching its flank with one paw, and has ripped and scored its body in easing itself. The *Macropus titan*, another inordinate roo, looks down from a height of eight feet. The bent bow of tail on which it balances is a rear phallus, and it keeps its testicles in a pouch the size of my head. A Pleistocene devil called *Sarcophilius laniarius* bats dainty eyelashes and bares its sharpened fangs, and as you turn away from it the *Thylacoleo carnifex* rears – a leopard-like marsupial with yellow shears in its mouth and hooked claws seeking your skin.

Even the rooms of extant fauna are eerie. Taxidermy suggests a creepily, suddenly stilled life: these exhibits were romping and feeding until you came in; they pause only to watch you, and will start up again the moment you leave. Possums are paralysed chomping on insects inside their cases, and the kangaroos with winking glass eyes are transfixed against a black-and-white photo-mural of dead trees. In their tank, fish swim on the spot without water or are tangled in curtains of leathery kelp. Snakes made of silicone ripple in arabesques, pausing at the moment of greatest writhing contortion. A masked owl is crucified against the wall, its eyes picked out to leave blank idiotic sockets. On shelves above the cases, eyries have been constructed for eagles, which stretch their wings and get ready to swoop. The bony abstract of a killer whale glides, out of its element, just below the roof. Insects are extrapolated into giants: a bull-ant, twenty-six times its real size, is built like a Volkswagen, and the Emperor gum moth, magnified six times, is a carpeted aeroplane with whiskers for propellers.

The worst frights lurk in booths which you press a button to light up. In one, the dark moonily discloses a tree full of possums, their red eyes glaring; they freeze as you watch, and when the time-switch clicks off they'll be back to their nocturnal business. In another, a coven of Tasmanian devils feasts on a dead wallaby, carving up a platter of green and yellow guts. A masked owl lunges, pinioned stationary in the air with a rat in its beak. Above the case, you're dive-bombed by a gargantuan leatherback turtle, which with slicing flippers is about to plummet to the floor.

Tasmania's most mythic animal – no doubt extinct, but kept alive by rumoured sightings and the tall tales of bushmen – is here too: the tiger. As constructed to life-size, it's a hyena dressed in a door mat, its mouth of course agape in a snarl. Its case contains the photograph of a specimen shot by a hunter and strung upside-down like Mussolini. The one human being in this room of carnivorous tableaux is a skeleton, who turns his wired neck to watch the possums nesting. Though all that's left of him is bones, he sprawls back to front on his black chair, with legs spread in the most aggressively macho of postures: a zoo-keeper who after long centuries at his post has died sitting there, and continued to sit while his flesh and sinew resorted to gas; the guardian of primordial, untamed Tasmania.

Tassie

The island has been made by a long series of alienating schisms. Tasmania first suffered disconnection from the mainland, which left its landscape buckled and eruptive; then it was singled out as a place of penance and the site for an experiment in genocide. The settlers pathetically strove to reconcile Arcady with Alcatraz; since then, the spoliation of mountains and the damming of wild rivers hint at a desire to punish the unyielding place into subservience.

Tasmania is Australia's pet Australia, doubly isolated from the world. When the Olympic Games were held in Melbourne in 1956, my father encouraged me to keep a scrapbook of clippings: his doleful reason was that 'they'll never come out here again.' I cut out the pictures of the tiresomely energetic athletes and fixed them in an album with some porridgy paste, but in Melbourne the games were as unbridgeably far away from me as if they had been in Oslo or Zanzibar or any of those other illusory destinations to which I despatched the apple cases. In Tasmania I paced the beach, scanning the horizon for a sail. Every January, the arrival of the yachts racing from Sydney to Hobart caused an outbreak of hysteria, and there were competitions to sight the first spinnaker in the blinding distance down the D'Entrecasteaux Channel. Perhaps this streamlined fleet had come at last to evacuate us? But after a few raucous days of parties in the dock, the yachties glided huffily away and left us on our own for another year.

Inside, such isolation produces an ache of self-doubt, a suspicion of solipsism. The enislèd ego bobs about on the ocean, like the bottled message of the castaway which no one will ever read. Outside, it begets a pride which is almost all defensiveness. When I returned to Tasmania for the first time, I went to visit some old friends who had turned themselves into swanky aesthetes. They lived surrounded by art books, and for a decade had been talking about a trip to Europe – but they hadn't made it, nor ever would. When they did, however, they specified that they wouldn't come to England. Why not? I asked. 'No baroque architecture,' they replied.

I muttered something about St Paul's, Blenheim Palace, Castle Howard. 'The wrong kind of baroque,' they quickly interposed. They're still in Tasmania, with their reproductions.

Australian nationalism is a version of this same bluff. The country's founders, unlike America's, endowed it with no ideology. How could they have, since they weren't there by choice? Rather than an identity, the nation has a temperament, which learned from the convicts to make the best of a bad job. 'Such is life,' as Ned Kelly grinned before the trapdoor gaped, or 'Worse things happen at sea,' as one of my unlucky aunts used to say whenever she burned the dinner / dropped a dish / scalded herself with the kettle / broke a limb / crashed the car. On occasion – Australia Day, for instance – the country makes valiant over-due efforts to equip itself with some motivating idea. I was there for the festivities last January. At the Sandy Bay regatta, plastic flags were handed out and a nationalisation ceremony was performed, admitting to citizenship four members of the Longo clan, a Mr Bahaa Samour and one Robert Lynch-Blosse Esq.; but when the band played the anthem no one sang, and the loudspeaker above the dodgem cars brayed out 'Born in the U.S.A.' all day long. The Prime Minister greeted the day with no rhetorical apothegms. All he could do was admonish his countrymen to 'spend time together . . . by joining in a favourite sporting event'. At Sandy Bay, those events included dummy-spitting and a pie-eating marathon. My father celebrated nationhood by ritually washing the car and watching the cricket on television.

The inward-looking continent used to regard the world which has exiled it with anger and envy. *On the Beach*, the book which catered to my adolescent sense of doom, is less about nuclear war than about Australia's fateful isolation. Moira rages against those 'other countries' in the northern hemisphere whose disagreements have sentenced innocent Australia to death; and yet her dying regret is that she'll never get to see any of those countries. She's broken-hearted because she won't be able to go shopping in the Rue de Rivoli. Her inferiority complex extends from culture to scenery. When she takes the American submarine commander to see the bush outside Melbourne, she's relieved that he approves. She was convinced, she says, that 'everything in England or America must be much better. That this is all right for Australia, but that's not saying much.' Dwight generously assures her that the gum trees pass muster 'by any standard that you'd like to name'. Shute's novel retrieves a Pyrrhic victory from the country's banishment: 'Anyway,' says Moira's father of the lethal fall-out, 'it comes to us last of all.' Finally, there was to be a bonus. Australia would expire a few months later than the rest of the world.

Moira lived and died on the mainland. More inured to isolation, Tasmania doesn't complain. Not long after its discovery in 1642, the midget island was established beyond the bounds of normality: Gulliver's map of his voyage places Lilliput to the north-west of Van Diemen's Land. Tasmania enjoys the idea of itself as Lilliput, and has even adopted an affectionately diminutive nickname. Those who live there are fond of referring to it as Tassie. It's a Lilliput inhabited by Robinson Crusoes, fiercely proud of their autonomy.

Tasmania learned to be self-sufficient early. Those huts on the hill at Risdon were constructed of materials scavenged in the bush, like Crusoe's humpy; only the nails came from Sydney. Since there was no glass, the dwellings did without windows, and for doors there were only canvas flaps. The same self-made world still existed when Ida West was growing up on Flinders Island. Utensils had to be fabricated before they could be used. Brushes and brooms were made from tussock-grass, sponges from the beach were collected for kitchen cleaners. Pots were scoured with ashes. Wallaby pelts were sewn into moccasins, mats, rugs and baskets plaited from reeds. Soap was made from dripping, and a gruesome wine squeezed from buzzies or burrs was believed to purify the blood and prevent boils. The oil from mutton birds made a chest liniment for rubbing on when someone had the 'flu.

Insularity is a Tasmanian creed. On the island, everyman is – or wants to be – an island. When I was back, the state resounded with a series of little agrarian dramas fomented by indigenous Crusoes or scions of the Swiss Family Robinson, fighting for their right to live outside society on their own desert island of the mind. In the Lemonthyme forest, when the bulldozers arrived to knock down the timber for the wood-chip industry, a female greenie shinned up one of the threatened trees and made her home there. She cried foul when a dozer nudged her leafy retreat. In Lenah Valley, one of the inner suburbs which runs off my main road, a woman devoted to animal liberation set up a backyard farm for free-range chickens in protest against the battery-hen industry; each week she sold her eggs on the steps of the government offices in Hobart, daring the law to a showdown by refusing to obtain a licence to market her produce. In Cygnet, down the Huon Valley, a flower-grower went on a hunger strike when government officials removed and burned four thousand of his chrysanthemum plants, which were suspected of having white rust. He subsisted for a week on cups of tea, and reported to the solicitous newspaper that the very idea of food now nauseated him: 'I seem to have gone past that stage.' He relented when he was compensated for the confiscated mums. Near Colebrook, in a tinder-dry valley on the eastern shore, an old-timer evicted from his stone cabin by a dam constructed for the farmers ostentatiously refused to be rehoused. He intended, he announced, to live in a cave – but disappointingly changed his mind when the government built him a new brick palazzo at the water's edge. In Taroona, a suburb for the newly affluent who hope eventually to move to genteel Sandy Bay, a resident planned to set up a piggery on his rural plot. When the council's zoning rules prevented this, he declared himself an independent entity, outside its jurisdiction. He stated Crusoe's faith as he promulgated his domestic economy: 'I have my own excavators and bobcat, so I can bury my own garbage. I have a septic tank, so there's no problem with sewage. I can soon get a water tank, and the council doesn't have to sweep my kerb and guttering, because I have none.'

These were islanders who had seceded from society, occupying tree-houses or settling down in the company of their chooks or porkers. Simultaneously, a letter-writer to the Hobart newspaper proposed the same alternative for the state: secession from socialist Australia (which actually keeps impoverished Tasmania in business, thanks to its subsidies). The writer was infuriated by the meddling of the federal government in the state's internal affairs – a directive from Canberra had overruled the latest scheme for flooding the south-west – and believed that sooner or later the country, with its redesigned flag, rewritten constitution and a citizenry regimented by new identity cards, would rid itself of the monarchy and become a republic. Therefore, he believed, 'it is time for Tasmanians to seriously examine the feasibility of seceding from the Federation and becoming an independent country, remaining within the British Commonwealth with the Queen as nominal head of state.' He had thought out all the advantages; this was a Crusoe with a visionary's mad gleam in his eye: 'We could have a vote at the United Nations, we could have our own currency, print our own stamps, have a flat rate of income tax to attract business registration, have a duty-free port and generally make the place a most attractive location for financial operations.' His conclusion was quite evangelical: 'I can see scope for Tasmania to become a sort of Switzerland of the Pacific.'

Or an Appalachia of the Antarctic? For inbreeding is another aspect of Tasmania's insular mystique. Tasmanians love to tell stories about the endogamic clans of the midlands, which have intermarried with their animals: I remember hearing when I was a boy about middle-aged women with the faces of pigs, sheep pushed in prams, and children with chains round their necks living in dog-kennels. Just off the highway, in the hills at Bagdad or Ouse or Black Bobs, this realm of genetic regression supposedly began. Of course – I suppose – the stories were fictions, but they were plausible enough to be thrilling. After all, a century ago white settlers kept aboriginal women on leashes outside their farmsteads for use when they needed sexual relief, and escaped convicts would sometimes stagger from the bush carrying raw gobbets of the companions they had cannibalised on their journey through the mountains. Tasmanians keep the legends alive by repeating them, and personally vouching for their truth. One classic tale concerns a boy and his father out hunting beyond Black Bobs. The father shoots a wallaby, then clambers down into a gully to fetch it. While there he has a heart attack and dies. The boy can't haul him out, so neatly sets about gutting him along with the wallaby, and takes them both home. A friend of mine, born at Moogara (one of Tasmania's notorious hillbilly havens) though now an academic in Sydney, relates a doctored version about his own family. In this variant, it's my friend's grandmother who dies; his grandfather puts her in a sack, slings her over his shoulder and takes her on the long hot dusty trek into town, where he goes straight to the pub and lays down his burden on the counter. 'What's in the bag, Bert?' asks the publican. 'The old woman,' my friend's grandfather replies. 'She croaked. I brought her in to be buried.' 'Blimey, Bert,' sniffs the publican, 'if I was you I'd've cleaned her first.' The fable has made one cautious concession to reality: this time the corpse isn't disembowelled; but public opinion still insists that it should have been.

There's a similar digest of tales about incest. At a family congress of pointy-nosed midlanders with receded eyes, a boy announces that he's found a nice girl, and they're going to get married: 'She can read and write, she lives in Ouse, and – you know what? – she's a virgin!' 'Bloody oath!' explodes the father. 'We're not having any virgins here. If she ain't bloody good enough for her own bloody family, she bloody ain't good enough for us.' Definition of a Tasmanian virgin: a girl who can run faster than her brothers.

Such are the tight little island's mythologies about itself. It likes the idea of families snugly bedded down together because its own structure is so tribal. Driving through the countryside, my parents will note of a side road, 'There's Heriots living up there,' or when someone from the Huon is mentioned they are likely to explain, 'She married a Crawford.' The same dynastic mode of thought operates at grander levels of society. I was taken to lunch at the Tasmanian Club, where the state's power-brokers do business. Introducing me to an amiable fogey, my host solemnly whispered that he was 'one of the Bethunes'. The society is so small that it seems to have total recall of all its personnel: hence the memorised lay-out of Cornelian Bay; and if, when I was back, I asked my parents' advice about finding an address, they never gave directions impersonally from the street map but always referred me to houses where friends or relatives had lived – 'You know Auntie Mary and Uncle Frank's old place? Well it's just round the corner from there.'

Tasmania has museums dedicated to this homy cohesion of communities. At Queenstown, for instance, there's a gallery of memorabilia assembled by Eric Thomas, born in 1906 and known as Shrewdy, who hauled the last load of ore from the open cut at Mount Lyell in 1972 and then retired to spend his time compiling the moribund town's family album. Inside its fence of mountains, Queenstown might as well be an island: when the first cars arrived from Hobart in 1932, their baggage racks loaded with provisions, all the locals turned out to greet them. Eric Thomas is the lonely tribe's self-elected bard and, in the mis-spelled captions which he has typed (in block capitals, because they sound more megaphonic) for the exhibits in his hoard of curios, he recites its history.

A gauche and porcine maiden with a frilled head-dress saying MT. LYELL and a costume allegorically festooned with mining tackle is glossed as follows: 'QUEENSTOWN 1911. SAID TO BE MISS ARCHER,

WHO FIRST WORE THE HAREM SKIRT IN QUEENSTOWN & RUN FOUL OF WATER-HOSE FOR LIFTING HER GEAR UP TWO INCHES & BEING NAUGHTY. GEE I BET THE CORSET LACES WERE PULLED TO BREAK-ING STRAIN AROUND HER WAIST. THAT'S WHY SHE WORE SPLITY KNICKERS SO THEY WOULD NOT HAVE TO BEND.' In this tiny settlement people assume legendary status as if acquiring girth; they grow larger as their exploits and attributes are bruited by Thomas the town-crier. He therefore adds, in appreciation of Miss Archer, 'SHE HAS A PAIR OF ARMS LIKE A LEG OF MUTTON.' Everyone is boosted by Thomas's characterisation, because the clan supplies all its members with a pedigree of extravagant exploits and idiosyncrasies. A man photographed at the railway station in 1931 has been communally renamed after the carnival he quit to join the tribe: 'MERRY MIX, HE CAME OFF A MERRY MIX THAT WAS IN QUEENS-TOWN AT THE TIME, LEFT THE SHOW TO WORK AT THE COMSTOCK MINE'; a jaunty bantam-weight, hand on hip and impenitently posing in front of a totalled lorry in 1972 is 'THE BOY FROM SYDNEY, APPRENTICE JOCKEY, PERFORMING FLEE. KEN LOVETT, FIRST MAN EVER TO BACK A FULL TRUCK OF ORE INTO THE CRUSHER OF WEST LYELL.' The accident is his entitlement to heroic grandeur, despite his size. The caption, a typed continuation of bar-counter teasing, asks Ken whether he still has to buy boys' boots to fit his tiny pins. There are memoirs of a brawling epic past, like rude Homeric tournaments – a tug-of-war at Zeehan in 1888 when all members of both teams were drunk and pitched, reeled and rolled over in the tangles of rope; the grave of someone slain in 1957, also at Zeehan, after a dispute over a skittles game. One of Thomas's prize items represents a fellow raconteur, dispensing the oral history which sustains another society. The photograph could show the boyhood of Raleigh: a wrinkly, pipe-sucking elder gripping a newspaper sits among his nets on a wharf, with an eager youth perched on a coil of rope at his feet; it was taken at Strahan on Macquarie Harbour on 1 September 1939. 'OLD TIMER WITH THE MERCURY,' Thomas ex-plains, 'KNOWN IN STRAHAN AS OLD BOB MUFF. INTERESTING YOUNG FELLOW WOULD BE REX WELLS OF STRAHAN, & I THINK IT WOULD BE MORE THAN A GOOD FISH YARN HE IS TELLING REX.'

Whitman, who took his bardic responsibilities seriously and acted as amanuensis for soldiers in hospital during the American Civil War, believed that every man's experience is of value to the community from which he derives it. Thomas's faith, unformulated, is the same. But he interprets it even more democratically than Whitman, apparently believing that any object which ever circulated in a community qualifies as a treasure because some memory adheres to it, like greying hair between the teeth of someone else's comb. Thus the shelves of his gallery display things which are precious in their ordinariness: beer bottles, butchers' bills, hospital records, old packets of Capstan cigarettes, Coronation mugs, petticoats, innocently smutty postcards, pen-nibs tipped with osmiridium, teddy bears with mange and a plate of salty face-powder. There are lives suspended here in anonymous limbo, waiting for someone to claim them. As at the apple museum in the Huon, a photograph of two snow-shovellers from the 1940s has a caption appealing for help in identifying the men: they have so far eluded Thomas's all-remembering census. One showcase props up next to a butter-knife a label worn on someone's lapel at a long-ago municipal function. The printed headlines boom, in capitals even more strident than those on Thomas's typewriter,

HELLO
MY NAME IS

and in an oblong box beneath, in tentative handwriting, the wearer has scribbled

Patricia.

Who? you feel like asking, startled by the button-holing bluffness of that capitalised greeting. But of course you know Patricia – or at least you remember her name. On the island, where everyone has been gazetted by Eric Thomas, there can be no strangers.

If Tasmania is Australia's Australia, then it has its own sprinkling of offshore Tasmanias in the islands of Bass Strait. Those who live here practise the reclusive discipline of Crusoe, who improvised his world from whatever flotsam he could find and called the roll of his few companions with a desperate retentiveness. The castaways on Flinders are scrupulous collectors of junk. They seize whatever rubbish hazard awards them, convinced that – since they're isolated here – it might one day come in handy. Derek Smith, the wizened wiseacre who has a preserve on Flinders for Cape Barren geese, fenced his sanctuary with plates of iron salvaged from a dump.

When we went out to see the place, two wallabies were posing against a section ripped from a derelict service station: on the windy plain the quivering marsupials framed one of those mercurial winged shoes which used to advertise Goodyear tyres. The top gear of Derek Smith's car is held in place by another of his serendipitous discoveries – a band of elastic: 'ex-bloody-WAF's bloomer elastic from the war,' he vouches; 'they used it to catapult Pommy agents into France off Dover cliff.' The island's doctor took me on a tour of his favourite tips in the bush, and then we travelled to Lady Barron to admire the two richest repositories of junk on Flinders. One man specialises in abandoned cars, which he eviscerates for spare parts and then parks in the ferns, waiting for the fronds to invade them and the lichen to crust their metal; creaking fleets of vehicles, smeared with green fish oil, go quietly to seed behind the house. Another collector's trophies, proudly paraded in his front garden, include six tractors, an Edison phonograph, a Hillman Minx which he uses to store bales of hay, and stacks of galvanised-iron fence-posts removed from the soldier-settlers' farms.

Flinders, like Queenstown, has its museum of elegiac scrap, locked in a one-time schoolhouse at Emita. A scrawl on the door names the place 'Dryazell': the teacher who came here in the 1890s, a remittance man exiled for his alcoholism, thirstily judged that Flinders was dry as hell. Inside are the island's garnered wonders, its humble equivalents to the unicorn horns, splinters of the true cross and carbuncular Fabergé eggs preserved by princes – bottled snakes in urine-coloured solutions, together with the skin one of them sloughed, still dusted with the sand where it lay; a fan-tail's nest, the straw matted by mucus; a crab claw eighteen inches long and a jar of purple spawn from a nautilus; a freeze-dried green turtle with a lustreless malicious eye. Linen table-cloths draped over the cabinets keep this unvisited past under wraps.

Most touching are the remembrances of ruptured communication – the wooden rotary blades of the first plane to land on Flinders, the old manual telephone exchange from Whitemark (where some gossipy female counterpart of Eric Thomas no doubt sat, interconnecting the community by way of her snooping earpiece). Seventy or more ships have sunk around these islands; planes from north-eastern Tasmania have crashed into them. At Emita, the wreckage disgorged by the sea and rained from the air is lovingly classified and shrouded in linen. Seat coverings from a downed plane, a fragment of wormy ship's mast, a porcelain toilet from another wreck, the sole of a child's shoe, copper-sheathed timber which the water has sucked hollow; a conglomerate of ornate glass smithereens, consolidated by corrosion and glued together underwater with a metal pulley frame and a spar of wood, melting into an inadvertent sculpture in which shells have embedded themselves. Outside are finds too large to fit in the hut: the white hooped ribs and cross-sectioned wheel-shaped spine of a sperm whale; the jutting, shafted propeller of another ship. They have grown alike in the sun on the grass: bone and steel, bodily architecture and engineered vane, beached and bleaching together. From such chance gifts of the elements, Robinson Crusoe makes his hermitage of art.

Tasmania's separation from the mainland occurred geological eternities ago, yet the mental fracture is recent history because something similar happened all over again in 1975, this time in the centre of Hobart. Early that year, an eleven thousand-tonne freighter with a cargo of concentrate for the zinc works rammed one of the pylons holding up the arch of the Tasman Bridge, which connects the city with its eastern suburbs. Four cars plummeted from the bridge, twelve people died; the ship is still on the river bed. For two and a half years before the span was rebuilt, Hobart was reminded each day of its bereft insularity. The city's museum has a model of the scene, with the perished freighter in a grave of grey plastic water among the columns it pulverised. In the same room stand some female figure-heads from the prows of whalers which used to dock in Hobart – Queen of the Seas, a classical actress in a ball-gown with jewelled wrists, pendulous ear-rings and a hand expressively pounding her heart; Mary Wadley, a Victorian virgin kneeling to pray; and Lady Franklin, starry eyes affronting the storm, who wears an off-the-shoulder dress buttressed under the bosom and has a gash in her wooden throat cleaving open to the chest. Landlocked now, these florid voyagers have joined the detainees, both living and dead, on our inescapable island.

IV

SPIRITS OF PLACE

The Naming of Places

One day when I was back I happened to be driving with my parents down the east coast. We had just passed Wet Marsh, a featureless fen outside Swansea; we next crossed Old Man Creek, a modest offshoot (I suppose) of Paul Robeson's eternal Ole Man River. My mother, who dislikes letting the landscape slip by unremarked, suddenly said, 'You'd wonder they could find names for all those there little creeks and rivulets.' I'd been thinking exactly the same. The wonder is that Tasmania names its places with such giddy inventiveness and such snatch-and-grab geographical eclecticism. This tiny triangle manages to contain – as well as the inevitable English Town and Irish Town – a Bagdad, a Nile, a Paradise and a Promised Land, not to mention the various spits and gulfs named in homage to the devil. The names in all these cases matter intensely, which is why so much exorbitant poetic fancy went into the act of assigning them. They are inscriptions on an unfriendly nowhere and metaphors of a cherished elsewhere; they plead for a spirit to inhere in this arbitrary place, and erect their sign-post as a hopeful altar. The map of Tasmania exudes a pathos which is almost unbearable.

New countries are liable to be named in a casual, hasty gesture of appropriation: New England, New Holland, New Zealand, New France, New Caledonia; the metaphor is tacked on, whether it matches or not. What connection is there between New York or New South Wales and the prototypes they claim to be renovating? Even worse, the new country can be named in description of its contents, which amount – for the first colonial appraisers – to zero. The Portuguese seamen trawling for cod in a frigid waste on the other side of the Atlantic dismissed the land mass behind the banks of fish. 'Cá nada,' they tersely said: nothing here. Canada has suffered the libel ever since. That's why the issue is so sensitive, and so serious. The name, as in Catholic countries where your infant is baptised in tribute to a saint, is a blessing, and also an experiment in predestination. I remember how depressed I felt when at Sunday school a canting teacher told me my own name stood for the saint's rock-like stability, which I didn't especially want to possess; and how I thought the petrific prophecy had been redoubled when the character I played in the film of *They Found a Cave* turned out to be called, bizarrely, Brick.

Adam in Eden was given the job of naming the animals and plants. It's the first duty of the poet, because it's his construction of the world. The unwritten map of a new country reverts to that day before things had been tagged with names, and to the childhood before we have learned language: Locke likened the *tabula rasa* of the young receptive mind to America; the world is our newfoundland. Since the space we're surveying is as flat and uninflected with meaning as the Nullarbor Plain, our first initiative in this world is therefore to declare our own centrality to it. This is the conceit of imagination: Kubla Khan's decree. Names of places, with truly quixotic trust, attempt to plant significance in a haphazard spot of earth by immortalising the namer. They all revise geography to establish the epicentre here, now, in me. I once travelled from London to Sydney on a Qantas 747 called 'City of Townsville'. That sums up the precious, necessary imposture. Townsville, on the northern coast of Queensland, is a town which adds a ville to itself and is thereby promoted to a city; the double tautology is then painted along the side of a flying machine which contradicts the very idea of rootedness and geocentricity, and will probably never go anywhere near the place with whose name it is emblazoned. Of course Townsville is not just town translated into French and thus accorded city status. It was named by Robert Towns, the English seaman who founded it in 1864 – but then what was he named after? And in any case, the -ville was at the time something of a presumption. Only after two years did Townsville even qualify as a municipality.

Tasmania's most touching place names are those which paraphrase the idea of the caption as a lucky charm, wistfully believing this to be the centre. Inland from Devonport, before the abrupt barrier of the mountains, is a settlement comfortably called Nook; nearby is Kindred, named after its own tribal self-cementing by intermarriage. Paradise and Promised Land are in the same area, ramshackle rows of huts mocking their messianic origins. The genial despair of the Australian character isn't deceived by such confident promulgations, which it knows to be no more than whistling in the wilderness. Close to these encampments, whose names have lighted solitary candles in the bush, is a place which gives the lie to them by admitting its own placelessness – its title is Nowhere Else. The same brutal humour requires the ground plan of paradise to be balanced by that of inferno. Beulah, which means the door to heaven, is just over the way from Devil's Gate (located, for an extra complication, on the Forth River, though even that, as I'll explain, is a pun or a mistake). The name is a calculated risk. Its owner may not deserve it (as I was made to feel when the etymology of Peter was explained to me at Sunday school), or may grow up derided by it. Springfield, one of the hastily sketched-in post-war suburbs near ours, running from the main road for a few blocks into the foothills, was laid out as a would-be Manhattan, with avenues numbered from First to Eighth. But the water-pipes ended at First Avenue, and the roads remained unpaved quagmires well into the 1950s.

The self-elected Adam of Tasmania, in days when it was more like Sodom than Eden, was Lachlan Macquarie, governor of New South Wales between 1810 and 1821. On sorties through his colony's outpost of Van Diemen's Land, he decided where settlements would be situated, and what they should be called. The map as he drew it was an orgy of self-congratulation. He it was who rechristened Glenorchy. The explorer John Hayes in 1793 had metaphorically annexed it to the landscape of the English lakes, calling it New Cumberland. Macquarie in 1811 shifted it north of the border. Henceforward it would be deemed a glen of rushing waters, because that was the name of his wife's home in Scotland.

Revolutionaries rename cities and monuments and even, in France, rewrite the calendar, because they wish to expunge history and begin time all over again. Macquarie high-handedly cleansed the slate out of mere uxoriousness. Touring the midlands in the same year, he spent a night beside Relief Creek. In this desiccated valley, the name was a sincere vote of thanks for water. Macquarie erased that, to compliment his wife once more: Relief Creek was promoted to the Elizabeth River. When he returned in 1821, he ordained a settlement there and ordered it to be called Campbell Town, which was the name of his wife's clan at Glenorchy. The previous day he selected a site further north and called it Perth, as a bread-and-butter tribute to his host in the area, who came from the Scottish town of the same name; and a few days later, on the same denominating crusade, he gave the town of Ross the name of a friend's residence on Loch Lomond. Earlier he had founded an Elizabeth Town on the Derwent, but it eventually adopted the name of New Norfolk. An up-river East Anglia, I always thought, with hop-fields and poplars. But in fact the Norfolk it renewed was Norfolk Island, the mutinous penal station in the Pacific halfway to New Caledonia; when it was closed down, some of the evacuated families transferred here to their new Norfolk. Macquarie and his Elizabeth drape themselves across the middle of Hobart, lying as if in bed at right angles to each other: they bestow their names on the two streets whose axis marks the city-centre. Elizabeth Street is indeed the first stretch of my main road; hours later, under the alias of the Midland Highway, it bisects Campbell Town.

The topographical vainglory is forgivable enough. The old plea to remember my name – spelled out by Eliza's tomb at Jericho and cheerily uttered by my murderer at Risdon – has been institutionalised. At least Macquarie didn't sanctify either himself or his lady, whereas when Hobart's cathedral was consecrated in 1823 as St David's, the locals maintained that the choice had less to do with reverence for the leek-eaters' patron than with the fact that the christian name of Collins, the colony's first lieutenant-governor, was David.

Macquarie invoked Scotland with a sense of hereditary entitlement; for others, its reproduction in Tasmania was pretence, using the southern hemisphere to redress the frustrations of the northern. In 1821, while Macquarie was on his hibernising binge in the midlands, a transported bigamist bought some bushland outside Hobart and called it Dynnyrne, referring to a Scottish property to which he had an imaginary claim. The area is now the suburb beside the university campus. All my life I've found it so unspellable that I assumed it to be an aboriginal word. The Scottish sheep farmers on the Fat Doe River rewrote the map to commemorate remote military glories: the river became the Clyde, their town Bothwell. Fingal, a coal-mining town in the north-east, was yoked to the caves Joseph Banks had visited at Staffa in 1792 – yet every time I hear the name I think not of Ossianic bards or Mendelssohn's music but of an idiot girl I saw in the bus depot at Launceston, her eyes crossed and her face blotched, convulsively sobbing over a cup of milky tea, rabidly biting her arm, then thumping the side of her head with a clenched fist to hammer sense into herself; she wore a National Coal Shovelling Titles T-shirt over a Hawaiian skirt. 'There's Sarah, doing her block again,' commented one of the drivers; 'she's waiting for the Fingal bus.'

The settlement of Tasmania coincided with (and morosely negated) the forays through uninhibited landscape of the romantic poets. John Hayes, annexing the colony to his native Lake District, named its river after Derwentwater and its mountain Skiddaw – even though Skiddaw is conical, contoured and mammary, not a hunched crouching lion like Wellington (as it's now called), and despite the fact that the Tasmanian peak is a good thousand feet taller than the English one it was meant to resemble. Thus Tasmania became a very approximate ideogram of Wordsworth country, all contemplative heights and glassy dreaming liquid depths. At the same time, the fancy-dress chivalry of Walter Scott was superimposed on it. Rokeby, now a resort just out of Hobart, was named after one of Scott's romances, and Deloraine in the north-west had as its parent a character from 'The Lay of the Last Minstrel'. There's a melancholy aptness to these Tasmanian mimicries of Scott, for his narratives record the historical defeat of a culture left behind by industrial modernity. His foggy north suits Tasmania's mood as well as Margaret Mitchell's malarial old south. *Gone with the Wind* was a powerful influence here, mythologising another contaminated, losing province. Driving back from the west coast, I passed a letter box on the Ouse road: an oil drum mounted sideways on some planks, open-ended so the motorised postman can hurl foreclosure notices into it. The name painted on its side was TARA. No willow-girt white-columned plantation house could be seen at the end of the dusty track.

Thomas Wood, during his tour in the 1930s, was teased and perturbed by Tasmania's glancing resemblances to England: 'You have seen it before, but where? The West Riding? The South Downs? Derbyshire? The Lake District?' Anxious to contain them all at once, Tasmania transforms itself into a garbled, compressed synopsis of the British Isles. On the west coast, you pass through Orford (extracted from East Anglia) on the way to Swansea (an excerpt from another new South Wales), with a turn-off to Pontypool. These Welsh towns are situated in the municipality of Glamorgan.

Devonport is in the county of Devon, and there's also a Torquay in the area. The north-west coast manages to sustain a likeness to England for miles on end, with pasture as smoothed and rounded and fecund as a human body. Then, just when the comparison fails, a swampy junction outside Stanley appears with the name Wiltshire. It consists of a railway line through the marsh, and a parked cargo of logs. The highlands contain a Ben Nevis and a Ben Lomond, though at Queenstown – in deference to the supposedly homesick Welsh miners – the twin peaks are called Owen and Jones. The east coast has its Irish Town (separated from Dublin Town by the hamlet of Cornwall); the north-west for good measure manages an Irishtown. There's even, in a scrubby unsacred nowhere, a Stonehenge lacking dolmens.

Tasmania keeps getting these spatial metaphors mixed, as if an atlas had been cut up for a jigsaw puzzle. The central plateau is known as our Lake District, though among the Wordsworthian vistas there's an interloper from the Bernese Oberland, Interlaken. The road across the mountains to the Gordon dam crosses a Florentine River, named by the surveyor Falkland because it reminded him of somewhere in Tuscany. His memory can't have been very reliable – seeping rain forests and shattered crags inside maelstroms of vapour in cultivated, amber-coloured Italy? But imagination will stop at nothing in its campaign to feel at home in Australia. The rivers west of the Tamar on the north coast had an even odder cartographic fate. At first they were merely numbered, like the avenues in Manhattan or Springfield, which confesses the provisional nature of the diagram: they were the First to Fourth Western Rivers. But since Tasmania was a white, radiant, empty page on which a world could be designed, when the time came to replace the numbers with proper names they were organised into a universal delta, radiating across continents. The First River was the Rubicon, the Second the Mersey, and the Third the Don. (This last was company for the town of Steppes behind the Western Tiers.) Imperial Rome and Czarist Russia were thus conflated, with romantic England in between. That left the Fourth River, which in a phonetic pun was hibernised as the Forth.

With supreme fantasticality, these streams were translated to three countries. Tasmania was also an area of polyglot dispute between the namers of three different national expeditions. The

Dutch came in 1642. Tasman entitled the island in tribute to his employer in the East India Company, van Diemen. On the way down the west coast he sighted the mountain at Zeehan, though its Dutch name was allocated later by Bass and Flinders during their circumnavigation; Tasman did name Maatsuyker Island, calling it a sugar mountain because the tea-trees were in bloom then – and as Derek Smith said to me, 'That's better than naming it after some bloody English earl who never fucking saw the place.' The French followed in 1792. Huon de Kermadec, captain of one of their ships, adopted my happy valley; the rear-admiral bestowed his christian name on Bruny Island and his surname on the D'Entrecasteaux Channel in which it lies. The east coast is their linguistic colony, with its Ile des Phoques, Cape des Tombeaux and Ile du Nord. But their expropriation has been undone by the local accent. The bluff above Clifton Beach, mined by the mutton birds whose nocturnal return to base I spied on, is called Cape Deslacs. From up there the circle of surf-skirted bays and slurping lagoons into which the Derwent spills does look like a pattern of interlocked lakes. My friends who live in the dunes behind the beach refer to the cape, however, as Deslax, which not only confounds the etymology but makes the place sound like a patent medicine for unclogging your internal drain.

When the English came to stay, a decade after the French voyage, they authenticated their claim by eliminating French tags, or naming places in sardonic competition with their predecessors. Battery Point, the jutting knob fortified in 1818 to guard the harbour, was planned as propaganda for the recent English rout of the French. Salamanca Place recalled one of Wellington's victories, and Mount Wellington – so called in 1824, to replace D'Entrecasteaux's flat-minded appellation of Montagne du Plateau – was offered to the victor. Napoleon was relegated to a street on Battery Point above the boatyards; towards it curved Waterloo Crescent. All the same, the miniature suburb squeezes into itself a sectarian muddle. It has a Cromwell Street, but along with this Protestant hero there are two allusions to successes of the French monarchy in suppressing the Huguenots: Montpelier Retreat refers to Montpellier, which retreated when besieged by Louis XIII in 1622; and Castray Esplanade, I suspect, has anglicised the town of Castres, whose Protestant republic the same king subdued in 1611. Perhaps, despite doctrinal contradictions, the romance of secession was even then dear to fledgling Tasmania.

Confronted by a new country, men are forced to recognise the quiddity and therefore the mystery of things. Ultimately, the place is unknowable – insentient rocks, frantically preoccupied water-courses, emptily smiling sky. Our only hope of partially knowing is by comparison. We conjure up in our words an alternative to the mute object. Hence all the metaphoric analogies to elsewhere in Tasmania. The most thoughtless, artless act of naming employs this verbal figure, because we must envisage something other behind the inscrutable novelty we have in view. Tasmania's mountains were named animistically – Dromedary, up the Derwent, with its two humps. Or else, with a Crusoesque ambition to make the world useful, they were appraised as utensils, like the sharp-toothed Saw Back Range beyond Maydena. The conquering eye takes a plane to them (as the pilot wanted to do when he proposed mobilising the road-grader against Mount Picton) and levels them off into furniture. There's a Table Mountain in the midlands, and the infamous Captain Bligh's first name for Wellington was Table Hill. In the highlands, even more commodiously smoothed and hollowed at the summit, is Cradle Mountain. John Hayes in 1793 found a heraldic iconography traced on the landscape, and called the inlet with the mud flats on which our suburb was eventually built Prince of Wales Bay, because its outline reminded him of the prince's floppy, feathery crest. The metaphor, as always, is a subjective illusion: to me the bay is a shapeless, malodorous blob. I prefer the utilitarian imagination of the unknown Crusoe, further up the Derwent, who decided that the pimple at the end of a thin causeway would be Frying Pan Island. Such images whittled and bevelled and moulded geography into a home.

At its most grandiose, naming is mythopoeia. Tasmania recon-voked the beginning of the world, and its taxonomic Adams did their best to write its terrain as the accomplishment of a scriptural prophecy. The Patriarchs, on Flinders, are looming forefathers of stone; Babel Island was so called because of the unclassified species of birds chattering orchestrally on it. With so many mountains to tabulate, Tasmania aspired to Olympian standards, and redrew the map of a classical early world to accompany the Christian one. The state has an Ossa and a Pelion, and at South Cape – recalling the poet who invented the rhetoric of high-altitude sublimity – there is Pindar's Peak. The most heart-breakingly irrelevant classical allusions are at Port Arthur. The children's prison was located at Point Puer, whose name suggests the sadism of precocious Latin cramming and at the same time nastily puns on a missing purity. Behind the commandant's cottage, a row of steps trails up to a barbed-wire fence and a plot of brambles and cow parsley. Here, once, stood Rose Cottage, the schoolhouse. The modest brow of hill was known, in its honour, as Mount Parnassus. It could make you weep to hear it. And yet how else can the constricted imagination cope? It must somehow devise and engineer its world, using like Crusoe whatever sullied facts lie to hand. A mound thus becomes a mountain, and a temple is raised in the backyard. The Tasmania which voted itself a Parnassus had the honesty to incorporate as well the classical underworld. One of the Derwent's tributaries is the Styx.

This relativity of its myths is another ironic romantic bequest to Tasmania. Romanticism, which converted religion into poetry, believed all mythologies to be interchangeable because – classical, Christian, Arabian or aboriginal – they were the dreamed cosmic patterns of the same human mind. A marine called Hugh Germain, arriving in 1804, set off to prove this true in the midlands. He carried with him in his knapsack two books, the Bible and the *Arabian Nights* tales, and drew on them both in creating his own holy land. Crossing the Derwent at Bridgewater, impeccably prosaic, you arrive in a jumbled·poetic fantasia, a double sacrament wished onto meaningless earth. From one of his texts Germain chose as place names Jericho and Jerusalem. At Jericho, where the church is becalmed in a dead yellow sea of grass, the metaphor still holds good. Jerusalem has since secularised itself as Colebrook, though the river beside it is the Coal. He called a lake Tiberias, after the capital which Herod dedicated to Tiberius; a river, while Germain was alliterating on J, was dubbed the Jordan. (When I was born my parents were living on a street in North Hobart which they always referred to as Jordan Hill Road. Its true title was Lower Jordan Hill Road, I later learned: the inner city was lowlier in its spiritual ambitions than Germain's visionary desert; there was no Upper Jordan Hill Road, and the street actually ran into a hill called Knocklofty.) From his profaner sacred text, Germain pulled out Abyssinia and Bagdad. Our version of the latter had neither caliphs nor flying carpets nor a minareted skyline; its only marvels were the moulting peacocks and dithery Swiss goats kept by Nan Chauncy, who wrote *They Found a Cave*, in her sanctuary there – unless you counted the incestuous hybrids we all believed to be marauding in the hills.

Beneath these literary glosses on the land are slangier attributions from local folklore: along the Tasman Highway, Mother Brown's Bonnet or, more dreadful in its metaphoric intimation of an orifice, Black Charlie's Opening. Sometimes the land is still indited with the heaved sighs, gratified curses and exclamation points of those who first crossed it. The east coast has a Bust-Me-Gall Hill, and a creek of the same ilk. Once at least a bosky pastoral place name is adopted with the bitterest Australian sarcasm. On the way to Cradle Mountain, in matted forest, was a logging camp known as Daisy Dell. Only the signpost remains, together with the community's single amenity – a tree stump which served as its post office. The marvel, as my mother said, is that the naming imagination could manage such feats here without flagging. Occasionally it has recourse to bland measurement or the skimpiest denotation – Seven or Nine Mile Beach, Sandy Point or Sandy Bay Beach, Woody Island – but then come the neologistic freaks, which lodge a riddle forever in the places they tag: Paper Beach, Squeaking Point, The Kick. One of the first maps on which Tasmania appeared was Gulliver's; it remains a catalogue of oddities.

The first namers scrawled their similes on a clean slate because they believed the aborigines incapable of christening anything. Recently the Hydro-Electric Commission has made restitution, using aboriginal words for its dams and power stations. Most of the titles chosen refer to the Hydro's sovereign god – Tungatinah is a shower, Miena a lagoon, Waddamana is noisy water and Liawenee is fresh water, Wyatinah and Liapootah are creeks – so the highlands resound with these cataracts of vowels, as thundery, gushing and spurious as *Hiawatha*. For though the Hydro's faith in inundation suggests some primordial cult, there's a grim historical justice to this use of native words for natural phenomena when naming structures which redirect the landscape.

The recovery of aboriginal words can't help but be ironic, because these are vocables plucked at random from perished dialects and applied willy-nilly by Europeans to sites they alone occupy. The suburbs adjoining ours are Moonah (meaning gum tree, of which the streets are bare) and Lutana (which, overlooking the midnight sun of the seething zinc works, means moon). The early colonists called one of the gullies climbing Mount Wellington's foothills Kangaroo Valley. Later they changed the name to Lenah Valley, since Lenah is the aboriginal word for a brush kangaroo. (The converse of my mistake about Dynnyrne, it always sounded to me as English as Ranelagh.) No doubt the intention was honourable, but it wasn't a readoption of the aboriginal name for the place. The usurping suburbanites had taken their own name and translated it into an alien tongue, thus ensuring that to most people – to me at least – it meant nothing. There's an avenue in Lenah Valley called Lumeah, and a street in Chigwell, another uprooted portion of outer London, called Allawah. Lumeah means 'I rest here', Allawah 'I camp here'. The quotations speak volumes about the emotions of pioneering, even as late as the 1950s when Chigwell was unpacked onto the hillside: they stake out terrain, rule abstractions on the sour clods and beg invaders to respect those frail borders; they know, though the sewage is connected and the antennae wired to the chimneys, that this is a camp. Yet these are European sentiments, venerating home-ownership and the privacy of property as our most invincible insurance against mortality. What could they mean to the aborigines from whose language they were borrowed? The Parlevars were nomads, wandering incessantly through the areas they hunted. They had no use for boundary fences and net curtains. Lumeah and Allawah are a jokey jabberwock, like Emohruo on the house near us or Haerami, the proud title of a bungalow in New Norfolk. Printing slogans back to front or mashing up and mis-spelling 'Here am I' makes English look like tribal baby-talk.

The solid thing needs the airy word which names it. Otherwise it has no identity, no resident spirit. And the word, when something or somewhere or someone answers to it, assumes the substantiality of the thing. There's a curious interchange in Tasmania between persons and places. People name places after themselves, or one another – van Diemen, the Macquaries, Wellington; Lieutenant-Governor Paterson founded a settlement in the north in 1805 and called it Patersonia (only to be trumped by his senior officer, Governor King, who named it after the Cornish town of Launceston where he himself was born). The place is personified. Once this happens, an individual can be the personification of that place. Australians, since their country was so recently invented, have enjoyed reinventing themselves as figments of it. Opera singers made a habit of this, since they were required to operate internationally: our Tasmanian diva Margaret Garde, who aggrandised herself in Italy as Margherita Grandi, is an exception, but Melba *née* Mitchell contracted and italianised Melbourne, while Florence Fawaz went overseas to sing as Florence Austral and in 1922 at Covent Garden substituted as Brünnhilde for a compatriot whose complementary sobriquet was Elsa Stralia; before I knew better, I suspected Joan Sutherland of taking her surname from that Great South Land which the European explorers had competed to discover. The parents of a girl I knew at school, refugees from Latvia, called her Austra when they arrived, petitioning the new country to be her patron saint. My apple-growing grandfather, whose orchard was at Castle Forbes Bay, had Forbes for his middle name; down the river, the Geeves family still owns Geeveston. Tasmania encourages this feudal practice. The farm boy in *They Found a Cave*, representing ethnicity, had to be Tas, and scanning the paper one morning I read in the register of driving offences about a three hundred dollar fine and an eighteen-month disqualification levied on one Derwent Tasman Gates of Lenah Valley, who – poor man – virtually was the state.

Imagination devoutly trusts the ordaining magic of the name, and when in 1853 the penal colony wanted to announce its moral uplift it began again as Tasmania, returning to first principles and honouring its discoverer not his patron. Port Arthur reformed itself as Carnarvon. With the same guilty misgivings, the settlement of Bismarck behind Glenorchy decided during one of England's periodic conflicts with Germany that it might be prudent to change its name to Collinsvale (though the potatoes it produced were still called after the Prussian war-lord); and the Konrads, anxious for anonymity, surreptitiously lowered their initial to a C. Every name on the map of Tasmania encodes a secret, or paraphrases a dream.

Devils and Holy Visitors

Tasmania wears its scars with a jaunty fatalistic good humour which is very Australian: the emblems of this gardened land, so blighted by its early history, are an apple and a fanged devil. Mark Twain, perplexed when he visited in the 1890s by the gap between the fresh grace of the scene and its vicious past, thought it 'a sort of bringing of heaven and hell together'. For me, it was a paradise I had to lose, inhospitable to slippery eels.

When I was at school and Tasmania was still bucolic, we used to draw it as a pristine, polished red apple. Now the fruity iconography has undergone a change. Today the official promoters of tourism hand out little business cards on which the Tasmania-shaped apple has had a mouthful bitten from its east coast by some greedy interstate Eve. Into the cavity is inserted the legend 'Tasmania. Be tempted'. Tasmania has grown to fancy the idea that it is a cursed or morally tainted place: perhaps this will attract tourists in search of sin. To help deprave the innocent orchard, a casino has opened in Hobart, though rather than raffish high-rollers from the gambling dens of Asia it attracts my relatives, who during the long afternoons fritter away their pensions in bouts of two-up. The trappings of Vandemonism, once so shameful, have emerged from hiding. At the Sandy Bay regatta a black tin stove for baking potatoes was trundled through the crowd. The lettering on its side announced 'Van Diemen Ovens'; underneath, a smirking spud brandished knife and fork, getting ready to eat himself.

Everywhere, on posters and postcards and envelopes and in cages, the Tasmanian devil snaps and snarls. It deserves its name. Satan in his manifestation as a snake was at least lithe and elegantly tortuous, able to writhe through arabesques of sophistic argument; if he'd chosen to arrive in Eden as a Tasmanian devil, Eve might have been frightened into good behaviour. It is the ugliest animal in creation: black eyes, the wet pink snout of a rat, a baggy unarticulated body ending in a flickery whiplash tail; it exudes a pong of sulphur, or the pit. All those I saw bore the wounds of war in their limping gait, tattered ears and ravaged fur. Herded into captivity, they scuttle about on their stubby rodents' legs doing single-minded demonic errands; when they collide, they rear at each other with scissory claws and sawing teeth. The sound they make is as toxic as their smell: a hiss ejected from some wind tunnel inside themselves, which slashes the air like a hook. Watching two of them exchange insults in a sordid zoo on the Tasman Peninsula, the mainlander beside me said 'The horrible buggers even hate each other.' Such is the state's unendearing mascot.

Being so demon-ridden, Tasmania from the first needed tutelary angels, spirits to replace the expelled aboriginal guardians of the land. The earliest settlers murmured devout spells against the wilderness, and pleaded with their god to include this place in his dominion. In 1804 the camp at Risdon was abandoned after the natives menaced it; the colonists retreated down river to the cove where Hobart began. Collins, the Lieutenant Governor, pitched his marquee on a slope, and Knopwood, the party's chaplain, at once conducted divine service. The knob of terrain they chose to bless remains as a phrenological bump under the pavement in the centre of town. The stop where I caught the bus home stood immediately beside it; around it, when I was a boy, were arranged the institutions which constituted the city – the Town Hall, the newspaper, the Post Office, the museum, the library and my favourite and most palatial cinema, all huddling within a cramped circle which marks the perimeter of Knopwood's first frail benediction. There had to be constant repetitions of this sanctifying charm. A settler in the east wrote in alarm thirty years later: 'No clergy at Prosser Plains. Divine Service has not been performed by a clergyman for seven years . . . Convict servants should not be permitted to continue longer without the Word of God preached to them.' As a result of appeals like this, a church was built at Buckland, though on the day I visited – with a summer gale rattling the slates on the roof and howling in the rafters, lashing the cord which pulls the steeple bell and flapping the pine trees – it didn't feel as if the heathen landscape had been appeased.

Derek Smith has installed an interceding spirit on the wind-battered empty acres of his Flinders Island sanctuary: 'Frank, the old Italian bloke who works for me out on the reserve. All I have to do is keep him in drink. He likes a drop of Marsala.' Frank is St Francis of

Assisi, in the form of a cheap bruised statuette. Outside Derek's impromptu A-frame cabin, Frank occupies his own A-frame chapel – two leaning boards roofed with flat stones, on an island in a dam built for breeding chats. The saint is mawkish and maidenly, his robe festooned with crucifixes and rosaries; he in his turn is guarded by the porcelain statuette of a robin, so out of proportion with him that it might be a bulbous red-breasted hawk. Beneath them both is a plaque spelling out a prayer of St Francis: 'Lord, make me an instrument of your peace.' Here Derek Smith practises a pantheistic gospel, hoarsely conversing with the wombats and pitying their mange or hanging on the fence a Goofy mask (scavenged, like Frank and the aquiline robin, from a tip) to warn the Cape Barren geese against braining themselves when they take off.

Mystic presences were always streaking across the Tasmanian sky during my childhood. Whenever a plane puttered over, we used to run into the streets and wave up at it, elated by this interruption of the blank blue quiet; once there was a sputnik, drilling through the night above Mount Wellington. Other emissaries from elsewhere actually landed, to assure us that the rest of the world existed. For me, the most consoling was the Queen, whom I saw for all of ten seconds in 1954. Looking the other way, she was driven past towards that bow-legged entomological arch built by the zinc works in her honour. She went on to make a speech (which I heard at home on the radio) outside the Town Hall, by that hump of sweltering ground where Knopwood first requested divine protection. Her accent with its throttled vowels was a sound relayed from outer space. She left her wrought-iron heraldic signature on a crisp page of the visitors' book at Parliament House, conserving her mystery by abbreviating her surname to R. Then she etherealised, as spirits are supposed to do. But she touched earth just long enough to embody the pale, sacred, abstruse idea of England, whose remotest annex we were.

In 1986 the Pope, allocating seven hours and ten minutes to the state, attempted all over again to sanctify outcast Tasmania. He did so on the race-course behind my parents' house, where the socialites in togas and Ruritanian army surplus gear congregated for the Hobart Cup. The open-air Mass was celebrated on the ruins of my old electric cathedral of light, the drive-in cinema. The white ruled screen which used to tantalise me all day in the sun, denying knowledge of the wraiths who came alive on it after dark, had long ago been dismantled. Now an altar was built in its place, on the foundation of the former projection booth, and the drive-in cafeteria was outfitted for the day as a vestry. Where the speakers you hooked to your car window once sprouted on the gravel, khaki tents were rigged up so communicants could confess before the Mass. To supplement the eucharistic wine and unleavened bread, stalls dispensed Dagwood hot dogs and treacly waffles along with the papal souvenirs.

Every effort was made to soothe the obdurate landscape and to pacify the wet, boisterous Tasmanian spring with words. A nun recruited to help out with the television commentary surveyed the scene and remarked 'Mountains provide that natural look that only God can give.' But Mount Wellington, steaming as the icy showers advanced down its gulleys, and sullen Mount Direction appeared to have other ideas about their teleological function. The local arch-bishop, sinister in shades, warmed up the crowd under its blankets and umbrellas by referring to himself as 'a citizen, proud of my island state – our beautiful Tasmania'; a sudden cyclone took the opportunity to slap and billow through his vestments. When the Pope arrived, the wind and rain briefly paused in their frisking. 'The sun's shining,' breathed one of the commentators; 'it's almost a miracle.' The Pope addressed God on the subject of Tasmania, remarking, 'All creation rightly gives You praise,' at which point a disrespectful gust threatened to knock his mitre off. He hastily straightened it, and two acolytes gripped his skirts on either side to hold him down while he read his homily. Once more the intention was to redeem Tasmania by making it the manifesto of some extraneous spirit. For me, that genius had been England and its writers (or sometimes America and its fleshy pagan gods, who cavorted on that metallic Cinemascope firmament above the altar); for the Pope, another agency deserved the credit. 'I know,' he said, 'that the church in Tasmania has a most interesting history, which shows how divine providence has been at work in your midst.' The colony which began in perdition was relieved by the Catholic faith, when its first bishop campaigned for an end to the transportation of convicts.

A bedraggled flock queued in the rain to nibble the wafers handed out by a troop of priests with yellow security passes tagged to their robes. God's emissary on earth, only too human, scratched his nose and even slyly finessed a yawn during the proceedings. The archbishop promised that the Pope would extend his blessing to 'any objects of devotion you may have brought with you'; the tourist bureau, as if to test the largesse of this grace, distributed sunglasses ornamented with Tasmanian devils. At the end, a froth of balloons was released, which the wind buffeted off towards infidel Mount Direction. The Pope followed them, grazing the edge of our suburb, crossing the river by the new bridge sliced through the rifle range and speeding on past the pink gaol to the airport.

He left a lot of Tasmania still unblessed. On the way to the race-course, as his procession crossed the city, the television comment-ator ventured, 'I'm sure that if he'd had the time, His Holiness would have liked to visit Hobart's historic Theatre Royal.' It's the oldest in Australia; Olivier had brought his troupe there in the year I was born, and was said to have politely remarked that it was the loveliest little theatre in the world – or one of the loveliest, or something like that. Thespian Hobart, at any rate, sustained itself on the compli-ment for a generation. The Pope didn't see it, just as the Queen omitted to inspect and rectify my humdrum stretch of the main road. Still, the state for an afternoon had been allowed to look at what the commentator called 'this holy visitor'.

As the phrase implies, in Tasmania all visitors partake of holiness, because they waft in from the supernature of interstate or overseas. When I was back, another of them breezed through for a day, less holy than pneumatic: Dolly Parton, who gave a concert on a sports ground a mile away from us. Thanks to the amplifiers, she might have been singing in my parents' backyard, under the shade of the rotary clothes-hoist. The whole suburb reverberated with Dolly's patter, blown in by the wind – appeals to sweet Jesus, commiseration with working folk, and tacky jokes about hillbillies peeing in their beds. I wandered across the highway towards the source of the noise, and found that everyone in Glenorchy had turned out to listen to the absent, booming goddess. Some had clambered in swimming trunks onto their sizzling corrugated roofs, and aimed binoculars into the distance; a congregation of oldies in bowling hats arranged a half-moon of garden chairs on their cement lawn, and sat there under the shelter of black rain umbrellas; a mile off in the other direction, as I later discovered, a nonogenarian aunt of mine – afflicted with a thrombosis, hiatus hernia, crippling arthritis and haemmorrhoids which required her to sit on an ice pack all day long, though still possessing, as my mother said, 'all her facilities' – had been wheeled to the open window and enthusiastically tapped her stick. Around the rim of the oval, a non-paying public clustered on top of parked lorries, or dangled from pine trees along the railway line. This was no specialised audience. Another of those starry, sanctifying passages of a comet was in progress, and the whole of the state had convened to witness it.

Manoeuvring myself into position at the gate of the oval, I could see through a gap in the banks of spectators. Far away in the centre of the arena, under a gazebo of loudspeakers, was the tiny owner of that omnipresent voice: a jiving avalanche of blonde hair, with some red legs holding it up. The coloured speck hopped and bounced in a frenzy; the voice explained that if she didn't keep moving, the wind – sneezing off Mount Wellington as on the day of the Pope's tempestuous Mass – would blow her away. Thus she didn't dare risk sitting down to play the banjo. 'I'll play it for y'all,' she promised, 'next time I come.'

I recalled long ago hearing someone else say something similar in this same place. When I was a boy, the circus came to town. One Friday night, while my father went to drink at the Returned Servicemen's Club, my mother brought me along to this oval to the canvas ziggurat where the clowns and lions and fire-eaters were to appear. But the wind was up that night too, and before the show could begin, it blew the tent down. As we filed out in docile misery through the gate, slatterns in quilted dressing-gowns – who should have been kicking their fish-netted legs as the trunks of elephants dandled them in the air, or hanging from trapezes by their sparkling teeth – handed us torn squares of coloured paper: pass-outs which, they said, would let us in free next time the circus came to town. I'm sure I still have the promissory chit somewhere in a drawer. I remember punctually thinking every January that maybe it would be this year that the circus returned. But no one passes this way twice. Dolly was one more comet in unpausing transit.

Some deposit relics of holiness without bothering to pass this way at all. As a boy I doted on a rotting, barnacled hulk moored in a bay across the river from our house, with a view of the tonsured rifle range and the sulphurous zinc works. This tub of scrap metal, slapped about by the tides, was the barque *Otago*, the first and only boat commanded by Joseph Conrad. He was entrusted with her in Singapore in 1887, and for the next fourteen months ferried teak from Bangkok to Sydney or sugar from Mauritius to Melbourne; he resigned in 1889, and booked passage on a steamer to England to launch a literary career. I always took the wreck's presence in our river to mean that Conrad had been here. Had he not, in a letter professing 'the warmest regards for Australians', deemed himself 'a fellow citizen', since the *Otago* was registered in Port Adelaide? Of course my namesake (who was known at the time as Mr Conrad Korzeniowski) hadn't been anywhere near Tasmania. The iron remnant of the *Otago* was no fond souvenir; it was merely junk, and its retirement on the Derwent had nothing to do with Conrad. In 1906 he wrote the vessel off, assuming it to be 'gone now from the face of the earth'. In fact it was already in Tasmania – did that mean the same thing? – being used as a coal barge. This grimy service lasted until 1931, when it was beached in the shallow bay under Mount Direction. There it decayed. During the 1950s a dotty hermit holed up in it; in 1957 it was gutted by fire.

Now all that's left is a marine cemetery of ribs and girders, stained white by the seagulls which occupy the decaying posts of what was once a jetty. The mud sucks on some strips of buckled boiler plate and a locker whose metal is eaten away to punctured skin; the red, broken anchorage is twisted among the stones like fossilised rope. The scene smells of stagnation, with the incense of ammonia exhaled from the zinc works. Nevertheless, the holy visitor who never came to visit is honoured here. Though the shrine is empty except for these molten twists of metal, the cove with its drooling drainpipe goes by the name of Otago Bay, and behind it a street which veers impulsively into the bush is called, in unreciprocated yearning, Conrad Drive.

Garden Gods

Tasmania was a Gothic society. The heroines of Mrs Radcliffe's novels shuddered deliciously at the thought of Italian monasteries, because they were closed-off enclaves of barbaric penance; Tasmania was such a psychic prison, expanded to fill the entire island. It also had a Gothic landscape. Marcus Clarke described the bush as haggard, hostile, spectral, every shape and sound the materialisation of a dread. The first prescription for civilising this Gothic place was therefore Grecian architecture. Neoclassicism would enlighten the benighted reserve of sin.

The early churches propound this sober conviction. The presbyterian kirk at Evandale outside Launceston, built in 1839, defies the romanticism of Scott and adopts a plain Attic rationality, with empty niches on either side of its yellow columned façade and a classical nymph decorously mourning the founding minister. Three years later Lady Franklin, wife of the governor, supplied Hobart with its own hortatory Greek temple. She owned a property in Kangaroo (subsequently Lenah) Valley, which, disregarding the marsupials, she renamed Ancanthe on an analogy with Greece. Here she began her campaign to construct an Athens of the south by building a Glyptothek – a microscopic version of the Temple of Athene – under the irate brow of Mount Wellington. The little sanctum was meant to house an ark of Grecian replicas. She wanted casts of the Elgin marbles – 'the Theseus, Ilyssus, Torso, and Horse's Head at the British Museum', she specified – and as well copies of the Apollo Belvedere, the Venus di Medici, the Laocoon and the Dying Gladiator. These imperturbable marble warriors and the chilly goddess, reproduced in chalky plaster, were to be prototypes for colonial behaviour. It was a touchingly out-of-date project. Two decades earlier, Byron had left his gloomy abbey at Newstead and gone off to die in the Greek war of independence, commissioning a suit of armour copied from neoclassical illustrations to the *Iliad*. Gothic was the style of morbid thought-haunted moral crime; Greece meant salvation. Lady

Franklin hoped the same charm would work for her husband's polluted subjects.

But her empty fane slid back from redemptive art to rude nature. Instead of the convoy of attitudinising paragons, it was furnished with monographs on mammals and local birds, and a collection of natural history specimens. Later in the century, the books were removed to a store in Hobart, where damp attacked them; the unrevered temple on its Acropolis of scrub became a shed for stacking crates of apples and sacks of potatoes. A local art club exhibits in it now. The earnest works on show – oily daubs of Coles Bay and inky prints of the wharves in Hobart – could well be the products of some Victorian sketching society, trying to educate the landscape by making imitations of it.

Lieutenant Bowen, protecting the settlement at Risdon which was his short-lived creation, too fondly described it as 'more like a nobleman's park in England than an uncultivated country'. Collins overruled him, shifted the site, and the presumptive park straggled back to wilderness again. Still, this vision of Tasmania as a tamed garden with attendant gods persisted. The village of Plenty, past New Norfolk, is named after that dream: plenitude, bounty, the blessings of Ceres. Around it is the usual tindery valley of stark gums and sparking grasses, the carious rooftops of gutted farms and the brick pyramid of a fireplace with no house belonging to it. Hawthorn hedges cordon off the plentiful, irrigated grove, devoted like paradise to fertilisation. It's called the Salmon Ponds, after an experiment in acclimatisation like those transplanted Windsor acorns at Lilydale. In 1864 the first trout and salmon eggs in the southern hemisphere – freighted from England in an ice-chest on a clipper ship to Melbourne, sent on by steamship to Hobart, then hurried to Plenty by river steamer – were hatched here. The place is an ovarian idyll, a sappy amniotic factory of kind. The eggs or milt are squeezed and tickled from the belly of the fish, then when fertilised held on trays in the hatching troughs, with water trickling through. Outside, pencil pines, Lombardy poplars, cypress and ash droop over the uterine pools. Their surface is padded with lily leaves, afloat on the gurgling tanks like a quivery armada of green fish. Snorkel-shaped buds sprout in sphincters of petals. Rainbow trout do circuits of the ponds, their scales glinting; among the mottled brown trout is a family of albinos, lemon with red eyes and a skin which looks like velvet under the water. In this small Eden, Adam and Eve could happily have overseen the foison of forms, and they'd have been secure so long as they didn't glance across the hedge at that flammable valley.

It is a vulnerable paradise, guarded from the wild by its fence. The best English hope was to plan a park inside Tasmania, as Bowen wistfully claimed for his stockade of huts at Risdon. It took a more intrepid, mountain-scaling Teutonic romantic, culturally accustomed to storm and stress and solitary forests, to live in this landscape rather than shutting it out, to trust it and pacify it with his love: this was the Austrian naturalist Gustav Weindorfer, who in 1911 cut and sawed King Billy pine in the highlands to build himself a cabin at Cradle Mountain, where he lived until his death in a blizzard in 1932. Around the chalet are conifers and moss-caked rocks which could be Tyrolean; a stream chuckles somewhere, and the hillside sweats cold mist. Wallabies suckle outside Weindorfer's door in the dew, the mother standing patiently upright, clasping its stumpy armless hands, while the child plugs its mouth to her, as if to a petrol bowser.

Here Weindorfer practised, for the first time in Tasmania, the romantic cult of communion with nature. He did so literally, by keeping open house for the creatures who were his only neighbours. In 1918 he recorded his habit in his diary: 'When the ground is all covered with snow, I do build a big fire, open my door, seat myself very, very quietly in front of the blazing logs and presently they come in one by one, the wild animals without their usual fear of man or one another, and share with me in stillness, the grateful warmth.' The 'very, very quietly' wills his own invisibility; in his absence, the animals could foregather again in the peaceable kingdom of old, where lion and lamb cohabited before they knew hate and fear.

Duterrau's painting of Robinson the reconciler tentatively extended the accord between races to the animals: a wallaby squats in company with its natural enemy the roo hound – though it does seem to be clenching its tiny flippers and retreating from the long-nosed dog behind a matey aboriginal. Weindorfer's dream of playing host to the fauna of the mountain has also been illustrated, in a mural by John Lendis which covers the wall of an old Masonic lodge in Sheffield, from where the road climbs into the highlands. The painting is a hyper-real hallucination. Weindorfer sits there, serenely unstirring, with his notebook and his hat on the table beside him. A wallaby and a wombat have already snuggled up on his hearth; the floor is occupied by a native cat, a kangaroo and that rodent-like mismatch of species, the potoroo. At the open door, a devil peeps in, its nasal whiskers bristling with suspicion of the armistice. The windows open, as romantic casements promise to do, onto vistas of impossibility: on one snowy alp, a black cockatoo perches unseasonably in a tropical pandanus tree and fluffs up its plumes; on another white hillside there's a sighting of Tasmania's elusive, non-existent wonder – the tiger, with its orange rib-cage of stripes. This Adam's beneficent at-home is framed by the corrugated roof of the lodge and the gravel of a parking lot, by public lavatories and a Bible chapel. A gaudy writing on the wall, its sentimentality is cancelled by its strangeness: here is a Dickensian Christmas for marsupials.

It's also still a vision of nature domesticated. The animals, house-trained, renounce wildness to move indoors. At the Cradle Mountain inn, near Weindorfer's Waldheim, its limitations are exposed. Here every night after dinner the scraps of left-over food are ladled out on a two-tiered trough behind the dining-room. Spotlights are trained on it to attract the scavengers from the bush; you can spy on them at close quarters from behind glass. It's not quite the peaceable kingdom out there. On the upper trough, stuffed with slices of day-old processed white bread, twenty or thirty possums jostle, their brushes coiled round each other. They are delicate eaters, clasping the squares in their tiny paws and systematically nibbling their way across them. Nuzzled companionably together, they look like a church choir ingesting its pages of sheet music. They gracefully grapple up the poles to this level reserved for them; below are the animals which can't climb – wallabies, potoroos, native cats and (lurking in the shrubbery out of sight) the devils. The segregation is social. The devils are filthy feeders, grubbing in the trough with their snouts in quest of meat and splashing among the milk slops, not prissily handling their vittles and posing upright to eat like the possums; they wolf rotten apples and snort in the mess with piggy relish. Their faces twist in a perpetual grimace: like the bums of monkeys, they represent the obscene, the unseeable. Their coats are ripped by vendettas, and one of them has a face which his colleagues have bitten bald. The storeys of the trough preserve a moral distance between upstairs and downstairs. The possums when they have polished off their papery bread swing away through the trees; the devils scuttle hissing into the underbrush.

Marsupials excite maternal feelings because they are themselves so maternally dependent. The wombat's worm-like infant spends six months inside the pouch, and feeds on its mother's milk for the first eleven months of its life outside that moist envelope. Tasmania abounds with women eager to adopt these somnolent suitcases of gritty fur. In the wildlife park at Chudleigh, a ranger hugged one which had been orphaned to her breast, wrapped in its own bunny rug; the doctor's wife on Flinders Island raised another on a water-bed, took it off the island by plane for holidays inside the ersatz pouch of her handbag, and in restaurants requested a baby's portion of milk for it. I find wombats difficult to love. They seem designed as diagrams of evolutionary retrogression. Their pouch faces back-wards, and opens towards the rear-end rather than being worn on the stomach like the wallaby's extramural womb; the arse is their lethal weapon, a cannon-ball of hard cartilage used to block the entry to their burrows, and with which they can crush a man's hand or a dog's head if it follows them in. Wallabies enjoy sitting under a tree and unfurling their tails in front between their legs for a scratch: they look as if they're delousing a stringy elasticised penis. And koalas, slumped in the crooks of gum boughs asleep, seem to have snored their way through centuries, waking from their stupor only to nibble leaves.

Weindorfer brought his gods with him to Tasmania. His idyll was a cultural import, like Lady Franklin's temple or those Atlantic salmon. Tramping the mountain tops, he might have been a mystic from a painting by Caspar David Friedrich. He worshipped in open-air cathedrals of dolerite, with rainbows as his testaments. Roman-ticism made him reread nature as scripture: hence that beautiful, improbable vision of the animals forgetting their feuds to share the affectionate warmth he exudes.

On Flinders, Derek Smith with his Franciscan crusade to save the Cape Barren geese from hunters lives by the same creed. Puffing on an acrid pipe and muttering from a corner of his mouth, this old man with the warty creased face as furrowed as terrain – a former baker who left school at fourteen, hasn't been off the island for seven years (when he took his stricken wife to hospital in Hobart, where he left her) and announces that it's his ambition to die here – talks like a Wordsworth given to expletives. At dusk we drove out across the wind-blown plain to his sanctuary, to chase the wallabies through the tussocks in his ramshackle unsprung car. On the way, he took me to meet his favourite grass-tree. It looks like a stilled fountain, its radial blades and soft spikes poised in the air. He rhapsodised over the exploding tuft of rushes: 'Bloody oath, will you look at that! To think something that transparent could be that solid. It makes you feel a bit bloody small,' which is exactly what the sublime portents of romantic nature were meant to do; 'three hundred and fifty, maybe a thousand years it's been standing there, watching the world go by. Bugger me.' From one of the peaks we saw the moon rise, floating into a sky turned metallic around it and quickening the lagoons beneath us to sheets of crinkled silver. 'It's like looking at a frigging birth,' said Derek Smith. And showing me the pond which is Frank the Italian bloke's moat, he reeled off the inventory of creatures living there – stick insects, green tree frogs, whitebait, after which I lost count – and added, 'Cripes! There's more hearts beating in there than in the whole of bloody Australia.'

Derek Smith's swearing is exactly that: it swears an oath and writes its name in blood to vouch for the truth of his emotion. It's far from lewd, because it's employed only in circumstances of matey solidarity. He was scandalised, he told me, when the local ranger 'effed' in front of some women at a social evening. Sometimes he means to call down an anathema – a bushfire on the island is to him 'the bloody bastard of a fire' – but more often his diction indulges lyrical enthusiasm while at the same time apologising for it: laconic Australians, with their side-of-mouth delivery, feel eloquence is justified only when it's abusive, so love must express itself in a cadenza of curses.

He doesn't mistake Flinders for Utopia. 'It would be a good place,' he says, 'if you could choose the people' – just as Coleridge and the other romantics fancied migrating to America to establish a pantiso-cratic colony beside the Susquehanna. As it is, the scant popula-tion of Flinders lives by farming or fishing, so has no patience with Derek Smith's concern for the protection of wildlife. He nettled the islanders when campaigning against their duck- and quail-shooting, or the slaughter of Cape Barren geese. Cruelty to animals is a national creed, continuing proof of our capacity to survive. I told him about a young cousin of mine, a gun-happy policeman, who'd asked me to take back to England the scrotum of a kangaroo. He had promised this tit-bit to an Englishman he met in Fiji, whose business was the distribution of pornography to south-east Asia. What better gift for a sleaze-monger than an emptied ball-bag which, strung tight with a thong removed from some other part of the roo, apparently makes a nifty change-purse? And, since kangaroos don't have antlers to cut off, what better evidence of human success in the daily battle against nature than this trophy of emasculation? Luckily my cousin didn't find a roo to geld, so I was spared the errand. Derek Smith favours poetic justice for all such hunters: 'I'd cut their trigger fingers and their dicks off' (which he also proposes as a political solution in the Middle East).

He has gone back to nature with exemplary squalor, and begins each day by sweeping away the overnight deposit of dung which his two pet Cape Barren geese have left outside his door. He disapproves of the flush toilet, which mediates between us and the earth. He possesses one himself in his plywood lean-to beside the water at Whitemark, but has installed it in a doorless room next to the kitchen, behind a filmy shower-curtain: you crouch there, inches from the breakfasting household, and pray that no untoward eruption will betray you. The same room contains an open wardrobe with Derek's funeral suit; until then, he wears cast-offs from St Vincent de Paul. The recycling of his smirched, ungainly garments appeals to him, I think: they too have been revolved in earth's diurnal, dirtying course, like the junked tin he fossicked for at the tip to fence his sanctuary and like the contents of his personal museum in a shed – gutted radios, legless teddy bears, shelves of caricatural clay faces he has moulded – which he says he will soon have to start carting back to the tip, where they'll await their own decomposition and reincarnation.

He takes the same pleasure in driving words into the ground, and describes frustrated efforts to educate the children of the island in etymology and environment at once: 'That mountain's made of igneous rock. What's igneous mean?' Blank stare from child. So he reasons back from mechanism to organism: 'When you get in your car, what's the first thing you do?' Child knows you start the ignition. 'Well, what does that mean? It sparks the motor, right? So if the ignition is a flame, how does an igneous rock get formed?' Child dimly perceives that it's treading on a volcano. With granite, Derek has had less luck. He quizzed a local kid about this, asking what chickens were fed on in the hope of leap-frogging by association from seed to grain to granular granite. Pert child's reply brought him to an abrupt halt: 'Our chooks eat Monds and Affleck fowl pellets.'

This is his despair – a world of substitutes, fakes, plastic unrealities. When I arrived, *Mork and Mindy* was on television, and he sat there beside the kitchen fire calling 'that silly bastard' Robin Williams a cavalcade of ignoble names. Nothing could be further from his desire to be grounded, planted in this stony segment of earth, than the manic somersaults and unhinged gibberish of Mork the extra-terrestrial. Unlike Lady Franklin, he doesn't want to civilise Tasmania. Civilisation is what he would like to save it from. Nor, like Weindorfer, does he sentimentally ennoble the animals he lives among. His wombats have mange, the wallabies have invaded the preserve he built for the geese, and the geese in turn express their gratitude by dumping on his doorstep. Islands are a refuge for mystics, and the mountains on Flinders have their share, apparently, of drop-outs in Afghan goat-skin tents; but an island is also a misanthrope's last resort.

Derek Smith feels a prickly affinity with trees, because he has given up on people. Explaining his attempts to threaten and cajole the islanders into respecting the place they exploit, he says, 'You've got to be a bit like this coastal tea tree – you lean a bit one way or the other, then straighten up when the wind drops; otherwise you'll be blown out of the ground.' The tree is embedded in that ground. Human beings wander about unfixed, waving their inverse mental roots uselessly in the air. I remembered the totemic practices of the aborigines, each of whose tribes selected a species of tree as the badge of its clan, and the pride the men took in their resemblance to red-topped gums. I also thought of some tree people I'd seen in a front garden outside Wynyard, on the north-west coast: a row of hirsute bristly man-ferns, their thick branches lopped off, dressed up beside the road like a ward of jolly amputees. Where fronds once grew, they wore panama hats or floral bonnets; belts were fastened round the midriff of their shaven boles. Bulbous streaky marbles had been stuck into the trunks for eyes. One of them, female presumably, had a mouth demarcated by a Cupid's bow of orange tape; her consort bit on a pipe. These, perhaps, are the gods most at home in Tasmanian gardens: not the nymphs and fauns Lady Franklin imagined in the bush, but ferns hacked into humanoids and put on display, like corpses dangled from a battlement, to signal nature's defeat.

Little England or Wild West?

At night, also unable to tolerate *Mork and Mindy*, my parents would take up their books. My mother's, borrowed from the library and jacketed in thick plastic, was one of the chronicles written by prim, pseudonymous 'Miss Read' about a cosy Cotswold village called Thrush Green; my father's, a much-thumbed paperback donated by a friend, was described on its cover as 'a tale of Larry and Stretch', two cowpoke pardners sired by the author, Marshall Grover. Its title: *Texans Walk Proud*. My mother read of hollyhocks and parish pumps, snowfalls and thatches, my father of rustlers, corrals, Colt .45s and swinging saloon doors.

They had retired into their separate, non-interchangeable elsewheres, each representing an Australian self-image. At first the country was to be an ancillary England; lately it has come to liken itself to brawling America. England, supposedly the mother country, is the matrilineal choice, America with its energetic violence is the masculine preference. Tasmania alternates between these borrowed identities. This tiny extradited England has suburban properties with names like Lazy Acres, suggesting a grandiose Texan spread. The myth of the big country is kept alive in Lilliput: the house beside the church at Richmond is entitled Santa Fe. In the midlands at Hamilton – whose river is the Clyde and whose manse is Glen Clyde House – the showground's stencilled motif is a cowboy flaunting his hat on top of a rearing bronco. At Queenstown, 'a good old country song' drawled from the car radio: Marty Robbins invited anyone who was listening to meet him tonight in Laredo, and promised they'd soon be in old Mexico; the announcer next advertised sachets of goanna oil, ideal gift packs for Australia Day. These are taunting illusions. The wild West existed to be subdued, like the broken-in steer. Tasmania's west coast, though wild, won't ever be conquered. And as for a frontier, where would the state have room for one?

Earlier, enclaves of Englishness were cultivated in the colony. In 1818 the Governor planted a garden. On the parched yellow mound of the Domain, a gully was trained to be a glade. Willow, laurel and ash were planted, and a dribbling creek was dammed to make a lily pond. Nature here wasn't left to its own haphazard devices, as on the ragged Domain; it was composed into views and vistas, with little useless bridges and tactically positioned benches. The pool of drowsing, stifling lilies has recently been re-landscaped into a map of Tasmania – a perfumed image to contradict the craggy silhouette of the state which the breakers obliterate at Remarkable Cave. But topographically, the Botanical Gardens evoke England: the park is laid out to admonish the informal bush around it, and even possesses its own juvenile ruin. An arch of stone, carved for an insurance office in Hobart in 1913, has been buried almost to the top in flower beds, with chiselled Ruskinian leaves twining over it. The fence debarring the local landscape nurtures a deciduous Arcadia: Governor Arthur in 1829 ordered the construction of a wall like those used to encourage English kitchen gardens, with fireplaces and air ducts in the brick so the plants could be pampered by heat from coal; and in 1878 gates of cast iron were shipped out from England to close off this lush oasis.

Beside the Botanical Gardens stands England's official citadel, the turreted folly of Government House, its windows criss-crossed with mullions like fretted pastry crusts, its steep rooftops bristling with an armed guard of chimneys. An émigré saint, overdressed for the climate, occupies a shallow niche on the front wall. The building should Gothically loom through mist; instead it's set in a shorn, tanned field beside the glittering river. Though sun demystifies it, it was to me the ominous beginning of England, and when I went there for the first time – in 1967, to have my table manners inspected by the selection committee for the Rhodes Scholarship, whose chairman was the Governor of the state – it was like crossing the border into my fantasy. The invitation to the dinner was itself a summons from another world: an envelope of starched linen, containing a card of impeccable white from which the embossed letters jutted like wrought iron; my own name was treated to curlicues I didn't deserve by a pen with a buck-toothed nib. On the appointed evening, my parents dropped me at the gate. We didn't have the gumption, collectively, to drive up to the portico, where the morning-suited equerry and the naval aide with the hyphenated name – wearing a uniform of the same crisp white as the invitation card – waited. I walked down the gravel path, and thought of Joan Fontaine in *Rebecca* fumbling through the fingering trees around the corner towards her own imaginary castle of Manderley. Of course here there was no spooky moon, only a fierce November sun; and I was no disembodied drifting voice but a boy in a tuxedo modelled on the Beatle suit, with stove-pipe legs pegged round the ankles, lapels slickly narrow, and a pair of spiky winkle-picker shoes which made the gravel (not meant to be walked on, except perhaps by the inmates of the Risdon gaol, who worked in the gardens) crunch like animals chomping in the shrubbery. But it might have been Manderley and its ghosts ahead, so far as my dry throat and jittery heart-beat were concerned: I was approaching a place of social terrors, the pinnacle of aloof England.

Inside, rather than the spiral stairs, cobwebbed vaults and crumbly masonry of Gothic fear, there were open spaces just as dreadful in their formality. I remember a room larger than any I'd ever been in, and the plain of empty carpet which had to be crossed to get to the Governor – a lame, benign soldier, sent out from England to spend his retirement administering us. When I went back there twenty years later to have lunch, I left that same room where I'd spent half an afternoon gossiping with the current Governor and glanced backwards to congratulate myself for not being afraid any more, as I was on my first limping pilgrimage across the floor: what I saw, with a flush, was the track the rubber treads of my shoes had left on that smooth golden fabric, as if I'd been trudging through wet sand. This was a carpet to glide over in patent leather; my every step had stigmatised me. Perhaps it's as well that you don't outlive your fears, or your shame. Later on the first night, two decades before, we had to show off our sporting graces by playing carpet bowls on that intimidating parade-ground. My bowl, biased against me in earnest, veered off on a course of its own around the room, while I could only watch in helpless anguish. Would it topple the spindly table on which the Queen's photograph perched? In the event it chose to thump the Governor's labrador, asleep under a sofa. The dog blinked at me superciliously when I went to rescue the bowl, then slept again.

The photograph in its silver frame and the gigantic oils of ponderous Edwardian royalty told all: these were the absentee tenants, making their presence felt on the walls, sideboards and grand piano. The house was kept ready for their occasional visits to it. They owned Tasmania; we merely lived in it. In the Tasmanian Club, among the halls lined with Victorian worthies who stare mournfully over hedges of hair, there's a print of the painting Tom Roberts made when the Duke of York opened Australia's first federal parliament. The ceremony appears to be happening in a cavernous, twilit Valhalla, with the Duchess aiming an imperially haughty glance aside at the artist. Beneath this print, the aged relics of Anglo-Australia reminisce. One of them, whose grandfather brought the blessing of Presbyterianism to Bothwell, told me how he had trooped through London with the standard of Empire loyalism after the First World War. His bent old body straightened at the thought, and his rheumy eyes gleamed. But there's no one younger to whom he can pass on the flag.

I can't imagine any child now looking forward to a royal tour as I did to that in 1954. For me, it was a day-long validation of our existence, an assurance that we belonged to something. That stiltedly waving figure in the passing car answered (during the few seconds she was visible) all sorts of infantile cosmic queries: why were we here? who made us? My own Empire loyalism in those days was not political but metaphysical. I had to supply the world with a centre, an omphalos, a mysterious and impenetrable place of origin; Buckingham Palace was it. I'd heard that, if you ever actually got there, you could walk up to the gate and, escorted by a policeman, gain admittance to a lobby where you were allowed to write your name in a visitors' book. Thus you reminded god that you were among his or her far-flung creation. When I arrived in London in 1968, I couldn't stop myself: I crossed the bridge from Waterloo and walked left down the Strand and the Mall until the grey façade behind the bars came into view. (I needed no map, having long ago memorised the lay-out of London from the Monopoly board.) There was my point of orientation. Content, without presuming to write my name in the book, I wandered off to see the rest of the world which rayed out from here.

Tasmania still locates its own displaced centre far away, but no longer at those palace gates. Woolnorth, the sheep- and cattle-station which occupies the north-western corner of the state, owes its land to the caprice of a royal charter. Yet there's no place in an imaginary England for its gale-scourged miles of gorse and prostrate shrubs, ending with a geological flourish on the dizzy cliffs at Suicide Bay. Woolnorth instead imitates the drawling hugeness of Texas. The top house, where the manager has his office on a lordly, windy knoll, is built of American cedar, with a shingle roof imported from Canada. The cowboys metaphorically adopt the same coinage Larry and Stretch slam down on the bar to pay for their shots of rye. Praising a horse for its turning circle, which enables it to round at once on a recalcitrant bull, its rider says, 'They can stop and turn on a dime.' For the cowboys, whose affectedly bad grammar conceals degrees in agricultural science from universities in New Zealand, the profession is a performance, consciously copying the already imaginary West of the films they've seen. They itemise their gear like finicky actors fussing over their wardrobe: the Western saddle with its double cinches, used for balance; the boots tapered to slither in and out of stirrups; hats streamlined to slice the wind; the jewelled swank of their belt buckles. Everyone must arrive on set properly outfitted: 'Where's your moleskins?' one of them sternly asked another, who appeared in the rodeo arena without the prescribed trousers. They carry off their charade with the help of the odd smirking alienation effect. The stockman, squeezing the last of the claret from a cardboard wine cask at lunch, said, 'Just like milkin' a cow'; squirting cream from another paper carton over my fruit, the station manager's wife announced, 'This is our cow.' Everything they handled, like that notional dime, was a theatrical prop.

Only their dumb accomplices sometimes forget the moves assigned to them. The virility of the stock bulls is enthusiastically vouched for by a cowgirl called Carolyn, who wears Fabergé jeans rather than the regulation moleskins: 'They're guaranteed to perform,' she vows; 'we deliver anywhere in Tasmania, and if the heifer's not satisfied, just send 'im back.' But when one of these meaty studs is called on to frisk round his corral in a show of fury so the horse can turn on that dime to restrain him, he resigns in disgust and concentrates on solemnly, steamily shitting. 'This shows the tremendous temperament we've got in our Hereford cattle here,' says the stockman in charge of the demonstration. Then the sheep ignore the kelpy which is maniacally yapping them into their pen: 'Jeez, them sheep get ignorant when they're worked too often,' sighs the cowboy with the New Zealand diploma; 'you wouldn't believe them mongrels of sheep.' These graceful admissions of defeat belong inimitably to Australia, not Texas. Ned Kelly shrugs again. The rhetoric of the place is bloodthirsty, as the borrowed ethos of the West requires. Carolyn describes the Caesarean sectioning of a cow – 'you should've seen the sausages that was pouring out of her stomach, and they was stuffing 'em back in by the handful' – or the freighting of sheep to the Middle East, where they're ritually slaughtered while their heads point towards Mecca. The Arabs believe in slashing the sheep's throat vertically not (as on Woolnorth) horizontally: 'they like to kill 'em,' says Carolyn with another of those philosophical shrugs, 'in their own special way.' The shearing sheds are touted as barbers' shops of gore. A shearer readying his razor calls for 'anyone who likes to see blood'. But sheep, so mild-mannered and timorous, don't belong to this particular theatre of force. The Western myth needs cattle – dangerous and difficult for the heroic rider to subdue. The lore of the Australian outback, from the ballad about the clicking shears or Tom Roberts's painting of the fleece-floored shed, is gentler, more abjectly pastoral. At Woolnorth, I watched a merino being shorn. The periwig trotting on stick-like legs is unzipped by the razor. His head and legs twisted elastically by the shearer, he lolls half-asleep; those milky eyes roll as he patiently awaits his metamorphosis from Louis XIV to a bag of bones in a loose shirt of skin. He ends sitting on the rug he previously wore. The fleece is grey on the surface, creamy within; the sheep has been turned inside out. Dazed for a moment, he soon stumbles away to begin growing another coat. Sheep are not fitted for Western battles between human courage and brutal, bullish power. Their easy-going fatalism is the essence of Australia.

Another American archetype stalks the Australian bush: Paul Bunyan the legendary axe-wielding giant, who cleared the land so men could build. Tree-slaying is the hard labour which makes settlement possible; since work is ritually celebrated as play, in Tasmania it's a sport as well. Every holiday in the Huon there would be chopping carnivals. The champion axemen, with beer bellies worthy of Paul Bunyan's bulk, gathered on a sports oval in their uniform of white trousers and singlets – dapper cricketers below the waist, shaggy centaurs above it. They'd bring out their box of blades like choosy executioners, spit on the wedge of polished steel they'd chosen, and hack at the trunks which were clamped in place to be massacred, sending blizzards of sappy chips whirring through the air. There was something ferociously primitive to these tournaments, as the sweating, gasping choppers worked off their rage against nature. Yet they slaughtered trees with the precise incisiveness of surgeons. The game was an epic trial of strength, and also a test of technical skill. To keep in practice, the prize-winners would knock down the tallest pine they could find, shave it and saw it into blocks, then set about systematically gashing it. Soon the tree would be no more than a pile of white and orange scales, useless even as firewood.

These athletic rehearsals are necessary because the battle with the bush is never-ending. The very notion of the bush suggests the indiscriminateness of growth, and its thick thorny obstructive texture; the history of settlement in Tasmania can be traced through this murder of trees. I went to see the loggers at work in the Lemonthyme forest. Paul Bunyan now has mechanical ogres to assist him – a dozer to bash down scrub and knock out stumps, a skidder to shift the logs along, an orc-faced excavator to pinion them in its yellow beak and load them ready for chaining on the lorries. The clearing was loud with the snorting and biting of these wood-eaters, and the snarl of the saw which slices the stringy bark from the trunks. Earth was a churned wreckage of uprooted grass, peeled bark, trampled eucalyptus sprigs; the forest gave off the aromatic oily stench of barbered timber. The felled trees were gouged with slits like the eye-holes in Ned Kelly's mask: toe-holds for the choppers, who clamber up on a shaky scaffold of clipped shoeboards to a height where the tree is narrow enough to be cross-cut, look further up to decide where the weight inclines so they can judge the angle of its fall, then slash a triangular wound in the bark on one side and a thin slice on the other. Now a fault line runs through the centre of the trunk, on which it begins to shudder and waver. Logging has its regular moments of truth. When the tree has been carved through like this, a tap with the axe will make the top of it, looming above, gyrate through the air; if it's leaning, a wedge slipped into the razored groove can cause it to snap and thud to the ground like a long lean homicidal cudgel. At this stage, the tree is deadly; once floored, it becomes the prey of the excavator, that tractor with the sharpened tusks and flexing jaws which pursues the clumsy length, scraping bark off as it snatches and gnaws.

The next scene is the sawmill, where the logs are rolled onto the whirring blade which rips them into flitches among a blitz of shavings and a bleeding of red dust from the core. A dockerman then planes them into planks, disclosing their white insides. Their career as trees is over; a spout behind the shed excretes a mound of sawdust. The wood's next incarnation is as lengths of weatherboard nailed together into houses like the one I grew up in. From the first, Tasmania has been axeing nature to raise a city, even if its location is elsewhere: the paling-splitters around Ulverstone in the middle of the nineteenth century cut the trees from which Melbourne was built.

Bunyan the American lumberjack, aided by his blue ox measuring forty-two axe-handles, fells trees without compunction. He is a man-machine, a locomotive slayer of landscape. Australian folklore has no such invincible hero because, in this arduous, wry, unself-pitying country, those who chop down the trees feel an affinity – hewn and hardened and stringy as they are – with their victims. Someone at a mill in Wynyard on the north-west coast said to me 'The poor old logs come here and go to be made into paper in Burnie.' Paul Bunyan couldn't risk such a commiserating sentiment. My mother, even more plaintively, likes to represent herself as one of those tender trunks bitten into by the nagging axes. 'You're always chipping at me,' she would say when I complained or otherwise vexed her; once, talking on the telephone to a sarcastic sister while my father grumbled some satire of his own in the room, she said to me, with a simultaneous giggle and grimace, 'They're chipping at me from both sides now.' She was the persecuted stump, clamped in place for the laughing choppers.

The cruises down the Gordon are manned by a family of loggers, who used to cut Huon pine in the rain forest and towed pontoons of timber back to Strahan to build their first boat. These men pay tribute to the trees they killed with a comradely personification: 'you cut him down,' one of them said admiringly about the Huon pine, 'and he'll float with a third of him above the water, he's so full of oil.' I'd first noticed this anthropomorphic matiness in our own vegetable garden. My father called me out one day to watch him cut a green giant for lunch. 'Nice cabbage, weren't he?' he asked afterwards.

Along the Gordon there are compliments for stands of King Billy pine – 'he's a lovely soft open-grained timber' – and for celery top 'which won't open up or move on you'. Always, with the foresight of Crusoe, the growth is appraised as the raw material of some utensil. The celery top is used for decking on boats because it resists the sun, and for telegraph poles 'because they grow so straight and beautiful'; as for the sassafras, 'he's a pretty handy old tree', made into pegs which won't stain your washing, into beer ('they reckon that's a good drop'), and 'a lovely black tea'; the blackwood is 'one of our best bending timbers – they use him for making beer barrels.' The loggers treat the trees as colleagues because the process of cutting them is a hereditary one, a game played inconclusively and passed on to the future by a smiling agreement between both sides. One of the woodcutters in the Lemonthyme told me that his father had logged this same area; one generation clears the land, then it grows up to be felled over again by the next. Both axemen and trees merge with their ancestry, and with their offspring.

My guide through the Lemonthyme forest was Darryl Stafford, descendant of a tree-felling dynasty who began steering log lorries out of the bush when a schoolboy. He worked alongside his father until the older man's neck was snapped by a ricocheting bough, then did a stretch as an interstate trucker, and now drives tourists from Devonport to Cradle Mountain in a bus decorated with Tasmanian devils, telling yarns as he goes. He remembers hurtling from a shoeboard wedged in the side of a tree he was cutting when a log split. He soared fifteen feet into the air and disappeared into a pin-cushion of prickly scrub. His father gulped, and was silent for a while. Then he tentatively shouted, 'Are you right, son?' Darryl answered from some hole in the shrubbery, and when his father heard his voice he began to bellow with mocking laughter. Such is the guarded fraternity of the bush, and its jokey confrontation of danger. 'You need the scares,' says Darryl, 'to keep you respectful.' He points out how stealthily loggers move, refusing to be hurried, always testing their ground or calculating how wind will alter the angle of a plummeting tree: they know the bush would enjoy killing them, and are determined to outwit it. Cunning is among their occupational skills. Darryl possesses it, though he deploys it for teasing people rather than levelling trees. He likes warning novices at Cradle Mountain about the dead bush-walkers they'll probably

have to step over on the track, and terrorised me by offering to
perform feats of bravado. When we passed a tiger snake coiled on
the road, lazily writhing and reorganising its circlets, he reversed at
once. 'Wanna see how to pick him up?' he asked, jumping out. 'You
grab him by the tail, then crack him like a whip.' Was he counting on
my refusal?

Like the Woolnorth cowboys, he knows he's performing a fantasy
– a playlet in which Australia imagines itself to be America. He urges
his four-wheel-drive van over ruts and ditches as if it were a bucking
mount: 'Git up there!' he growls when it demurs at a ridge or a
toppled tree. Australia peeps out from behind the American mask
only when he admits his unease, and laughs about it. He was
running in the van on the Lemonthyme's slippery slides of mud,
bordered by precipices. 'It's me maiden voyage,' he said; 'hope it's
not like the *Titanic*.' After we'd jolted down a mountain, with the van
leaning out at sick angles to admire the drop, he asked me, 'Was you
frightened?' 'Er, no', I said deliberately. 'I was shit scared!' roared
Darryl. Since he's playing a bushman, he conscientiously dresses for
the part, and likes to tell you how much the moleskins, the hand-
made boots and the cabbage-leaf hat of leather cost him. When we
parted, he hauled a tanned executive briefcase from its hiding-place
in the back of his jalopy, fiddled with the combination lock, and gave
me as a souvenir a sheaf of press cuttings about himself – mentions in
Time magazine, and a write-up by a Canadian female journalist he'd
squired around Tasmania. He was planning a self-promoting tour to
North America next year, and his Canadian contact had made him
promise to step from the plane wearing his bush outfit, whatever
the season. It sounded familiar. Where had I come across this plot
before?

Then, flying back from Sydney to New York, I watched Paul
Hogan flying from Sydney to New York in *Crocodile Dundee*, the film
which rejoices in Australia's impersonation of America and which
supplied Darryl Stafford with his saleable persona. It's an artful
exercise in comparative mythology, and a sly admission that myth
means fraud – the sustaining lie, without which we can't live. Here
once more Australia's self-mistrust is appeased. Moira in *On the
Beach* worried that the indigenous landscape couldn't compare with
those of England or America. Crocodile Dundee soothes these fears
of inferiority, and by the same relativistic means: just as America

could export Kirk Douglas to play *The Man from Snowy River* in a southern Western, so Australia can export Hogan to Manhattan, where he accommodates himself to the city's municipal myths. He grins gamely as Australia is colonised all over again by a new cultural empire. America can only comprehend him, of course, by treating him as an epigone of itself. 'The man from the backwoods' is how he's described by the snotty journalist whose girl he steals: a down-under Natty Bumppo, the morganatic offspring of Fenimore Cooper. 'It's like living with Davy Crockett,' remarks the girl reporter he takes on safari in the Northern Territory; 'a regular Tarzan,' say the New York whores when he roughs up their pimp; and the Crocodile's launching of a tin can, which zooms through the air supersonically to brain a mugger, is a stunt he might have learned from another interplanetary crusader in the same city, Superman. Oafishly pursuing the beautiful girl through those streets and winning her by his virile primitivism, he resembles one more of Manhattan's rampant out-of-towners: King Kong, house-trained by the bidet in the Plaza Hotel.

The easy-going hero – named oxymoronically after the union of a town in Scotland and a tropical saurian – minds none of these inflictions, because his own Australia is patched together from imported, incongruous symbols. An aborigine on his track through the bush to a corroboree is daubed with warpaint and totes a spear, but wears blue jeans and a gold watch. The Croc, camping, alarms his American guest by offering her goanna, yams and witchety grubs; then he opens a can. He unashamedly joins his personal mystique to the other myths with which Australia is littered. Is he afraid to die? No, he says: 'God and Jesus and all them apostles – they were fishermen just like me. God 'n me'd be mates.' It's as impudent a piece of bricolage as the fabrication of the platypus, which the first English observers thought was a hoax, sewn from a rat's head and a fish tail. America believes its own national propaganda with the puritan's fanaticism; Australia, flashing a characteristic twisted grin, concedes that its legends are threadbare fictions. Crocodile Dundee, like Stafford in his expensively casual costume or the Woolnorth cowpokes turning their mounts on a dime, ventures to 'make meself more colourful for the tourists'. In the pub, he wrestles a crocodile. 'It's stuffed,' sneers his friend Wally. 'Me too,' Dundee agrees. The fiction isn't only for consumption by credulous Americans, or bemused expatriates: these people colour themselves in for their own benefit. They dramatise this suburban country, whose cities cling to the shore and look nostalgically across oceans, as an outback of intrepid pioneers. Having unlearned its deference to England, must Australia now play a surrogate America? Will it never belong to itself?

Or was I complaining because I didn't belong to it, or it to me? Bumping through the air towards New York, thinking already of another life to be resumed in London a month later, I was the symptom complaining of the disease. Perhaps Australia arrived too late in a contracting world, when even its isolation was no guarantee of autonomy, and even its insularity couldn't protect it from bombardment by images of other, prior cultures. Perhaps that isolation was to blame: in my childhood the cast-off country, subsisting on remittance, longed for recognition by and assimilation in the world which had sent it to the antipodes. Thus I turned out to be the composite of my parents' reading matter, travelling between their imagined realms as if exchanging disguises – villagy, snuggling, sympathetic England and liberating, aggressive America.

Thinking back down that day-long vapour-trail over the Pacific, I could see that my emotional business with my native land would always remain unfinished. Was it the fallen continent, unappeased by gods and unconquered by axe-men, whose punitive harshness drives away its sons? Or a sunny, simple paradise, too contented, which you must lose by choice before you can become yourself? Growth means, after all, a series of rejections. When I went back I was young enough still to feel the necessity of my ingratitude, and old enough to regret what it had cost.

V

IMAGINING TASMANIA

Cabbala

How can we exist in the world without representing it? Its contingency and its brevity alarm us. I bawled precociously at the showground that day, I'm sure, because of this perceptual terror. Why had our lives been absent-mindedly blown into this landscape? What relation could there be between the running races and chopping exhibitions we had come to watch and those sulking mountains, unmoved by small human ambitions? Why was everything – the gritty wind, the announcer's voice which it plucked away, the wasted effort of the puffing athletes, the cars hissing by on the highway – merely passing through? Phenomena are unshaped, imperfect, as involuntary as a life you haven't requested but must somehow make do with. The representation, however, charms chance into orderly choice. It imposes a spatial centre, a temporal plot. It makes a pattern or tells a story, and soothes the fractious, querulous child to sleep. Then when you wake again you recognise, cheated, the falsity of the tale you trusted. Representation is derided by the gap which always yawns between the obdurate thing and the word or image. No matter how many adjectives it's coated with, Mount Direction will still slump there and lumpily disdain them all, amorphous and directionless.

Yet the place which moved me most in Tasmania was a site where I recognised this primal pattern-making at work. On this spot, centuries ago, someone had felt the same disorientation terror as me, and had set about figuring an imagined world to which he could belong, mapping a universe for Tasmania (though it wasn't called that then) to be located in. The place is Tiagarra, a cliff jutting into Bass Strait outside Devonport, where an aborigine has hacked and hammered his own narrative version of emergence *ab origine* into the rock. I'm assuming one man made this global history, though the job was no doubt plural: there are 240 engravings in the dolerite, so the labour – anonymous, collective, age-old – seems the effort of an entire race, the scratched monument to a perennial human need for organised space and plotted time. Tiagarra for all its world-creating confidence also admits the futility of representation. You describe only what eludes you. If reality were satisfactory, we wouldn't have grown an imagination. This geological folio of graffiti invents art in Tasmania.

George Augustus Robinson, roping the natives of the north-west inside his cordon of protection in 1830, reported that he had seen a rock carving of a circle inside a perimeter of dots. Though he had no idea what it meant, it seems to signify an act of delimitation. Art yokes life into unity: that zone is sanctified, and guarded by the stake-marks around its edge. The world is not everything that exists, but everything that is included by the circle. The enclosure is our defensive definition of completeness. After it come the paling fences and herbaceous borders of the suburbs, and mis-spelled talismanic spells like Emohruo.

Tiagarra's story of formation begins with a grounded sky of such circles, lariats which desire and pursue the whole. One of them is a bud blooming concentrically outwards, opening from its little node of certainty into ever larger and more courageous containers. Another is an impregnable double circle, a fortified belt which sketches security not, like its partner, expansion. In a third, the circle has been rewritten as a coiled snake, a whorl curling outwards from the head to wrap things inside an embrace meant to comfort not, like the boa's, to constrict. Inside a fourth, there is already dissension. A truant half-circle with a dotted nucleus of its own is nudging the rim of the oval. It wants to escape: instead of the ovoid shelter, it longs for the unrolled straight line of personal discovery; the main road to somewhere else. Another image catches the convulsion – the split atom, the sundered home – as it happens. The baggy circle is halved by a border drawn through its middle. To one side is a somnolent embryonic comma, which won't quit the nest; yet the ruled road can't be hemmed in by the circle, and the cliff at Tiagarra is the starting-point for the track it inscribes across the world.

This design has a representational reference too. The enwombing circle or world-egg is an abalone shell, one of those sea-ears whose flesh the aborigines ate. The abalone is a compact cosmos. Under the dry sea-bed of the shell, caked with calcium and dirty ridges of moss, you can drill your way to a layer of pearl; and prised apart, the shell discloses a panorama of rainbows. The real and ordinary object opens into a symbol of the world's bifurcation. The abstract diagram precedes the figurative replica: first comes the theorem about fission, and the circle's impalement by that travelling line; only later do you see that the myth has been lodged in an abalone shell, exactly and beautifully drawn. Then a bestiary starts to prowl over the rocks. The rounded arcs and runaway lengths of straightness, used in the beginning as metaphysical fences, now find they have the magic power to conjure up live creatures. Two narrowed sickles and two more tapering parallels catch the fragile head and muscular neck of an emu in stone, and in another hollow of rock a seal – marked by an equine elongated face and the relaxed curve of a body – bathes out of its element.

We need words only if the things we want to call aren't present. Hence all those far-flung Utopias named on the map of Tasmania. And the representation too fills up a vacancy. A representative is a stand-in, a substitute, a second-best, doing duty for someone else who remains absent. So it was, presumably, with the seal. For the aborigines, seals were a source of protein. Those who caught them on the boulder-strewn beach under this cliff didn't need to draw them. The artist seceded from the chase. He watched the beast from his perch up here, let it escape and then chose to remember it with his tracery; or else he didn't see it at all, which is the best reason for designing a replica of it. The outline is the husk of that slippery living thing. Emu and seal are departed spirits, wished into a retroactive captivity. At Tiagarra, art makes its first boldly fictitious attempts to rationalise Tasmania.

On the mainland, the Gumatj people painted their ancestor Wirrili on bark, as he trudged over the scorched, ochrey plain in quest of pigments – clays or soft stones – which he bequeathed to the tribe for ceremonial adornment. Even the nimble Crusoe on his island couldn't manufacture ink for the pens he whittled, but the aboriginal artist derives the means of his art from earth, or at Tiagarra scrapes his testimony into the hard surface of the land. The carvings are like the ornamental welts the aborigines raised on their own flesh: sacred scarifications, maiming reality into meaning. Arranged in a sequence, they narrate imagination's gradual gaining of freedom. That tight, enclosed circle unloops and begins a calligraphic dance, contorting itself into an emu or elongating itself into a seal. The line has an infinite number of identities. Yet its skittishness is a shadow-play, not a hunt. It mimes experience rather than mastering it. The artist has etched here the confession of his own inadequacy.

Art's mission to accuse and then replace reality was passed on to the convicts, whose only liberty lay in vengeful imagination. At Ross in the midlands in 1836 a transported signwriter turned stonemason carved a cosmology of his own beneath the parapets of a bridge designed by John Lee Archer. Tiagarra is our first scrawled experiment in signification, the geometrical discovery of categories for our understanding – maternal circles, ambitious pioneering straight lines. It begins by trying to comprehend creation; when it arrives at the two animals, it ventures a human robbery of that godly creative power. At Ross, the image-maker has grown more insolent. Now his creativity derides and deforms the official creativity of god. Daniel Herbert, convicted as a highwayman, covered the façades of Archer's bridge with a teeming herd of mongrels and mutants – dogs with antlers, thin-snouted pigs, owl-headed or rat-faced or feline-whiskered men; a vision of society from underneath, and a visual curse on the figures they represented. The carvings at Tiagarra scratch the idea of form into the irregular rocks. The masons at Ross chiselled the stone punitively, hacking it into a gallery of caricatures. Art which at Tiagarra sketches planetary motions and the serene cycles of nature has at Ross turned into a bad dream, a nightmare whose ogres are regurgitated by the mind and released defamingly into the world. At Tiagarra, the rock is written on, taught a graphic alphabet; at Ross, the rock has been mined and undermined, excavated to set free the mongrelised men and beasts who were locked up in its depths. Art has passed from the irradiation of reality – as when the abalone shell opens into a sky – to a grimacing, insurgent surrealism.

The seal at Tiagarra was preserved from the hunt, studied as an icon not marked down as prey. The Ross bridge, however, is a jungle of unleashed predators. Crowned lions feed on woolly lambs as if in one of Blake's cabbalistic songs. A horned ram, the beast of some unorthodox apocalypse, pounces from the undergrowth. A snarling hound has its mane dressed in a pompous baroque wig. The animals intermarry with the gremlins of legal and religious authority – bowler-hatted magistrates and snub-nosed mitred priests, diademed queens and pantomime kings with side-whiskers and spiked helmets. Tiagarra began with elementary abstractions, and at length redesigned them to represent figures. The Ross bridge reverses this rational evolution. The disfigured faces are squeezed into vertical panels between abstract reefs of orange coral, tangled weeds and tendrils, tubers and mollusc fossils: the ocean underneath consciousness, from which the monsters emerge and into which they dive again. A king's face is surmounted by what appears to be a knotted bundle of thick leathery intestines; the viscerae take over from the head. The stone looks as intricately wrinkled and folded as a cerebral cortex, and its submarine imagery dredges the river, luring hidden fishy phantasms to the mental surface.

A face supposed to be Herbert's own, struggling free like Blake's tiger from a shrubbery of fronds, bears witness to the oppression of these dreams. Its eyes are agonised, its mouth taut. It has been placed directly under one of the arches, as if to hold up the bridge. Archer believed he had engineered the crossing of a stream; in fact the structure depends on and riots from the brain of Herbert. The carvings contrive to keep themselves a secret from those who parade over the bridge and use it as a sensible extension of the roadway (for until the highway by-passed it, it lay on the main road between Hobart and Launceston). They're invisible from on top, and from the banks they're a messy, foreshortened jumble. They can only be read from a boat on the river, because they conspire to view a society jeeringly from below and to expose the underbelly of imagination. The final irony is that Herbert earned a free pardon for depicting Van Diemen's Land as a lair of sanctimonious brutes. Art had already learned double-tongued deception.

In 1830 Herbert was working on a chain gang at Bothwell. Archer had built a church for the town, and Herbert was engaged – it is thought – to carve two stone bosses on either side of its porch. As he was to do beneath the bridge, he pronounced his own verdict on penal society by sculpting gargoyles. The tiny pin-heads hide on the front of the church, just as his leering villains at Ross lurk under the bridge; their stony faces, hardened in prim disgust or solemn disapproval, glare down and classify all who pass below them into the church. The woman's mouth is pinched and turned down at the corners, as if tasting something sour. Her face has the shape of a clamped bud which refuses to bloom. The head-dress she wears is no flower but a fluted insignia of rank, with a repressively tightened fringe of curls beneath. The man on the other side of the door has the same thin acid lips, and a hierarchical head-dress of his own. Like a Victorian Nebuchadnezzar, he's piled high with symbols of state: a mattress of braided hair, below it a head-band of officialdom hung with a drooping jewel, below that another curtain of locks to guard his forehead, and then on the next tier a sombre plantation of eyebrows. The eyes are small, unseeing, wearily lidded, and the face is edged by a stiff patriarchal beard. In profile, you can see a hooked nose and the nasty black aperture, like a plug-hole, of his ear. These severed heads, the size of clenched fists, are Herbert's symbols of petrified self-righteousness – a smug, tyrannical prophet and a vinegary sibyl.

At Tiagarra, the image gestured towards an unseizable subject. Here it has claimed for itself a new and dangerous power: it incriminates the actuality, and takes a long slow pleasure in torturing it. Art which begins as compensation ends as revenge.

Scenic Schemes

Once art has learned how to represent the world, it advances to the greater glory of misrepresentation. Robert Dowling, the Launceston painter whose speciality was taxidermic groupings of Tasmanian aborigines, showed the process at work in his picture 'Early Efforts – Art in Australia'. A gaggle of schoolchildren watch a boy with an easel sketch a black man, who poses stoically with his spear and a boomerang. Of course the nascent artist won't be able to paint what he sees. The black man will either be sentimentalised as a guileless primitive or satirised as a degenerate throwback; by Dowling himself he's treated as an ethnological specimen, embalmed in academic paint. A chubby infant in the foreground of Dowling's picture idly hacks at a stick: art was another of the white man's weapons against the black, conquering by misconstruing.

Critics of colonial art complain that the painters, bringing their cultural assumptions and scenic schemes along in their luggage, couldn't even see the anomalous facts of Australia, let alone represent them. Take, for instance, the iconography of eucalypts. Spindly and shaggy, they conformed to no European preconception about trees. They had curious habits – leaves which dangle vertically and decline to give shade; bark which is sloughed all the year round in coarse dry strands, undressing pale flesh beneath. With their pink or orange or scarlet stamens, they were flowering plants which had somehow managed to grow, if they tried hard enough, three hundred feet tall. They had an Australian suspicion of elegance, but though they slouched, their posture wasn't relaxed. They grew branches at odd spasmodic angles, and twitched nervily in the air.

The first painters got them wrong on purpose, trying to train them in picturesqueness. John Glover, passing from the romantic landscapes of Europe to Tasmania in the 1830s, choreographed the gums. In his painting of the aborigines mustering at Risdon, the eucalypts preen in a rubber-limbed, double-jointed dance. They writhe, they wriggle; their jerky boughs unwreathe into those ample S-curves which Hogarth defined as the signature of beauty itself. Even their bark – intact, of course, not peeling, except for a few uncombed stringy curls – grows up from the ground with the same serpentine grain. The mustering aborigines have merged with this elastic ballet of rippling form. One of them has slithered far up a tree to trap a possum; he grips the trunk with arms and legs extended in boneless variations of the letter S, and the crozier-shaped tail of the possum is purest rococo. Nor will Glover consent to paint the scragginess of Tasmanian bush. His vegetation is meticulously dotted, so the marsh of ragged grasses is tidied into a green and yellow meadow by the act of painting. And the light which smiles on the scene – golden, with none of the harsh local brightness; mitigating things, smoothing their contours or drowning them in amber – is one that never was on sea or land in Tasmania.

I didn't mind the infidelity. In fact I derived a certain comfort from watching Tasmania misrepresented like this. It proved that reality needn't be taken as given: it was manipulable, according to your own compulsive way of seeing. And it promised a heady relativity, replacing the single inescapable world with a kaleidoscopic array of images, all of them different. At Tiagarra, the artist's subject is an unattainable object – the elusive emu or seal. But in these early paintings of Tasmania, the object has capitulated to the subjective I or eye, which revises it while purporting to represent it. Tasmania is put through a prism of impressions.

Stalking the boundaries of my small world, I thought I could enlarge it by finding new places to look at it from. That's why I loved travelling into Hobart on the slow, wheezing train; and when a metal footbridge was propped across the highway outside my first school, I didn't see it as a protection from the traffic but as a dizzy perch on which the world could be studied, ironed out, from above: another angle had been added to my repertory. I went back to the bridge when I was home, to test whether it still possessed its alpine exhilaration. The clearance, I discovered – that elevation which used to shudder thrillingly as the trucks sped beneath – was all of 5.4 metres. Hardly a Pisgah sight. My new points of vantage mostly brought disillusion with them. The footbridge surveyed a frontier I'd rather have forgotten – the humid mud flats and a few nosing tugs, the frayed rifle range, the frothing bay and beyond it the barrier of Mount Direction. When I pleaded my way onto the roof terrace of the new Commonwealth Bank in the centre of town, all the view did was belittle Hobart. The block of shops, seen from up here, lost its covetable allure; it was a tawdry scaffold of verandahs, slick plastic fronts belied by Victorian chimneys and callous ancient layers of brick or pock-marked plaster.

In my disenchantment, the paintings of Hobart in the museum cheered me, because they managed to achieve what I couldn't. They altered the reality, and they variegated it. They estranged what was familiar (which it's the metaphoric duty of art to do), and showed that there was more than one way of looking at Hobart. Or at least, to be cruelly precise, there were four ways of looking at it. Three of these chose to see the city from the middle of the harbour. William Duke in 1849 painted a whaling fleet offshore in a skirmish of up-ended skiffs, razory jaws and flailing tails, all foamy eruption and vicarious danger. Henry Gritten in 1856 took inventory of a stabler fleet – paddle steamers, hay barges and galleons, one of them unloading a steer. Haughton Forrest in 1882 calmed the agitation of Duke's whalers. He saw the harbour as a placid mill-pond, with a grey frigate anchored in it: a scene of mercantile peace and imperial protection.

These painters placed themselves on the water for prosaic reasons of their own. They were reporting on the town's commercial prospects. To Duke, Hobart is a boisterous sea-port, to Gritten a marketing haven, to Forrest an outpost of empire under naval guard against competition. For me, this documentation didn't matter. The wonder of the pictures was that they observed the city from an angle unattainable by me, and that they reached such divergent con- clusions about it. The sky above Mount Wellington was a Turner- esque pageant of elements in Gritten's painting, its mauve and yellow fires tinting the stone hills, dazzlingly reflected from the snow. Haughton Forrest forbade any such display: his sky was coolly, implacably blue, as severe a uniform as the battleship-grey of the frigate. And for a fourth artist – Knut Bull, painting the view from the suburb of New Town in the 1850s – the mountain burned an incense of stormy clouds.

Bull also painted an impossible view from the Domain over Hobart and down the D'Entrecasteaux Channel. The quarried earth of the Domain, scooped out to make a twisting path for a woodcutter's cart and for the travelling eye, is russet; at the end of the ocular tunnel, the sky in the south is the fizzy colour of lemon rind. Between the red, edible earth and the fresh effervescent sky, Hobart with its few sails and steeples and windmills swims on fields and waves of bluish green. Landmarks can be made out – dour Trinity Church wearing a crown of spikes, the classical campanile of St George's Church in Battery Point – but they're not enough to ballast the picture in the world I knew. Bull painted a vision not a vista: Hobart alight with paint.

I loved the imperativeness of this artistry, the way it could amend the data supplied to it and reconstitute the world. The poet Vivian Smith describes Tasmania as 'watercolour country'. Its winter tonalities are an overcast white and foggy grey; it's damp and drizzling. The Bristol watercolourist Skinner Prout, who spent the years between 1844 and 1848 in Hobart, adapted it at once to his medium. He sometimes painted in oil, when his subjects were muddier and more bituminous – natives wallowing in a bog of the Cascade rivulet, murky crags around a waterfall at Lake St Clair. But mostly he used the mirage-like liquidity of watercolour, with its pools of colour draining into the paper, to wash away the stark facts of Tasmania. His is a watered-down country. Mount Wellington above the Cascade rivulet in one scene is a puddle of washy purple. Mount Direction in a Derwent Valley landscape has desolidified, blurred its ribs of rock and its quill-like bristling timber into a blue haze – which in almost two decades of looking at it, I never saw it do. Brushed in by Prout, the dead gums on Mount Wellington look moist not haggard; his Moss Fall at Fern Tree rids the ferns of their musty earthy brown and fertile green, tuning them down to the insipidity of grass. Colour is anaemically denied, so that the subjects, hushed and made gentle, fade into the paper. Port Arthur – with a spire, a turret and leafy walk between them – could be a cathedral close: no orange brick, no olive-drab hill of gums, no yellow-jacketed convicts. Small flecks of brilliance atone for the half-light in which this Tasmania drowns. Chalky tombstones gleam in St David's Park; a stroller on the Domain is wearing a red cape, someone else is flying the white tadpole of a balloon. Otherwise things recede into a mist of indirectness and a muffling pallor.

On the paper, Prout frames the wilderness within a border of gentility. A view towards Hobart from the brickfields in Sandy Bay sets a thatched hut in the foreground as evidence of domesticity; far beyond is snowy, unaccommodated Mount Wellington. 'Our

Tasmanian Home' repeats the spatial rule, as Prout finds a mediating home for his vision in this new world: a shuttered, shaded cottage, positioned so he can look out on the mountain from a distance. Once he reverses the relation between aesthetic frame and natural phenomenon. His scene of Lady Franklin's museum places the midget temple beside a bush farmstead. Its stilted verandah parodies the Glyptothek's colonnade, its peaked roof with a smoking chimney laughs at the useless triangular pediment. The museum, meant to lodge Hobart inside its cultural frame and establish it as a castaway Athens, is itself marooned inside a fringe of heedless gums and collapsed logs.

Watercolour depends on dilution, and Prout can cope with Tasmania only by neutralising it. The eye's inroads are tentative: the track on which a cart wends down from the foothills towards the Derwent, through an obscuring tracery of trees, is a tube for vision, a perspective intended to keep objects at bay. Wherever possible, he pictures a shelter for that dazed, exhausted eye – the dark triangle of a native humpy; the white palisade of sheets hung over a bough at a camping spot near Lake St Clair; his own house with its face averted from Mount Wellington.

By contrast with Prout's disorientation, John Glover rejoices in belonging to Tasmania. 'My Harvest Home' in 1835 paints a golden repast of light, as willing oxen drag a mound of grass which gleams from within like coals.

Nevertheless, Glover imported this vision, and fitted Tasmania to a preconception. His view of landscape as fecund Arcady or beatified Eden derives from Italy. There classical temples decompose into nature and are absorbed by a new romantic religion, with trees for cathedrals and errant clouds or wavering rainbows as spiritual apparitions. Prout shows how Lady Franklin's dishonoured church was rejected by the valley it wished to convert. But when Glover paints Paestum or Tivoli, the ruins are earth's consumption of the cult, which it transforms into a serene pantheism. The pink Italian sky glows like warmed skin; stone crumbles as if it were bread. Glover saw England in the same way, painting Durham Cathedral rosy in the sun beyond a field where the cows are being milked, or Kensington Gardens with a population of figures – boys dreaming beside a pond, couples flirting under a tree – who seem to be vegetating there, lazily adjusting themselves to the organic peace of the place. Meditating on those scenes, art digests them. In Glover's painting of Snowdon, an artist on the river bank sketches the mountain, while a rustic elder studies him. Or the landscape reflexively studies itself. Glover's view of Ullswater from Patterdale, painted about 1820, inverts the hills in the lake so that, like Narcissus, they can muse on the conundrum of their own being. By this calm exercise of contemplation, nature is recreated as pastoral. As it ponders the world, the fretful consciousness is quietened, even mystically sedated. Like the good shepherd or the drowsing flocks he tends, the artist has merged with the inert, sleepily sentient land. A picture is a place made safe by its motionlessness, where no disturbance can ever occur: Keats's bower of beauty. This is how Glover paints Tasmania – gums at Bothwell which have learned to flex rhythmically; the Ouse River with every tree delicately dabbed in and some rabbit-like kangaroos posing on the plain as tutelary residents. There is always the sense that unsatisfied life and restless process have paused in order to be painted, and always the same syrupy golden light which, too dense and clogged to move through, seals things in stillness like resin.

Thus Glover, by applying paint as a soothing spell, manages the benediction of gruff antagonistic Mount Wellington. In 1837 he painted it with the orphan asylum in its foothills. The stretched-out range of turreted, crenellated rock has lost its bareness. It's furred over by green; the bleached dead trees poking from it are disallowed. The asylum is a speck with a spire planted in the velvety bush, and above it shines a rainbow. The curved trickling streams of colour which moisten the air stain the side of the mountain. The sky sheds brightness. This is no view: rather it's a fable, the appeasing answer to all my wary glances at that mountain as I left the house in the morning. Glover has designed an allegory, the altarpiece for some alfresco romantic church. The asylum recognises our sense that we are orphaned in the world – the ailment of such romantic characters as Blake's little boy lost in the dark miry night, of Wordsworth's lonely wanderers or of Dickens's Oliver Twist assailed by bogeys; the lament as well of infant Australia, deserted by its parent country. The romantic orphaned child is reclaimed by maternal nature. Protectively bent like an augury between the asylum and those furrowed organ pipes, which carve a mind in obtuse stone and impute a meaning to landscape, Glover's rainbow radiates this hope.

Of course the blessing is illusory, a refracted aureole. Later painters make more strenuous efforts to exalt local nature. W. C. Pigenuit, the first native-born Australian landscape painter, worked as a surveyor for the Tasmanian government between 1849 and 1872. Resigning his job, he exchanged topography for the stern sublime moralisation of mountains. His Kosciusko in 1903 is circled by high-born clouds of metaphysical vapour, and he treats Tasmanian peaks with the same rhetorical vehemence. When he paints Mount Olympus near Lake St Clair, the abrupt height does look Olympian. Inside grey fog – its nimbus of intellection – the pinnacle glares white and lucid: thought banishes confusion. Pigenuit constructs platforms for gods. A painting entitled 'A Mountain Top, Tasmania' places its standing stones in a Celtic ring as a rough geological sacrament, and when Pigenuit delivers the accustomed view of Hobart from across the water at Bellerive, Mount Wellington is an eyrie of inspiration, obscured in mist lower down but alight at the summit and semaphoring uplift.

Photography, for all its pretence of candour, contrives fictions of its own. The globe-trotting English photographer E. O. Hoppé toured Australia in the late 1920s, in quest of 'pictorial possibilities' for a book called *The Fifth Continent*. His friends doubted that he'd find any; determined to prove them wrong, he appraises everything he sees as if its ambition were to have its picture taken. Sailing into Sydney Harbour, he assumes the irregular coves and bays exist for the sake of a cultivated artifice: 'truly the landscape gardener has ideal material in Sydney, and he makes the most of it.' The harbour bridge, then new, is complimented for its decorative completion of the view, not for any utilitarian function it might be serving: 'its sweeping lines link together the rhythm of curve and inlet, and where formerly the line of vision was broken by a gap, it is now carried right round this most beautiful of harbours in harmonious continuity.' After the mainland with its simmering flatness, Tasmania gratifies him because it might have been laid out according to the precepts of those English connoisseurs of the eighteenth century – Uvedale Price or Richard Payne Knight – who favoured generous mounds and umbrageous clefts in picturesque landscape. 'The whole is broken up,' he says of the state's terrain, 'in heights and depths of surprising fairness.' His surprise at encountering beauty here is worthy of note.

The cities are seen to be posing for Hoppé, angling their best features towards the camera. Hobart's harbour 'is a fitting preface to the beautifully situated capital', and Launceston 'may well boast of the Cataract Gorge as its "pièce de résistance"!'. Lake St Clair is also allowed to have 'justly acquired its reputation for beauty'. Is it right to hear again the note of begrudgement in these little courtesies? Launceston is indulged by being permitted to boast of its gorge, and to do so in outlandish, arriviste French; Lake St Clair has its reputation scrutinised, and after due consideration is decreed to have deserved it. Hoppé knows that the beauty he commends is an illusion. It depends on the suspension of disbelief, and the erasure of memory. Thus he can say that time (aided by two episodes of cauterising arson) 'has softened the harshness of the prison at Port Arthur into the mellowness of a ruined monastery': Wordsworth's Tintern Abbey, that site of romantic nature-worship. Looking down the avenue of oaks, he reports that 'all has the aspect of a peaceful English village.'

The fairness which surprised him is language's imposition. For all his pictorial muting and amelioration, the penitentiary he photographs doesn't look at all like an abbey gone to seed and given over to pantheism. Its walls haven't gently, dustily succumbed; they stand up straight, intact but burned out from within, and they're matched by the unfallen leafless trees stuck into the hill behind them. The ruin is no place for wandering or rumination. In Hoppé's photographs, it has been fenced off. And though he arranges some leafy gums in front of it, he can't avoid a pile of chopped, uprooted stumps at the water's edge – more evidence of human intervention, to contradict the myth of time's absent-minded kindness.

The state which Hoppé calls 'a scenic jewel' doesn't live up to his fulsome verbal imagery. He speaks of the sun coming out to banish Port Arthur's shadows and reveal 'the brighter and laughing face of Tasmania'; but the broadest smiles he photographs are those of two devils in their den, baring their teeth to bite. His Tasmania is bleakly black and white – charred gums, dully glittering ingots of zinc stacked beside the river at Risdon, grey wharves smudged by smoke in the centre of Hobart. Black and white suit photography because they set the terms of our existence at its sparsest and starkest: a battle between gloom and hope, inconclusive because the negative switches these opposites into reverse. Hoppé's preface uses the extremes of his own monochrome spectrum to measure Tasmania's mood. The past is black. The place's penal history, he says, 'has cast so deep a shade on the annals of the island'. Colonisation means the advance of whiteness into the guilty dark – or at least it ought to, but Hoppé regrets to admit that after a century 'there are still 6,000 square miles in the south west of the island which never have been traversed by the foot of the white man.' The black man's nomadic traversal of them does not, of course, matter. Hoppé sees Tasmania with a morbidity induced by his medium. The Isle of the Dead burdens the water across from Port Arthur with its cargo of un-named corpses. Black is the encroaching shadow of the past; but white is a winter's tale too, of misery and advancing age – the snow drift through which a flock of sheep stumble, the snowy flesh and hair of a nonogenarian fruit-grower.

When colour arrives in this photographic Tasmania, it is as a second coming, a sunburst. For the state's hundred and fiftieth anniversary in 1953, the photographer Frank Hurley compiled a determinedly optimistic report on Tasmania. He called his 'camera survey' a 'Joy Book', and declared Tasmania 'a Happy Land of Golden Opportunity'. His capital letters made a fairy kingdom of my drab, dun world; his photographs gilded what they claimed merely to be representing. The joy was applied like a cosmetic. The violently roseate tints, as detachable as adjectives are from the stolid nouns they prettify, quiver on the page like clouds, ever so slightly overlapping the object to which they belong. The flaming red of suburban rooftops seems about to lift off from the tin oblongs of the houses; the poplars at the Salmon Ponds are the wincing yellow of mustard; Pigenuit's favourite eminence, Mount Olympus, has had its purple flanks touched up. Every landscape contains its resident admirers, like a claque to cue our response – honeymooners in chaste swim-wear of the period on the beach at Coles Bay, a man in a pin-stripe suit feeding non-existent gulls at the Victoria Dock in Hobart and again (now jacketless in collar and tie, with the addition of a back-pack) gathering wild flowers in a meadow at Port Arthur.

Hurley's is an iridescent Tasmania, and where the camera can't manage the necessary Technicolor his flushed prose makes atone-ment. The last photograph in his book is of Frenchman's Cap, and it's black and white. But in a caption he remembers hiking to the summit at sunset: 'The last rays were turning the lakes far below to chains of glittering gold; mists were screening the valleys with purple veils; the full moon was rising full and clear – I doubt if the conquerors of Everest looked down on anything more inspiring or sublime.' The language mines the landscape imperiously for riches (golden lakes, and presumably a silver moon); it links the flattering obliquities of beauty (those veiled valleys) with the more brazen might of sublimity (the hike as a mountain's conquest); and it offers up this natural majesty to its British owner and ruler, since Everest had been conquered just months before as a gift to the Queen on her coronation.

It's not that these observers couldn't see actual, irreducible Tasmania. Rather they decided not to see it. They preferred their own fabulations: Tasmania as Glover's abundant granary, as Prout's tear-stained aquarium, as Pigenuit's cloudy upland, as Hoppé's homespun frieze of verbal colour where in the Huon Valley 'the russet and gold of the orchards, the deep crimson of the fruit, weave themselves into a gorgeous tapestry', or as Hurley's golden province, luminous with cheap electricity. These capricious substitutions taught me how reality could be transcended, or at least circumvented.

On the bus, as rain and a riotous wind marred another day of putative summer, I heard a weary old man say to his neighbour, 'I don't know who's in charge of sending the weather along, but I reckon we've just got to take it as it comes.' Who does send it? – those my parents used to call 'the heads' or 'the high-ups'; the warders, or perhaps God. Ours not to reason why. My own instinct was more rebellious. The spirit of contradiction entered me very early, perhaps the day of my gratuitous tantrum at the gymkhana. And if there weren't visible alternatives, there could at least be imagined ones – for instance, those schemes for revising local terrain as scenery. We are given art, it is said, so that we shouldn't perish from the truth. Long before I could think in these terms, or had heard of the wise madman who uttered the words, this was my faith and my daily policy in Tasmania.

Seeing Tasmania

The art I liked was an appeasement. It rendered Tasmania habitable by depicting a fiction. These were the alluring shadows which the fire cast on the cave wall, contradictions of abrasive daylight. I was happy with these deceptions until, two months before returning, I came upon the untreated truth of Tasmania. At last I found an image of the desolation I had always felt there, baring the dust and mire beneath the streets, the ragged bush beyond the buildings, the wet throttling jungles which men had to hack their way through, that white sullen wintry sky like the film on a cataract-occluded eye. The revelation stared out of three dozen photographs, taken a century ago. They made me shiver. It was like watching a comfortless dawn reinvent the world in all its shoddy, short-lived newness. They almost made me wail, as on that first day of awakening at the showground – except that the illumination happened in a New York auction room, and by now I knew how to conceal my feelings.

Here was a Tasmania I recognised, without the cloyed, varnished composition of those paintings. In an ancient landscape, with the menace of bad weather on the mountain, a tentative society proposes itself. Hobart's façades are freshly chiselled, its unsure fledgling parks haven't yet had the chance to grow; railways thrust strict straight lines through the scrub, and bridge rivers on wobbly trellises; cartwheels and ploughs scar the soil, and – in some of the photographs – the filaments of electric wires tenuously brace the houses. It reminded me of that contraption in the packing shed on the orchard, which slapped planks together, fastened them with some hastily banged-in nails, and made a box as you watched. The camera recorded the raising of ramparts, the act of exclusion which declares human dominion, the fortifying of little islands in this congested, impassable emptiness. Yet the colonists who cleared these swathes across the matted hills and plotted towns with their set squares had eerily disappeared, deserting their creation. Except for some phantoms in Victorian top hats, or a few defunct children wearing laundered pinafores, the photographs can find no people to pose. The walls and fences have been left to fend for themselves. No one believes enough in their substance to be seen manning them. Everywhere the insulted bush grows back, sending its shadow ahead across the photographic paper, while the split, spilt, seismic rocks of which the place is made disrupt a level human topography. Mount Wellington lolls enormously above crouching Hobart; outside Launceston, the sharpened slope of the Cataract Gorge ignores the stilted boardwalk treading on its base. This Tasmania hasn't consented yet to civilisation, and doesn't answer to its name.

The photographer's nonentity admits his helplessness. No vision imposes itself, managing to make the trees undulate and the sunlight turn to nectar as Glover can do. This witness works no visual coercion. He's as nameless and remote as the carver at Tiagarra – more so, since he has no preconception about the place, and no myth of wholeness in which to set it; and whereas the engravings at Tiagarra, though primordial, exist outside time and could have been scraped there yesterday, the photographs are time's leftovers, dead like everything in them, their paper as brown and creased and thin as fallen leaves. Windblown by time, they had been shunted through space as well. How had they come to land here, in this cardboard folder in New York? What story of homesickness – or perhaps mere geographical curiosity – did their provenance have to tell? And by what stealthy stage-managed chance had I found them? I respected the coincidence, bid for them and bought them. For the next two months I pored over them, asking them questions which I knew they would eventually answer; and I took them with me to Tasmania, holding them up against the same places now.

They infallibly sorted out reality from appearance. The Salmon Ponds for instance, to me a lavish liquid seedbed, appeared here in an ashamed original nudity: one hut above a stagnant pool, with lawns of weed and twitch grass and a random fringe of saplings. Or Government House, at a loss in its dry paddock, its flag limp in the heat, its serried line-up of chimneys teased by the glaring sun. The haughty social terrors it contained made it truly a castle for me, a shrouded pinnacle of privilege. The photograph discounted all mystifying atmosphere. The baronial toy had been dropped here, suddenly uncrated in the wrong landscape and climate, with only a low hedge and a fence of wooden stakes to protect it. With its usual cruel instinct, the camera chose the angle most likely to expose deceit. It's positioned on the other side of the road over the Domain, which passes the gate of Government House; in the foreground is another fence and, beneath it, the rubble of a quarried trench. The castle has its foundations in a culvert.

The photographs were a memento mori for every view – a memory of origins but also the premonition of an end, since the long-ago moments detained on paper were present then, and now are irretrievably past. The camera is a killing chamber, which speeds up the time it claims to be conserving. Like coffins exhumed and prised open, the photographs put on show what we were and what we will be again.

The collection began with the inevitable scene of Hobart across the harbour from Bellerive. The painters in the museum had all chosen that angle; here it was bled of picturesqueness. The sky emulsified on the paper was a dull, sour, eggy yellow. The harbour, over-exposed, might have been an iced lake, with none of the neat ruffles the painters traced in for waves. The distant town was a litter of masts and mill chimneys. No painter's eye picked out the church spires: the photograph disallowed such visual favouritism, and such a glib assurance of redemption. The settlement above that dazing sheet of water has no centre, and the foothills interrupt and scatter it. Disparate white dots, like specks on skin, stand for houses brave enough to occupy the slanting gullies behind the town. Then the scrub – coagulated black – resumes. The colonised strip is pressed between rocks: the foreground of Bellerive (though no beach is visible, only the cusps of boulders like a serrated battlement), and the background of Mount Wellington sprawled along the sky. A human eye, in its own interest, would equalise things and solidify the town by holding it in focus, imagining details which the painters solemnly point up. But the lens is as cynically neutral as a lizard's eye. It registers only what is there, or not there; it makes no affectionate adjustments. In one of the views towards Mount Wellington, the camera's bland honesty has proved too much for the photographer to bear. Some chemical disease on the paper has freckled the mountain side, giving it the look of a threadbare leopard's pelt. The effect is inadvertent: the mishap of the medium doesn't intend to create beauty. At the organ pipes, however, a human eye and hand have intervened, to supply the dark squelching blot of stone with feature and identity. The pipes have been scratched in on the photographic plate; the metaphor, so important because it redefines the monolith as a musical console, is added after the event.

In the centre of Hobart, photography catches the awkward impromptu fabrication of a town, trusting in formalities for which the camera has no respect. The government buildings seen from Macquarie Street are quaintly asymmetrical, rhyming a staircase with an archway and uncertain which side is meant to be the front. Their sedate Georgian classicism arrives ready-made in a world still unready. The street they survey is a sandy track corrugated by deposits of horse dung; their blinds are pulled down as if in discreet avoidance. The thoroughfare has the idea of becoming an avenue some time in the future: shrubs on the sidewalk peep over square paling fences. At right angles, Elizabeth Street sets off on its long journey towards North Hobart, New Town, Glenorchy, Launceston, the mainland, the world. But as it does so, it exposes the effrontery of those Georgian offices around the corner. Elizabeth Street in the photograph is a glimpse behind the scenes. Its façades wear the proper uniform of useless Doric pilasters, augmented by verandahs of tin and barred windows. Behind these architectural alibis are stables, inns, the Tasmanian Pale Ale Stores and, as the street begins to amble up the hill, a furniture warehouse – depositories for filling out the propped-up walls, which still remember their first shaky incarnation as canvas; watering-holes to dispense conviviality and the bleary contagion of fellow-feeling. A city has been provided for, but where are the citizens? Only some stray shadows of men dematerialising as the camera eye blinks, or spirits walking out of their bodies on the pavement.

Then, gradually, more human lives emerge from this albumen autumn of sere brown. A woman on a bench in Franklin Square reading a book, the white feather on her hat camouflaging itself as a flower in the hedge behind her; a boy beneath the statue of Franklin himself on his plinth of palms, leaning over the glassy water; a bowler-hatted guard outside Government House, or perhaps a passer-by halted forever, with the clock in the arch above the front door at 3.40 and no wind to make the standard billow. On St George's Terrace in Battery Point I could see at once the boy standing beside his penny-farthing bicycle, the smaller wheel reaching his ankle, the larger touching his shoulder. He had dismounted so as not to be a streak in transit through this street of sun and silence. The tin rooftops of the cottages burned; the trees in their wild backyards stood still too; the photograph was an oven of stuffy air through which you couldn't move. The boy had the enervated suburb to himself. Or did he? Weeks later I noticed the stumpy blobs in front of a white picket fence further down the street: two girls – no, three – in sun hats and aprons, peering on tiptoe over the fence into that garden, looking away from the photographer at something hidden by the trees. The photograph had gathered them in too, but as soon as it released them it engulfed them again, curtailing lives it refused to be responsible for. What was it in the garden that mattered more than having their picture taken? Every photograph tells a short story. Each is foreshortened by time, like childhood. After what seemed to be hours of scrutiny, I discovered two more hostages in Cataract Gorge. Skulking in a corner were two young men in boaters, fishing from the perch of a boulder. Could that white spot beside them be their dog? Once more, the photograph wasn't telling. Their rods extended over a gorge which contained no cataract, only a smooth unreadable surface frozen by over-exposure. Fishing was the right occupation for someone arrested in the temporal frame: an eventless vigil which will last until eternity. This explained the verisimilitude of mood I felt in the photographs. They transfixed people in those suffocating moments, or hid them in a pointillist mesh of brown dots; like Tasmania, they were a space for detention.

Among the collection was a series of Fern Tree, the drizzly arbour under the mountain through which the road passes on its way to the Huon – a jungle of wet crumbling humus, exactly the tone of the photographic paper; pubic groves of fronds with spawning shadows; tiered cascades from the summit drenching the moss. Darwin, pausing in Hobart on the *Beagle* in 1836, toiled up to the pinnacle from here, grumbling that his stupid guide chose the damp southern side 'where the labour of ascent, from the number of rotten trunks, was almost as great as on a mountain in Tierra del Fuego or in Chile'. To him the place was a clammy tropic, the vertical struggle as long and obstructed a march as evolution. He did his best to establish human ascendancy, commandeering the vegetation as protective headgear. The man ferns, he thought, considerately unfurled into 'elegant parasols'. The photographs see them less daintily. They're a choked basement of hairy roots and spore-studded stems, growing in lateral prongs from the hillside to poke at the sunlight far above; they flourish greedily among gums dead on their feet, imbibing and exuding moisture. Once more the photographs seem to record a time more distant than a century ago. Despite the milestones, the hunter resting on his gun and gazing up through the multiple ceilings of forest, or the schoolboys in pork-pie hats squatting among some man ferns which twist like the trunks of elephants, this is an atavistic lair. The photographer has intruded on a heart of darkness.

Mount Wellington shows itself here as it is, as I saw it every morning when I left the house. The painters can't help transforming and placating it – smoothing its flanks like Glover as if stroking the fur of a pet animal, portentously exalting it like Pigenuit, reducing it to a blue, wishy-washy haze like Prout. In the photographs it does without the dance of wavelengths which create colour. It's either a black smudge on the sky or – with snow along its crest – a chilling stripe of whiteness. Nor do the photographs bother to seek out its profile (except for the one which scrapes in the would-be organ pipes). It sprawls as stolidly as a sack of potatoes: a geological accident not an intention of harmonising nature, as it is when Glover invests it with that rainbow. The Huon road, in some photographs taken in winter, is a rutted path newly gouged through the bush, slipping out of sight into a gulf between palisades of gaunt black trees; further on it's blocked by a diagonal barrier of gums which have slid down the collapsing mountain side. Beside a mill on one of the road's sharpest bends, the camera catches another of the human incidents it observes but refuses to explain: a woman, whose hat trails muslin veils and whose clean skirt drags in the mud, has stepped out of her carriage. She's alone on this precipice of skeletal timber, among those clustering, fanning ferns; you have no sense that the photographer is nearby. What has happened? Has the road turned boggy ahead? Is she about to wander off into the seeping undergrowth? The camera, with its reptilian squint, couldn't care less.

Nor can it account for the oddest human tenants of this wilderness, when it stumbles on them higher up the mountain beneath the brow fissured with the organ pipes. In a clearing near the springs are two teetering huts, roofed with shingles. On some rough benches outside sit a quaint congregation – hikers, or hermits? – who suspiciously outstare the camera: a Victorian worthy in a stove-pipe hat, with a bib of white whiskers half way down his chest; a woman in a mob cap, hands folded on the apron in her lap, houseproud in this forest of upright bones; a schoolboy, too young to be their child, neatly combed and dressed as if for Sunday school though lost in the bush; and a yokel with mouth agape and idiotic grin, who doesn't belong with them even though they don't plausibly belong together. I'm sure there must be some banal reason for their presence on that edge of rock, in this casually crazy photograph. A painting could pass them off as Wordsworthian solitaries, mystically cloistered in nature. But the photograph notices too much which is absurd, or excessive – the vine (a tomato plant, perhaps) crawling up one of the outhouses; the gas lamp with its fretted iron trimmings, salvaged no doubt from some Hobart street and rigged to the roof of the hut so that it juts pompously over the door; the gum tree, tilted at an angle of forty-five degrees, which appears to grow through the roof; and behind this draughty rickety incongruous idyll, established on a shelf of the dormant volcano, the hump of sheer cracked stone which goes by the name of the organ pipes. These photographs sum up the quixotic madness of settlement in Tasmania.

In the same series there's one last tribute to the fanciful human desire to domesticate an alien planet. It shows a hillside of oxidised boulders growing dry scabs of moss, with the battered limbs of trees slashed off by gales twisted between them. I recognised it at once: a landslip you can still see just as the road bends round to the summit; it's even visible from the back steps of my parents' house as a moulted patch on the mountain, where the cladding of vegetation has been peeled away to leave this wound of teeming pebbles and careening slabs like runaway tombstones. The photograph spies on the ancient upheavals which deformed the mountain and gave shape to Tasmania. And yet on the back of the print has been written, in a spidery hand which leads the capitals astray into twirls, 'Ploughed field, Mount Wellington'. Was a metaphor ever more pathetically hopeful? If only those churned, tumbling rocks had been clods turned over by the plough! Then this land would be arable, not the devastated site of some long-ago geological war. The mind imagines pastures on these sterile heights, and inseminates the jagged infertile rubble. But the camera doesn't know about the dreamy caption, and has seen the truth in all its rigour: this is a place unfit for habitation, or for comprehension. Here, once, the elements did battle, and earth tore stones from itself to hurl at a sky which couldn't be punctured, and was too insentient to be hurt.

I Find a Cave

Twenty-five years before, I had found my own dim, comforting *camera obscura* in Tasmania: the roofless shell of that cave on the showground, containing a delirium of false, entrancing fires. This was no truth-teller, like the mechanical optic which blinked at a flinching country in the photographs I bought. It was a capsule for fantasising in, as impregnable as the outdoor privy converted to a fort and wrapped by a clambering vine of passion fruit in our neighbours' backyard. Once the clapper banged, we could begin to perform our lives instead of living them; and Tasmania itself became a meretricious actor too. The intoxication of the film was to see the place traduce itself. My suburban scenery – plastic flags flapping above the used car lots, the reek of Chico rolls puffed onto the pavement, the slick Laminex kitchenette suites in the windows of the furniture shops – was magicked away. Instead there appeared a Tasmania gamely impersonating somewhere else: a place already as deceased as childhood (the film was supposed to be set during the war), when steam trains puffed along coastal tracks, draught horses nodded and clopped through country towns of golden stone, and fat red-faced bobbies kept genial watch. It was almost quaint enough to be England.

This, needless to say, isn't what Nan Chauncy intended. For her, *They Found a Cave* was about acclimatisation to Australia; only for me, thanks to the film, did it become an experiment in artistic maladjustment. The book begins with the young heroine Cherry – evacuated along with three brothers from the blitz in London, to be looked after by a Tasmanian aunt – comparing landscapes. As her body drowses in the Tasmanian sun, her thoughts vault home to England, and the untidy gums (accused of course of bad manners for shedding their bark, not leaves) wither into the memory of beech trees spilling their nuts on a smoothed English lawn now pitted with bomb craters. It's this nostalgia which Nan Chauncy's story sets out to cure. Tas the farm boy, son of the villainous Pinners who by maltreating the children when their aunt goes into hospital provoke the escape to the cave, at first taunts the newcomers as Pommies, and is aghast at their queer names: Nigel, Brick which is short for Brickenden (and who was me), Nippy which is somehow a diminutive of Anthony; he doesn't think his own name is odd 'because he lives in Tasmania'. But he makes common cause with the runaways, and by the end the roles have been reversed. A family reunion at Christmas dinner celebrates the imperial extended family. Cherry toasts the New Country, while Tas loyally proposes the health of the Old.

Finding the cave does not mean going bush, or turning native. On the contrary, since this is a colonial fable, it counsels the subjugation of wildness. The story concentrates on the exiguous housekeeping of the children. Cherry skims cream from the milk of the goats they take with them to the cave, and uses it to make butter. When their supply of meat runs out, Tas traps mountain parrots. A murderous recipe for making them palatable is included: you stew them, taking care to cut off the tails and to gouge out the grease bag. There are also instructions for serving up jays, and for making rabbit taste less rabbity by frying it in onions then cooking it in milk. 'Go easy on the onions till we pinch some more,' someone warns: this is a life which, like that of the colonists, must be stolen, if not from nature then from the larder down at the farm. The children reconstruct home in their den of rock, and never for a moment consider sleeping rough. They make mattresses with ferns and dried leaves; Nigel with the same Crusoesque ingenuity repairs a bicycle whose tyres are worn out by stuffing the tubes with grass, reeds and straw, also pinched from the cowshed. They learn the craft of that omnipresent Tasmanian frontiersman, the logger. When a huge gum keels over, there's a discussion about what to do with it. Brick suggests cutting the branches and stacking them in the cave for winter firewood; when Nigel – the eldest brother, and therefore the sage – advises delay, Tas says, 'It must be cut green or it'll be like iron.'

As a do-it-yourself kit for young settlers, They Found a Cave supplies an anthology of bush lore. Tasmania is here, among other things, a lost world of zoological curiosities; the colonist inherits and assiduously catalogues a society of throwbacks. The children meet a recluse known as Mad Dad, who scavenges in pools. His madness is methodical, scientific: he's searching for a rare species of inland crustacean. 'I go wherever the anaspides – the mountain shrimps –

are to be found,' he explains. These creatures are supposed extinct, 'yes, dead and done for twenty thousand or so years before our time,' but all that while they have been quietly swimming in the tarns of 'our own wonderful little Island'. Though camouflaged as a local, Mad Dad is an English figure, last in a sequence of curators and custodians which began with Joseph Banks and his definition of Australia as a museum of recondite specimens, its first landing stage situated at a place called Botany Bay. Even his eccentricity has its English prototype, in the hermit-like leech-gatherer Wordsworth meets stirring a pond with his staff in 'Resolution and Independence'. Mad Dad, talking about his pursuit of the anaspides, almost paraphrases Wordsworth's old man:

> Once I could meet with them on every side;
> But they have dwindled long by slow decay;
> Yet still I persevere, and find them where I may.

The difference is that the English solitary scans a destitute moor, whereas the fossicker in the bush roams an island abounding in wonders. Romantic England was a depleted place, too civilised and industrialised to tolerate the chimerae of imagination; the poets had to search for splendour in the grass, a world in a sand-grain, a nightingale in the garden. The leech-gatherer laments a reality no longer sacred. But England's loss, when Nan Chauncy's fable brings romantic escapism downunder, is Tasmania's gain. Here there are anaspides everywhere, even if nightingales and skylarks are scarce.

The shrimps turn out not to be extinct, but Tasmania's other defunct populations find house-room in the synoptic story. Tas warns Pa Pinner against stealing Aunt Jandie's sheep, and threatens that he might 'go . . . where the convicts used to go in Hobart – ter prison!' The cave was once the hide-out of a bushranger, the profession adopted by many escaped convicts. In the film, the evocations of convictry are much more graphic. Pa Pinner supervises a scrub-clearing work gang consisting of Tas and Nigel, while a bloated Ma Pinner, photographed between the verandah railings from an imposingly low angle, is the sadistic commandant lazing at ease as her childish captives chop wood (which gave me the opportunity for a prized close-up, as I paused with the axe in my hand and mouthed some silent curses I had scripted myself). Another episode in the film evokes the aborigines, when the children black their faces using pot-char in preparation for a nocturnal raid on the farm larder. The book, in a denouement which the film omits, turns up an ethnographic specimen even more precious than Mad Dad's shrimps: the skeleton of an aborigine, discovered by Nigel – 'one of the rarest things in the world' because the Parlevars cremated their dead. This one has his tools and weapons by his side, and must have suffered an accident while out hunting. 'He's all complete with not a bone out of place,' it's reported. Now comes an inspired piece of colonial profiteering. Nigel sells the skeleton to the men from the museum for £500, and uses the money to fly his parents out from warring England to the safety of Tasmania. The slaughter of the first Tasmanians results in an imperial profit. Nan Chauncy's children achieve more than acclimatisation to the new world; they buy and sell it with the confidence of fledgeling Crusoes.

The book ends with news that the war is looking better, only the Japs remaining a problem. The last word is Jandie's, censuring primitive food fights around the Christmas table: 'You are back in civilisation now. This is the end of the cave stuff, please.'

The film did away with the book's discreet ideological designs on Tasmania. It made its own propaganda, which was touristic. It advertised Tasmania's scenery, as we processed through country towns in our dray or scampered through orchards. I had one emblematic little scene in which I reached up for an apple – polished in advance by the props lady – and bit a chunk out of it, unable even then to wait for Eve to take the initiative. The cave, like Tasmania itself, was here represented as a place to spend a holiday (of the self-catering kind). Nan Chauncy's book concludes with 'the end of the cave stuff', because 'civilisation' has at last abolished the native frontier; the last wistful shot in the film, an epilogue to the riotous Christmas dinner, wanders across the chipped rock of the abandoned bungalow in the hills and fixes on a childishly lettered sign announcing 'CAVE FOR RENT'.

To me, this trailer for Tasmania didn't matter. I had my own private scenario. The film wasn't about settling down to a practical accommodation with reality, as Nan Chauncy had counselled; it was about contradicting that reality, or stepping out of it into the fourth dimension of licence: art. Nan Chauncy's characters were English children learning to love Tasmania. I was a Tasmanian child already discontentedly in love with the idea of England (or perhaps, less specifically, with anywhere which was elsewhere). The film wrote a fantasy of mine into truth: the children are said to be disoriented, as their train fumes into the station in the bush, because they're 'used to living in a big city like London'. Since we were all internees of Hobart's northern suburbs, that introduction had a dreadful irony; but the film allowed us to pretend that our existences were otherwise. The locations too, though near where we lived, were changed when we assumed our false identities in front of them. A tumbledown farmhouse off the Huon road, reached across a bridge of rickety planks, was chosen as Jandie's farmstead. The impoverished farmer, his depressed wife and their squalling babies stood aside as we briefly occupied their domain and transformed it into the happy valley. Some humble ledges on the lower slopes of Mount Direction became a sheer cliff face where we clambered in search of the cave. Closest to home of all yet mentally furthest away, the cave itself hid across two lanes of highway and through the showground fence inside a shed now jointly occupied by Cadbury's and Schweppes. Three minutes after leaving the house I was in it, having prised open the concealed, overgrown door of a dream, which admits you to a secret recess within yourself.

It was an intoxicating time. Finding a cave meant for me, I now see, an evasion of ordinary life: getting off school and out of uniform, wearing a baggy green shirt and patched, fraying shorts – my costume, which for six months I had to battle to prevent my mother from washing – and growing your hair. Even after I returned to school, I kept the lank untidy mop, and whenever a teacher remonstrated with me about it – this was three years before the Beatles invented sexual intercourse and long hair – I'd say importantly that I couldn't have it cut because there might still be retakes to do. Back at school, there were other withdrawal symptoms. On our make-do sets, I'd always admired the habit of the camera man and the director, who screwed one hand into an eyehole-shaped aperture and squinted through it as if down the tunnel of a viewfinder, or made a rectangle with the extended thumbs and forefingers of both hands and surveyed the scene from inside that. They were framing life, composing it; I used to do the same from my desk in the back row of the class room, directing the teachers as they toiled through their explanations of algebra and French genders.

None of them appreciated my placing a frame round them, and I can't imagine why I wasn't expelled for obnoxiousness.

At the end of the year, the film opened at the Odeon in Hobart, with an honour guard of scouts to salute the arriving municipal dignitaries. I saw it once and soon forgot about it, embarrassed by its childishness and by those short trousers. I had no dreams of my name grandly stamped on a deck chair somewhere across the Pacific; it was an episode only, and it was over. There weren't even any souvenirs. I was given a record of the theme tune, written by Peter Sculthorpe and played by Larry Adler on the harmonica, but we had no gramophone and I knew nothing about the properties of vinyl. I left it in the sun on my bedroom window ledge, so without being played it erupted in ripples and pimples like a frying egg. I did have a poster, with the five of us perilously clinging to the side of Mount Direction; unable to imagine the past or the sad value of its leavings, I must have thrown it away.

I should have realised that no experience is ever laid finally to rest. Everything has its eternal return. Twenty-five years afterwards, on the day of my dazed arrival in Australia, *They Found a Cave* rose ghoulishly up to greet me. I had come from New York with its muddy snow to Melbourne, where the streets were dusted with jacaranda blossoms. My friends took me out, stupefied, for a walk. On the pretext of renting a film overnight for their daughter, they led me into a video store. I browsed through the racks, and began to wonder about an item called *The Long Swift Sword of Siegfried*, with Heidi Ramshorn as a nubile, non-Wagnerian Brünnhilde; my friends as we left confronted me with a cassette containing, like a bottled genie, my short-trousered self. It was the fated, unexpected start to my journey backwards.

We watched it that evening. Already deconstellated by twenty hours in the air and the plunge from one hemisphere to another, I now had to face this jerky, nervous, long-lost stranger who was me. It was childhood too instantly recovered, and against my will. I had to admit that I recognised this person, even though only the body was mine (or once had been): our voices were all dubbed after the event by plummy middle-aged contraltos, specialists in the archly eager inflections required. The frown was mine, fending off the daylight; so was the awkwardness, which brought back to me all the cringeing dread of that age. When we climb from the train and are greeted by Jandie, my hand out of its turn darts forward to shake hers, then retracts as if bitten. The sensation of that moment returns with sickening vividness, like regurgitated food, and along with it every social miscalculation I've committed since then. Why did they leave that in? It's a truth from which there is no appeal. More and more, watching, I realised that I still was this uneasy creature, somehow no part of the playful group. The other four were archetypes, with all their defining attributes on show: Cherry was the girl and thus the maternal provider, milking goats, cooking dampers and refusing to run away until she had stolen enough canned meat; Nigel was the eldest boy and therefore the chieftain; Nippy was the youngest and therefore the weepy homesick baby; Tas of course was Tasmania. But Brick wasn't anything, unless he was me – a child without qualities, an empty space unsure of what to do with its hands. The name is supposed to suggest practicality and solidity, but the two occasions in the film when Brick displays these virtues are the moments most uncharacteristic of me then or now. One is when he demonstrates a rabbit snare which he has rigged up with some twine. 'We haven't got a steel trap,' he says, 'so this one will just have to do'; he smirks that he read about it in a scout book. The second comes at the Christmas dinner, when everyone is allocated a job on the farm to replace the gaoled Pinners. 'I can do the wood!' volunteers Brick, with a hypocritical enthusiasm which makes me wince. Neither rabbit-trapping nor wood-chopping were avocations I fancied for myself. I would never accustom myself to this rough frontier.

My friends told me, when it was over, that I hadn't changed a bit. The intervening years, and the distance they put between me and Tasmania, compressed like the cell walls in the horror story, which move in to crush their occupant. In my own version of the fable – still only half-formed at the time I acted it out on those strips of accusing, confidential celluloid – I didn't run away to a bushranger's den in the hills, to test myself against the wilderness and learn the techniques for managing it; I fled to some dim, absconded attic where the mind could look down on the strange agitations of experience far below in the valley, hearing only echoes or words ripped apart by the wind, as in that scene from the film when the tiny quivering blob of Ma Pinner wobbles out of the farm-house, visibly dilates to take in air, then screeches the dread word, 'Tas-man!' Spying from our height, we were safe: I wanted an eyrie like that. *They Found a Cave*, I saw, was the premature, proleptic story of my life.

'So men write poems in Australia'

My cave was made not from gooey plaster slapped on a skeleton of wire-netting but from words; the fire tended in its furthest recess was language. Scuttling into that darkness, I repeated in my own time the earliest impulse of settlement in Australia. As soon as the scrub is cleared, the houses built, and the natives dispossessed, a new country must set about furnishing itself with a literature. This is the surest of moral supports for evicted Adam or shipwrecked Crusoe. Writing implants a spirit in place, subdues things by describing them. And what is written should not be a tally of facts. Frederick Sinnett, an English journalist who moved to Australia in 1849, declared when assessing the literary possibilities of the land that 'man can no more do without works of fiction than he can do without clothing.' Fiction, like the holistic diagrams at Tiagarra, pretends that an unintelligible terrain is orderly; it replaces crude, cruel accident with beautiful design. Australia is ordained from inside a book.

In 1789, a year after arriving in their forgotten continent, the military guards at Sydney Cove organised the performance of a play, the first ever staged in a place which till then had known no feigning. It was Farquhar's *The Recruiting Officer*, chosen because there happened to be two copies of it to hand. Thomas Keneally's novel about this catastrophe-prone amateur night in the bush, *The Playmaker*, describes the making of both the play and Australia. For Australia is the play – scripted in advance by the penal necessities of the Home Office and the imperial stratagems of the Admiralty, yet amended by those sent out to realise it in performance, just as the convicts acting in *The Recruiting Officer* alter Farquhar to suit their own circumstances, changing grenadiers to marines and substituting for his French campaigns some up-to-date jibes against the traitorous colonists in America. Fiction improves on facts, and enactment on the ground gradually did away with the tyranny of the English text: the place of banishment and penance relaxed into a newfoundland of liberty and ease. In deserting the pre-emptions of

Farquhar's play or reading subversively between its lines, Keneally's characters rehearse the social and sexual revolutions which will constitute Australia. The director Ralph Clark – Keneally's playmaker, a marine lieutenant – abandons the memory of his wife in England and takes up with a convict actress, enjoying 'a willing commonwealth' of equality. The fiction sponsors new, illicit truths, and also serves as their alibi: Ralph and Mary live together under cover of the pretence that she's his servant.

Playmakers are recruiting officers. They must conscript reality, teach people that life is acting, deem an empty open space to be a stage. Keneally sees colonisation as the raising of a theatre, transforming a deadly uncharted vacuum into a social arena and a legal forum. Sydney is less a settlement than an improvised set. In this endless horizon, there's a single staircase with nowhere to go, emptily symbolising gubernatorial authority. As yet no church exists, and during services it has to be imagined. This stranded stage has its prompt and off-prompt sides: to the east of a certain stream live the more yeoman-like, industrious felons; west are the unregenerate cases. The space beyond the camp is fabulous, exotically fictitious. The convicts believe that China begins forty miles inland over the Blue Mountains. When one of the thieves paints a lying backdrop of 'great oaks and parklands and country houses' to hang behind the stage, he's merely formalising the effrontery. The play educates all its performers in the flimsiness of their own existence and the frailty of the social experiment they are sentenced to act out. Clark's paramour specialised in stealing clothes. Is civilisation any more than the theft of mendacious coverings from naked nature? The natives believe the white invaders to be ghosts. Made up for the play with faces of floury pallor, that's what they become.

Clark treasures the plotted symmetry of drama, and laments untidy actuality. He hopes the play will create goodwill and fellow-feeling, soothing the quarrelsome prison into a genial community. Of course that doesn't happen. The play is interrupted and very nearly aborted, while Farquhar's engineered blessings have no power offstage. But these mishaps are prognostications about Australia, whose foretold plot goes miraculously astray. Keneally's novel contains several hangings – judicial performances too, requiring the bluff of stoicism or impertinence from those on the platform – which are twisted awry and given happy endings. Isn't Australia as well a doomed place which escapes from its fate to live happily ever after? The performance was a constitutional convention.

Keneally prepares a dramatic scenario for Australia. Peter Porter and David Malouf find the country predicted in classical poetry – Porter in the pastoral verse of Hesiod, Malouf in the political chronicle of Horace. Porter's 'On First Looking into Chapman's Hesiod' is a work of knowing second-sightedness, seeing the Elizabethan translation of Hesiod by way of Keats's 'On First Looking into Chapman's Homer'. The translation literally translated Keats, making him travel mentally, as metaphor (the carrier) always does – transporting him through realms of gold, setting him beside Cortez on the peak in Darien. Porter's experience too, when he buys a copy of Hesiod's *Works and Days* for fivepence at a village fête, is to find himself translated, repatriated from a cosy English village to the primitive husbandry of smallholders in the south. 'Yes,' he decides, 'Australians are Boeotians,' tough and taciturn citizens of an iron age, castrating their cattle by hand, philosophising over their billy-cans of tea, preaching to the stringy barks, inscribing country wisdom on fly-spotted dog-eared calendars like those I found for obsolete years under the floorboards of my uncle's farm in the Huon Valley. Porter accustoms himself to Australia by finding a precedent for it in literature:

> Some of us feel at home nowhere,
> Others in one generation fuse with the land

He can feel at home there once the book has explained the place to him. For Porter, Australia's prototype is rustic, exiguous ancient Greece; for Malouf, it is imperial Rome. His poem 'Reading Horace outside Sydney, 1970' begins by conceding that the literary perspective distorts reality. 'The distance is deceptive,' he says, because he's at a double distance – spatial and temporal – from his subject. Sydney, molten in a heat haze, is thirty miles off, Rome two thousand years away. But the poem equalises those different distances. Malouf by means of his book is translated to a point equidistant from nearby Sydney and vanished Rome. He can look down on history, as if from the vertically remote Cessna biplane which he sees crop-dusting lucerne; and from here he sees Horatian Rome with its corporate feuds and its embattled empire as a metaphor for Sydney, where decline and fall are charted by the noiseless crash of mineral shares.

Keneally's novel and the poems of Porter and Malouf afford Australia a literary genealogy. It is a melodrama acted out by liars trained in perjury and dissimulation; a hard-bitten pastoral whose music is 'the sonata of the shotgun'; an epic of one civilisation's demise and another's resurgence as those Malouf calls 'barbarous northern people' – Rome's Goths, or Australia's chained and reluctant founding fathers – push 'south into history'. But the beginning they invent is a belated, retrospective one. The new country had no knowledge of this inheritance.

America from the first possessed a literary form corresponding to its new social and economic conditions: a mode of documentary sublimity, cataloguing an expanse of truths which were stranger and more abundant than any fiction – Whitman's burgeoning metro-politan statistics, Melville's heroic engineering works on board the ship in *Moby Dick*. The whole country turned out to be composed like those non-fiction novels eventually written by Norman Mailer and Truman Capote. For Australia, literary acclimatisation was harder. The American land was there to be exploited, and the imagination as it eagerly accumulated data could join in the venture of conquest; but Australia was a place of punitive exile, and the earliest songs of its unwilling settlers recoil aghast from the penal colony to yearn for 'that isle of great contentment which we shall see no more'. They are caught between an old world which is lost to them and a new world which they refuse to recognise; the first subject of Australian literature is therefore the indescribability of Australia.

Watkin Tench's journal of the settlement at Port Jackson in 1791 surveys a place profuse only in negative attributes, 'a plain country, apparently very sterile, and with very little grass in it'. The natives have laid no imaginative claim to it: Tench is astounded by what he takes to be 'their total ignorance of the country', and their lack of interest in expeditions through it. They represent, like their barren surroundings, life at its grudging minimum. 'A less enlightened state,' Tench decides, '. . . can hardly exist.' Barron Field, exploring the Blue Mountains in 1822, dismissed the drab, metallic vegetation as 'unpicturesque'. Nature here was of no use to art. 'New South Wales is a perpetual flower garden,' Field admitted, 'but there is not a single scene in it of which a painter could make a landscape.' It's a terrifying embargo; Australia is disqualified from ever being the material of art. Field's poem 'The Kangaroo' was equally disconcerted by the fauna. Its couplets extol the Miltonic equilibrium of creation, yet they find the kangaroo – in this world where all discords must be harmonised – unrhymable and thus irreconcilable. Field lamely concedes, 'To describe thee, it is hard,' and can comprehend the beast only as a hybrid of squirrel and hart, or 'converse of the camélopard' (the giraffe, assumed to be a cross between camel and leopard).

Description remains destitute in Peter Carey's story 'A Windmill in the West', the demarcation of space still – in contemporary Australia – as confused as when Tench clambered through a terrain he called 'very bad' or when Field wearily surveyed the acreage of 'eternal eucalyptus, with . . . its scanty tin-like foliage'. In Carey's story, a soldier guarding an electrified fence in the desert has been instructed that 'the area to the west could be considered the United States, although, in fact, it was not; that the area to the east of the line could be considered to be Australia, which it was.' The barrier of wire like that stream in Keneally's Sydney Cove is the ordering imagination's initial mark on an unwritten ground. But for Keneally's warders it works as a sanitary cordon, segregating two species of offender. Carey's soldier has no context in which to place it, and so can't understand its function. His job is to keep intruders outside that abstractly fanciful line, but because he doesn't know what's inside it, he can't judge who should be debarred. This minion of the nuclear age is even more discomfited than Tench with his compass, steering 'from the governor's house at Rose Hill . . . for a short time nearly in a north-east direction, after which we turned to north 34° west.' Carey's character has 'no orientation brief, no maps' – and no literature to justify space by reorganising it around him.

Describing Australia didn't mean adding up an expansive plenum of facts, as in Whitman's America. It involved cancellation, denial, killing. The first professional describer and depicter of the land, the botanist Banks on his voyage with Cook in 1770, was an Adam who stalked through Eden armed with a musket. For him, taxonomy and assassination went hand in hand. 'I made a small excursion in order to shoot anything I could meet with,' he reports, 'and found a large quantity of quails.' The birds were obliging targets for the analyst, since they hadn't yet learned fear: 'I might have killed as many almost as I pleased had I given my time up to it, but my business was to kill variety and not too many individuals of the same species.' Botanising in the woods, Banks is one of those intellectual viziers William Blake derides – demons of the romantic age, who murder to dissect. He turns up again in Rex Ingamells's *The Great South Land*, where his rituals of spoliation are play-acted at a native corroboree. The dancers chant

> *I am Banka Banka.*
> *I am the Hunter of grasses and flowers.*
> *I dig up anything that grows in the ground.*

Stooping to collect a specimen, Banks looks to the blacks like a moribund kangaroo. He was himself puzzled by the quiddity of the kangaroo (which he classified as a mouse-coloured greyhound) and was satisfied only when he killed 'a very large one'. He consummated the act of enquiry by dining on his prey, disillusioned by 'the total want of flavour, for he was certainly the most insipid meat.' Banks gunned down parrots, preserving the gaudy skins and excavating all the innards for pie; Tench on his excursion records, in the same spirit, 'We saw many ducks, and killed one'; and the explorer Edward Giles, thirsting in the outback, achieves the twin consummations of knowledge and description when he keeps himself alive by ravening on an infant wallaby, which he ate 'living, raw, dying – fur, skin, bones, skull, and all'. This remains the story of settlement in Australia, punishing a landscape which won't consent to being loved. Peter Cowan's story 'The Tractor' is about the vengefulness of clearance, the erasure of countryside to construct a suburb. 'He hated his land,' the wife reflects as she watches her husband's mechanised assault on trees, flowers and wild life. Adam cultivated the garden; his Australian offspring replaces it with a concrete backyard.

The only way literature could understand the place was as a bereft, inadequate version of pastoral. Robert Lowe in some squatters' songs enumerates more of its negative properties: 'The gum has no shade,/And the wattle no fruit'; unlike the inhabitants of Philip Sidney's mellifluous Arcady, 'the shepherds won't sing.' Lowe winced that 'the cockatoo cooeth/Not much like a dove', and Emilie Heron heard the forest as a jeering onomatopoeia where all song is devalued by mocking kookaburras. For Ingamells, the magpie makes at best an 'atonal music'; Christopher Brennan records the strident drilling which is 'the cicada's torture-point of song'. At last Henry Kendall's bell-birds dispense a silver-voiced enchantment, and seem like Shelley's skylark or Keats's nightingale to be sponsors of poetry, but when the suburban ornithologists in Patrick White's *The Burnt Ones* try to capture that song, they're left with a crackling and hissing which might be the noise of the bush but is in fact the exhausted protest of their tape machine.

There were conscious efforts to establish Australia as a latter-day paradise. Mary Gilmore, offended by the caricature of 'a land of songless birds and scentless flowers', derived that blessed state from her childhood and lapsed into a paraphrase of Traherne, who celebrated his immortal, angelic youth in jewelled fields: 'In spring the bush used to be a constant choir of song; . . . In every bush I dare affirm there was a pigeon or a dove.' Does the need to dare so innocuous an affirmation hint at a doubt? She annexes the entire continent as her secret garden, and bans anything noxious: 'there were no bad smells about the bush when the kingdom of the wild was its only kingdom . . . Once Australia smelt like the Spice Islands.' Wordsworth tranquilly, regretfully recollected the lost Eden of his infancy, and surveyed a world where the rainbow had come and gone. Furnley Maurice exchanged Wordsworth's decayed abbeys and ruined cottages and wintry thorn trees for a brawling Melbourne bazaar of produce in his poem 'The Victoria Markets Recollected in Tranquillity'. Wordsworth's pastoral is messily democratised down under: the cornucopia of skinned rabbits and water-melons pours its goods 'from Earth's mothering soul'. A lyric anecdote by Francis Letters treats the case of a mute Australian Milton, elated by the continent's free central spaces but unable to praise them aloud because 'the Muses gave him everything but song.' How does a shy, laconic antipodean Orpheus gain the courage and conviction to sing? The myth of a transplanted sub-equatorial Arcady comes to his aid. The 'inglorious Milton' of Francis Letters, disabled like the silent sleepers in Gray's country church-yard, can be nourished into eloquence. Kenneth Slessor summons up an edible pastoral plenty in 'Five Bells' by means of a pun: someone is babbling 'of Milton, melons, and the Rights of Man', but the words interbreed

So Milton became melons, melons girls,
And fifty mouths, it seemed, were out that night;

while more recently a tropical rhapsody by Richard Tipping reconstitutes the lush garden of Marvell, which with its luscious succulent ornamental fruits is a symbol of poetry. Milton is squeezed into melons, Slessor's rights of man into mangoes, and Tipping can announce that

mangoes are a positive good in the world
mangoes like poetry.

Despite this glutted joy, the pastoral remains an import, the evocation of elsewhere. Australia is always the distorted replica of another ideal place. Mary Gilmore delighted in it as 'this the last of the Wonderful Lands', but Allen Afterman in 'Van Diemen's Land' ravages her myth and sees Tasmania as a malevolent boneyard, a 'world no one wanted to live in' where the flora of Eden has been uprooted:

Land without a fruit-bearing tree,
as though Truth were exiled and the lie remained.

Afterman's Tasmania belongs to 'the lost, the fallen continent', whose citizens are not aboriginal Adams but the last, victimised men on a derelict planet. Australia is still seen by way of metaphor, and disoriented by the verbal device. Metaphor promises transference; it does a vehicle's work, carrying one agent across space to join it with a distant other, and in Australia it is the reflex of a helpless homesickness. The convict woman in her ballad laments 'that wretched place Van Diemen's Land, far from our native shore'. The genteel versifiers who follow her adapt recalcitrant Australia to a pastoral setting they have left behind. William Woolls, who arrived in 1832, saw the 'sweet retirement' of his haven 'far from Sydney's dusty ways' as a metaphoric compound of other literary gardens – Jonson's plenteous Penshurst where you can fill your bag with game, Marvell's hermetic Appleton where you can sweetly retire from the sound of drum and fife or cannon, Gray's wistful Stoke Poges where in silent evening you can watch the labouring oxen bow towards home and the twilight fade. Richard Whateley, having taken inventory of Australia's wonders (marsupial monsters, black swans), sums up the place as an image only of itself, an unreciprocated simile:

> Now of what place could such strange tales
> Be told with truth save New South Wales?

Yet here too there is an echo, a precedent to gainsay the novelty. Whateley has paraphrased the self-reference of Marvell's garden, which computes time on a floral clock:

> How could such sweet and wholesome hours
> Be reckoned but with herbs and flowers?

Though praising the idiosyncrasy of New South Wales, he must do so in imitative cadences.

The muse, as Charles Harpur says in one of his Wordsworthian ballads about the calamities of settlers, is Memory. Harpur's own verse variously remembers and collates the pastorals of Marvell (when he slavers over oranges as 'gold lamps in a green night of shade'), Keats (when he calls plums 'the language of lush summer's Eden theme' and anticipates their 'juicy comfort'), or Shelley (when during a storm in the mountains he appears to be studying Mont Blanc, and asks how in this elemental riot he 'may find/ . . . the light of Mind?'). These mimicking deceptive memories call up momentary Edens for Australian literature. Imagination, Keats said, is Adam's dream of Eve; he awakes to find it gratified. Poetic imagination in Australia dreamed of England, and awoke to a different, depleted truth. Francis MacNamara has a vision of his own apotheosis as Frank the Poet until 'I awoke and found 'twas but a dream'; Emilie Heron in the rustic setting of Comerang imagines herself in an English village, an insular valley so 'English-like' that we

> . . . half believe ourselves again at home,
> Or think this were a memory, taking form,
> A reminiscence sweet, or waking dream!

Even a poet as redoubtably nationalist as Les Murray can't help writing revisions of incongruous elsewheres. This is the case with his pastoral domain in 'A New England Farm, August 1914', where the New England within New South Wales is measured against America's New England, even more estranged from the English original. Murray's poem begins a yeoman-like correction of

T. S. Eliot's *Waste Land*. Instead of Eliot's dryness and disgust, a Georgic poet readies his plough:

> August is the winter's death,
> He dries the rotted June rain in the earth,
> Stiffens fat roots, ignites within the peach tree
> Flower and seed. August is time to think
> Of facing ploughshares, getting out new boots,
> And of the first calves shivering in the grass
> Still wet with birth-slime.

Eliot's poem, with its cruel lashing April, dreads spring. In the southern hemisphere the seasons happen back to front, and attitudes are reversed; Murray's farmer has no leisure for despair, and must resume his battle with the land. But his August remains a comment on Eliot's maimed rite of spring, as that in its turn was a satiric footnote to Chaucer's inspiriting, showery April, moving men to go on pilgrimages, at the beginning of *The Canterbury Tales*; Australia, like Eliot's puritanical America, is one more belated renovation of England.

Down below the rest of the world, Australia metamorphosed reality by standing that world on its head. Thus its early literature transposes the moody mysteries of the Gothic from northern Europe to this remote, inverted south. Marcus Clarke in a preface to Adam Lindsay Gordon's poems argued that spooky Australia might have been hallucinated by Poe: the 'dominant note' of its scenery is 'Weird Melancholy'; the bush is 'funereal, secret, stern'. The cockatoos shriek 'like evil souls', and Clarke recites the legend of the Bunyip as if it were one of those krakens with which the Scottish highlands are infested in Collins's poem about their superstitions. The gum trees are tortured and twisted, the wilderness keens curses in its 'myriad tongues'. This is no Arcady or Boeotia. It is a haunt of grotesquerie, a 'fantastic land of monstrosities'. Adam Lindsay Gordon agreed that the eucalypt trunks had been carved 'like weird columns Egyptian', inscribed with cabbala; Henry Lawson described the bush as 'nurse and tutor of eccentric minds, home of the weird'. Travelling as far south as you can go, you arrive in an imaginary north – the gnarled, skeletal Hartz mountains of Goethe's Mephistopheles (which have their upside-down Tasmanian replica behind the Huon Valley), the white desert of ice through which Mary Shelley's Frankenstein pursues his brain-child (and where Sir John Franklin perished, seeking the North-West Passage after his posting in Van Diemen's Land).

C. J. Koch's novel *The Doubleman* treats the antipodes as a world entered through the looking-glass. Set in an 'upside-down frame', Tasmania 'duplicates the Atlantic coast of Europe', climatically separate from the parched, dazzling mainland. Its atmosphere is once more that of Gothic obfuscation: Koch's characters grope through London peasoupers, and the clouds draped along the hills are 'straight from the Hound of the Baskervilles'. The island here is the victim of Manichean geography. It's a sombre, misty England displaced in the lower hemisphere; it's also a dualistic society, in which you can step out of humdrum reality into an ulterior dimension of strangeness. Behind Tasmania, in the shadows, is the 'other island' it had once been – feared, hated Van Diemen's Land. Koch's Tasmanians conceal this prior identity as if it were the guilty secret everyone guards in a Gothic novel. But for Koch, the state's official schizophrenia makes it the point of access, like the green door I used to ponder on the main road, to a 'Faery Otherworld'. He transplants to Tasmania the Celtic preserve of elfs, imps and ethereal female magicians discovered by Spenser in Ireland during the sixteenth century.

In the process he manages one of those small metaphoric miracles which are literature's brand of sorcery, enticing a genie to take up residence in a blunt excrescence of the known world. He achieves the sublimation of Mount Direction. For his hero, it is a pinnacle looking into Tasmania's numinous faeryland. He sees it glowing mauve in the afternoon from his house in New Town, 'sleeping at the gateway of light'. Magic seethes inside it, as in the Venusberg: it has 'a musing air of marvel', and behind it the green tinge in the evening sky is a membrane veiling – perhaps – the face of God. 'No one,' enthuses the boy, '. . . has ever loved a hill or a mountain as I do; Mount Direction is not just a mountain.' He has cajoled a directionless nonentity into meaning, manipulated the lump of rock into shape with words. Metaphor is the object's vanishing-act. But meanwhile, unmoved, Mount Direction still sprawls along the horizon behind my parents' house, and still in memory looks to me incohate, opaque, gracelessly dumped there. Was it ever mauve? Or did I simply lack the courage or the concentration to be entranced by it 'for an hour at a time', like Koch's boy? The colours I remember are khaki and carbon, which the sun could never excite. For evidence of the transcendent in that valley, I suppose I looked to the zinc works or the celluloid sky over the race-course: that was where, on a Cinemascopic membrane above the car park, my supernatural faces materialised.

The religious motive of Koch's fable is clear. In Australia, the purpose of literature must be consecration, tracing pattern and value – as at Tiagarra – on unhallowed ground. Here too, Australia inherits a romantic project. Cardinal Newman in an essay on poetry in 1829 wrote that Christians had a duty to see things poetically, to colour them with the hues of faith, to discern divine meanings. During the nineteenth century, literature took over from scripture as the ground of this faith. The romantic vision was the desire to see through and thus beyond things. Metaphor translates object into subject, natural phenomenon into supernatural augury. Thus Koch renders Mount Direction transparent, glimpsing through it an 'amazing Beyond'; on those untidy slopes I knew so well, he has pitched his heterodox altar. As it reads Australia and fantasticates its facts, literature can't help seeming like a surrogate theology. It argues the landscape into significance. 'Here is the symbol,' says Judith Wright of a cliff called Nigger's Leap, and she might be echoing the formal decision of the carver at Tiagarra. The precipice becomes a moral portent in her poem, lecturing her on the need of 'a time for synthesis'. Meditating on the place, she works out a truce between historical guilt about these dead black men and a compassionate envy. Suicide like Mount Direction is the route to a beyond, merging us with Jung's oceanic life:

> Night floods us suddenly as history
> that has sunk many islands in its good time.

With the same mobile metaphoric versatility, Wright can extradite the driver of an outback bullock-train to the sacerdotal setting of the Old Testament:

> The prophet Moses feeds the grape,
> and fruitful is the Promised Land.

A. D. Hope's poem 'Australia' longs for such symbolic progeny, 'if still from the deserts the prophets come'. But the prophetic function devolves here on the writer.

James McAuley designs his own map of similitudes for the 'mythical Australia' discovered by Quiros. His metaphoric geography establishes here the ancient icons of religious assurance, catholic in their global relevance. The cockatoo, for him as for Marcus Clarke, 'screams with demoniac pain', but there are other serene remonstrances to faith: the pollen of wattle inseminates 'the doubting heart', the angophora 'preaches . . ./With the gestures of Moses'.

The technique of ascription can seem opportunistic. This is Australia moralised – or, in the poem 'In the Huon Valley', Tasmania medievally allegorised. The apple industry is here an exercise in garnering experiential fruits, gathering in a wisdom 'worth the lifting and stacking'. The harvest of ripeness persuades McAuley that

> Life is full of returns;
> It isn't true that one never
> Profits, never learns.

Yet I wonder whether my aunts and uncles, dragging their leathery cement-like sacks to the tractor or toiling over the grader until midnight, ever saw the season this way? Did they learn anything from their work, or salvage any spiritual profit? The cyclical return was for them the revolution of a treadmill, not the reliable comeback of juicy Dame Nature. They lived in a Tasmania impervious to poetry (except perhaps for the cheery songs which crackled from a transistor radio above the rumble of the grader, to numb the aching head while the body packed stupid apples). Only when the trees were grubbed out could the farm become a playpen of bric-à-brac, with three-horned beasts of the apocalypse nailed above the barn doors. Sometimes, though, McAuley's scriptural gloss on Tasmania overlaps with my own observation of it. 'St John's Park' is about a street running off my main road, opposite McAuley's house and also opposite that towered folly with the tantalising green door. Here a sports field and an old folks' home abut. The coincidence allows McAuley to medievalise society, as two opposed ages of man conjoin in his allegorical almanac:

> Old people slowly rot along the wall.
> The young ones hardly notice them at all.
> Both live in the same picture-book of hours.

I see my parents in his illustrated panel. Because life in Tasmania is so compressed, so coincidental, St John's Park happens to be the setting of both their youth and their old age. My mother left the farm to nurse at the hospital there. My father used to walk her home from the tram stop up the long leafy avenue, and when he was shipped off to New Guinea during the war she wrote to him winsomely saying that she didn't like to walk up there alone without an escort after dark . . . He gave her a comforting hug in his next letter. It was a scene for loitering, a street to be taken as slowly as possible because at its end they had to part. The same street is now the scene of a later biological hour. They go there two or three times a week to play bowls, pacing out their retirement as they traipse up and down the green. They're not exactly rotting, but bowls is a game meant to slow the organism; and the young ones who shout in the avenue outside are their sloughed younger selves. For once, reality obliges by matching the image.

McAuley admits that the quest for meanings in Australia is urgent just because they're so sparse. Remembering his fascination with a backyard wistaria vine during his childhood in western Sydney, he reflects

> The soul must feed on something for its dreams
> In those brick suburbs, and there wasn't much.

Despite its flimsiness, he poetically nourishes the growth as one more testament to faith, and it soon garlands an iconographic shrine with 'crossed flags at the back', poised 'between the brass cross and the Union Jack'. McAuley's literary mission was to fabricate a symbolism for Australia. The land, however, resists these rationalisations. Stone didn't soften because of those graffiti at Tiagarra. Perhaps the braver duty of Australian literature is iconoclasm. Randolph Stow's missionary Heriot in *To the Islands* destroys the symbolic fiction which mediates between him and the country's nothingness. Dying in the outback, he breaks his crucifix and decides that 'my soul is a strange country' – an internal Australia, a dead heart not of darkness but of searing, scarring light. Is literature a homecoming, or the outsider's report on a home he can describe but not belong to? In Australia, is everyone an expatriate?

Porter in his poem about Boeotian Australia notices the split. The settlers have fused with their land; others 'feel at home nowhere' – or only in poetry. Les Murray in 'Noonday axeman' listens to the 'unhuman silence' which follows the axe's bite and its echo in the bush. He wonders at his own capacity to tolerate the stillness, and knows he possesses a hardihood some cannot share:

> It will be centuries
> Before many men are truly at home in this country.

This is a poem of quiet self-congratulation. Chopping wood, Murray remembers an ancestral line of 'axemen, dairymen, horse-breakers' who have preceded him in the silence. He is again the Georgic poet, the husbandman who writes between bouts of 'clearing, splitting, sawing', whose songs accompany labour. 'Noonday axeman', with its stanzaic refrain of 'axe-fall, echo and silence', adopts the rhythm of work. In meditative rests between swinging the axe, the poet rolls tobacco and considers what he's doing; after a spell, he resumes. The typographic silence between the verses resounds with the thud of steel into the red gum. But two ironies unsettle Murray's conviction that he belongs here. He makes himself at home in the bush by destroying it, and though he respects the silence and comments, 'Things are so wordless,' as he looks at beady sap in the tree's wounds, a poem is speech which disrupts that peace.

Poetry constructs a home, and it does so by slicing down trees, replacing their muteness with the sociable noise of language. Australian literature has its origins in this motive: the letter sent to Banjo Paterson by Clancy of the Overflow's shearing mate, scribbled with a thumb nail dipped in tar; the communal yearning which immortalises the Man from Snowy River, kept alive by epic recitation when 'the stockmen tell the story of his ride'. John Manifold, at a friend's tomb in Crete after the Second World War, performs the same ceremony of commemoration. Building 'a cairn of words', he remembers the dead John Learmonth's own invention of an Australian literature:

> Schoolboy, I watched his ballading begin:
> Billy and bullocky and billabong,
> Our properties of childhood, all were in.

In Rosemary Dobson's 'Country Press' that bardic, mnemonic function has been assumed by the rural newspaper, in whose roll-call of the race she wants to be entered. Type-setting her own obituary, she requests

> When I shall die
> Set me up close against my fellow-men . . .
> Jostled and cheered, in lower-case italics
> I shall go homewards in the *Western Star*.

Letterpress grants her, even if posthumously, the comfort of companionship.

But beside this crafting of society by Banjo Paterson's oral sagas or Manifold's upright stones or Dobson's village of cramped columns, there's another explanation of literature in Australia: as the product of rage and madness, an urge towards deracination; something lateral to reality, literally outlandish like the country itself. Kenneth Slessor in *Five Visions of Captain Cook* defends poetry by seeing Australia as a supreme, perverse fiction. The mariners before Cook, like Tasman and Bougainville, 'paused on the brink of mystery', but chose to heed a wind which was 'blowing home, blowing home'. They turned to the north towards that home, and missed Australia. According to Slessor, Cook was more foolhardy, driven by a poet's visionary fanaticism. He chose to sail 'over the brink, into the devil's mouth', though he hadn't enough food and his crew was mutinously homesick. Slessor conjectures a remote sequel:

> So Cook made choice, so Cook sailed westabout,
> So men write poems in Australia.

The leap from Cook's crazy detour to the writing of poems is inspired. Men write poems in Australia so they can imagine and then explore elsewhere. The art estranges reality or deranges it, metaphorically questioning the idea of a home. It dares to be disaffected, like the man in Les Murray's 'An Absolutely Ordinary Rainbow' who weeps inexplicably in a Sydney street, causing scandalised crowds to gather and traffic to pile up. Australia has hurt him into poetry. My tantrum at the showground is a footnote to the scene.

So, too, men scribble in notebooks in Tasmania. At the time, I felt the activity to be somehow shameful, clandestine. 'Collecting information?' said a custodian at Port Arthur, staring me out when I enquired about those fading extra-territorial murals on the commandant's house. 'Is this for a school project?' asked the mystified old lady at the apple museum as I listed the labels of the packing cases. Who but a pedagogue or a suspicious policeman would observe things for a living? Other ways of preserving experience seemed more innocent. People taking snapshots at Port Arthur or making their families perform for the video camera as they boarded the Gordon River cruise boat provoked no unease. What they were doing was forgivable because instantaneous, unreflective; a notebook, however, was the equipment of alienation and espionage. Inside it, experience was broken down into subjectivity, as if in those industrial processes which fascinated me – rock reduced to zinc, water churned into electricity then dismissively dewatered. Or else experience was translated, enciphered, obscured by a hand jerking over the page unreadably in cars, boats and bucking aeroplanes. An album of photographs is a journal, meant to be shown and shared. My notebook was a soliloquy, like those unvoiced, unprintable words I mouthed when made to chop the wood in *They Found a Cave*: the secret language of someone who couldn't converse with the country.

Even with all that literature can do, it will take centuries – as Les Murray calculated – before some men are truly at home here. I know I won't have that long.

VI

AT HOME AND AWAY

In the Family

Fatherland, mother country. They are two different images of parental Tasmania, whose runaway offspring I was: the grumpy mountain, with the happy valley lying behind it; a place which threatened and tested you, trying your fitness for membership of it, and a place which called you home without asking questions.

Edmund Burke thought that landscapes made infants of us again, because we revert in our feelings about them to our earliest memories: fear of the intimidating father, dependence on the cossetting mother. The landscape we are born in has our childhood inscribed on it. Burke's categories – the sublime and its bracing terrors, where every crag and thunderclap stands in for the retributive father; beauty and its tender contours, announcing the mother – fit my Tasmania. Sublime Tasmania, the paternal land, is made of unapproachable alps and looming trees: Mount Wellington and all its kin, once fulminating volcanoes, still frowning through their brows of cloud; those forests where the axemen persist in the old masculine drill of conquest. Beautiful Tasmania is made of maternal nests: the orchards of the Huon, the amniotic ponds with their germinating salmon. On Flinders Island, the profile of the Patriarchs; on the east coast, the welcoming calm of the Friendly Beaches. The little state maps a mental condition.

It grew symbolic for me by association. From our back porch, what I saw was inside me: the virile overbearing mountain, and the thin fruitful crevice of apples and aunties I knew was hidden on its other side. In the foreground of the view, summing up its contradictions, was an apricot tree on a triangle of lawn, its roots tangled under the cement paths of our backyard. I hated it and loved it through my childhood. When I remember summer, the season consists of afternoons spent looking up through the leaves of the tree at a sky which beamed, and biting into the oozy flesh of the apricots as I did so. But in winter the branches battered the walls and windows of the house. The friendly tree became an ogre, trying to break down our shelter. Blameless itself, it came to signify the punitive starkness which terrified me in Tasmania. The branches when the fruit was eaten and the leaves had fallen were gnarled and knuckle-like, with a coarse mottled rind; every winter my father would choose one with pedantic care and pull off a length of it, to be kept admonishingly on top of the refrigerator for when I played up. Switches of apricot made the best canes, because the knobbly wood was guaranteed to raise a ridge on your legs. The tree delivered pleasure and pain, the knowledge of good and evil. It grew in both the fatherland and the mother country. It died a few years ago, and was cut down; when my parents wrote to tell me so, I wasn't sure what to feel. Should I mourn the loss of a friend, or rejoice that I had outlasted an ancient enemy?

My father's job was building Tasmania. He worked for the housing department; the new suburbs of the 1950s, bulldozed into the bush or run up overnight on squelching fields of mud, were his handicraft. He began by painting the lookalike crates, walled with weatherboard and roofed with lids of corrugated iron, and ended by overseeing others – mostly gangs of 'new Australians' – who did the same. He was proprietorial about the shaky, provisional estates. On Sunday afternoon we'd often go on tours of his building sites, to look at the timber struts and asbestos ceilings and cement paths: Chigwell clinging uncertainly to its hillside, Risdon Vale cowering under the walls of the pink prison. The paling fences seemed too frail to keep uncolonised space out; the wrinkled rooftops with their skins of colour were no security against the enormous sky. The thought of living where no one had ever lived before alarmed me. But to my father, these wooden containers signified safety. They dealt so negligently with the landscape – felling trees, creating a waste and calling it a vale – because they were his escape from it. Here where all was new the old miseries of a poor rural childhood could be forgotten. Once the bush was abolished, you could cultivate a garden.

My mother's job was tending that garden. The man builds Tasmania, the woman decorates it. At first my parents grew vegetables out the front: rows of cabbages and trellises of beans, trenches of onions and potatoes. Behind the house, they planted three fruit trees – apricot, nectarine and peach. On their little lot, they instinctively recreated in microcosm the farms they had quit.

There were even hens, cackling and crapping in their coop beside the back fence. Gradually they did away with these recollections of the agricultural past. The vegetables went into hiding beyond the woodshed, and the front yard was grassed. Between the paths, my mother planted thickets of flowers. The house retired behind a red gum and a willow tree, which clutched at the water-pipes and had to be cut down for its greed. My father took to cultivating cacti in a hut of glass. The move from vegetables to flowers was a historical victory, completing that first conquest of the wild when the houses were set in their foundations. 'They make a lovely show, don't they?' my mother would say of her hydrangeas and flaunting gladioli. This was her creation, enticed from the dry black soil; her art, and her own floral barricade against the world.

My father built the house, she made the home. When he had a shower each night after work, he'd leave an anthill of silt in the tub, trophy of his day's labour among the grime of an unmade world. My mother meanwhile crusaded against dust indoors while grubbing outside to plant her seeds and bulbs and crying if they didn't grow. They made themselves at home in the country and with the land by virtue of their daily, soiling struggle with it. I lacked their courage, and ran away.

One night I was sitting with my parents in front of the television set. No doubt the programme was *Mork and Mindy*. Restless, I glanced at my father to the right of me, my mother to the left. They had settled almost sculpturally in their chairs. This evening was the exact facsimile of every previous one; for almost twenty years, with the house to themselves, they'd been fixed in their routine and in physical attitudes which summed them up. In repose, their characters were written on their unguarded expressions and in the disposition of their limbs. They occupied eternity, as in a photograph or on a tombstone. My father had one brawny leg cocked over the arm of his chair; my mother held her chin, a finger in the groove which carved her cheek between the nose and mouth. The postures were confessional. My father's sprawling leg expressed a boyish disregard for furniture and for social niceties. It was the surly statement of a larrikin who didn't like being indoors, assertively casual. My mother's hand, with her thumb propping up her chin, her index finger tracing that furrow of flesh and her forefinger lying along her lips as if to silence them, had set into an emblem of unprotesting stoicism. It held the line on her face as if comforting a pain.

Then, suddenly ashamed of being the observer looking in at their lives, I became aware of myself doing the looking, and noticed with a shock what my own body was up to. My right leg was cocked over the leg of my chair, and my left hand was holding my chin, with a finger in that same crevice on my face. We made the perfect genetic triptych: I was the superimposed image of these two people from whom I had spent so long apart, to whom I was almost a stranger. Shiftily I withdrew my leg and found something for my hand to do inside a pocket, but within that moment I had aged several years. At long last I resigned from the adolescent rage to invent myself, and quietly capitulated to a predestining chemistry. Losing faith in your own singularity is the start of wisdom, I suppose; also the first announcement of death. The recognition spread like a stain soaking outwards through the skin. And as I wriggled there in my chair, I understood that my personality was as much a compound as my posture: an unstable merger of my father's aggressiveness and my mother's nervous qualms, of paternal gruffness and maternal worry.

I apologise for the obviousness of this domestic epiphany, but until then it hadn't been obvious to me. If you are the only child in the family, you imagine yourself to be the only person in the world. Solipsistic islands and anti-social caves were my habitat. After half a life, I had to admit that I was no self-created foundling, but a haphazard amalgam of other flesh; not even the mind had been left to my choice, since it was pressed into form by the landscapes I tried so hard not to look at. Tasmania reappeared under cover in the literary scenery of England: from where else had I derived my liking for Celtic faerylands and Gothic fogs? When you leave home, it travels with you; the parents you think you can reject dictate from within your every action. You serve your sentence for the term of your natural life.

A few days later, a genetic coincidence – accidental or designed? – occurred on the mantelpiece. My father had come home from bowls, and unpinned the badge he wears on his shirt with his surname and initials. He set it down on the shelf above the fireplace. When I came into the room, I noticed it at once: it was placed in front of my framed photograph. My face wore his name as identification; I was a caption to his existence. It didn't matter that the photograph was taken among the piled snow of an American winter, and sent home to demonstrate how I was flourishing in this cold remote climate my parents would never see. Again my freedom was abruptly rescinded. I shuddered at the justice of it.

Next time I passed through the room, the badge which tagged me had gone. But the face in the photograph looked older than it did before, and no longer belonged to an individual. Behind it, pressing through the skin like a mask embedded there, was my father's, and behind that the face of his father, who died in alcoholic dejection long before I was born.

This grandfather always intrigued me. His seemed to have been a very Tasmanian fate: trapped at a dead end, imprisoned and killed by circumstances. He's supposed to have had some artistic talents, but since no one ever spoke of him it was hard to discover what they were. In any event, there was no call for them in the Lachlan Valley of the 1920s and '30s. He painted houses instead, produced children, and committed slow suicide by drinking. Though the family was silent on the subject, he was its missing link: the source of all our faces, for neither I nor any of my cousins resembled his fragile, put-upon wife, who died babbling Swedish during my adolescence. The square Germanic features we all had, and those gloomy eyebrows, must be his. Yet he was a nobody – as extinct as a Tasmanian aborigine, as non-existent as one of those convict ancestors whose names were removed from the record by Hobart's burghers when they made good. He was the denied past, returning to haunt us physiognomically. I had never even seen a picture of him.

Then a cousin found two photographs to show me. They told his story in a drastic, deathly abridgement. In the first, he's dressed up for some rustic operetta, with false moustache and shiny thigh boots, posed next to the chair of a ringleted actress: one of his enthusiasms was the theatre, it seems. He and the woman stand on a ruffled flowery hedge of carpet, with a painted curtain behind. He was a Konrad then, play-acting a Bavarian or Tyrolean peasant. The second photograph abruptly drops him in Tasmania. He and my grandmother stand in their Sunday best against a row of shrubs in an unkempt garden. Over the fence, the bush begins. Their faces are bisected by dark, shadowed under the brims of their hats; their eyes can't meet mine. Only his jowl and jaw reveal what has happened to the dapper amateur actor. His cheeks are puffy yet hollow, his mouth set in a grim, terse straight line. There's no moustache to conceal the collapse of his features. His stance is the same as in the charade, left hand in pocket. But the posture the first time is foppishly lax, calculated to show off an inch of starched cuff. Here it's uneasy, awkward. The listless weight makes him buckle at the knees. In the other scene, his right hand grips the wicker chair in which the woman sits; now it droops, making no effort to touch his wife, whose own worn hands hang in front of her imploring to be occupied.

The fantasist has been trapped in reality, locked in the shabby thorny yard on the edge of the bush. There were no caves for him to find. The face erased by the hat decomposed, and then in a second biological gamble was put back together as me.

I had placed my trust, mistakenly, in the myth of self-invention. You created yourself, and did so out of nothing. The past was permitted no claim. I learned this faith in New York, where it's the local ideology. The buildings attest to it, growing recklessly away from the earth and pretending they're suspended from the sky; so do the people, attitudinising behind their shades, treating the street as their stage, each equipped with his or her own home-made mystique. Seen in Greenwich Village recently: a woman whose T-shirt loudly declared 'I'm a legend in my own mind'.

The return to Tasmania rid me of this notion. I could feel myself disappearing into the people and places I'd been made by. The person I thought I'd elected to be was an incident in someone else's mind, a convergence of other bodies, a figure grown by the landscape itself. I had no siblings to teach me that identity was shared and derivative; my tutors were my tribe of cousins. One of them, a childhood favourite whom I hadn't seen for more than twenty years, promptly co-opted me. Her every observation annexed me to the family, of which I was one more unexceptional offshoot: 'All the Conrads are stirrers' or 'All the Conrads are great readers', she would say; and once again a casual stance was classified – 'All the Conrads stand with their arms crossed like that.' I was the image, she assured me, of her youngest son.

There were other claims from the competing side. When I

protested that I couldn't drive because it took an effort for me to tell left from right, my mother triumphantly seized on that as evidence for her contribution: 'Your father always said the Smiths was a bit slow.' The local paper published a photograph of me scowling in the sun beside the plane which was about to take me to the south-west. An auntie told my mother that I looked just like their father, the old man who all those years ago had chased me through the orchard, convinced I was a stranger and a trespasser. I was being taken into biological custody.

I even learned that I had a double – a cousin I'd never met, son of a sister of my father's who had gone to live in Sydney before I was born. A photo album was produced to convince me: the impersonator sat in a backyard, brandishing a glass of beer. The man wearing my face was what I should have been, a me without maladjustments. He worked, I learned, in a Sydney post office. I hatched a plot, wondering whether it might end in a life-swap. I'd go to the post office, patiently queue at his window, watch for him to notice his alter ego advancing towards him; when I got to him, I'd innocently ask for some stamps. . . . He didn't know of my existence: would he recognise himself in this anonymous walk-in? In Sydney, I did go to the post office, and paced up and down outside debating the wisdom of the experiment. I even peered in through the door. There I was, amiably selling stamps and manhandling parcels, grinning behind the counter. The sight from a distance was enough; I left without joining the line, absurdly pleased to think that someone was enjoying – as if on my behalf – the life here that I had denied myself.

The most difficult thing was learning not to be afraid.

One night a friend was driving me back from a dinner at the beach. We were talking, and didn't notice that we had edged into the eastern suburbs. A police car crossed in front and waved us over. My friend realised he'd been speeding. My first thought, in a hot spasm of confusion as the policeman grinned through the window: I don't have my passport on me. Why do I always guiltily assume I'm in a foreign country?

Another twilight, having been to see the cemetery on the headland outside Strahan, I was walking back to town along a grassed-over railway line, with darkness clotting in the hedges. As the little settlement came into sight round a few more bends, I felt someone padding along the track behind me. An urban panic stalled me; I stopped myself from wheeling round to look and willed myself ahead, ashamed to run. The footsteps closed in. I tried not to glance sideways. A loping youth drew level with me and in profile – without looking at me, not needing to because his intention was so impersonal – asked, 'How's she goin', mate?'

'OK,' I said, aghast at sounding so nervous.

'Startin' to cool off a bit,' he drawled. His pace had already overtaken mine; on he strode to the pub. My absurd fearful seizure relaxed into an equally silly bliss. This world was friendly after all. But by then I was alone in it again.

My own fraught feelings dramatised the landscape. Since I felt it to be antagonistic, it became sublime. Father-fixations bristled and glowered everywhere. When I relaxed, so did Tasmania. The obstructive peaks retreated; I saw at last the beauty of the place.

On my last weekend there, I drove back down the centre of the state from Launceston to Hobart at nightfall, watching it all pass in review outside. At Oatlands, halfway through the journey, the sun lunged to eye level and stared from a ground of sizzling gold. Everything it looked at – the sandstone cottages, the weedy lake, the blue unrolling ribbon of the main road – flared with a last infusion of light, which burned into the rock, the water and the metal to be exhaled again as heat. There was a pulse in objects. Then the hills sliced through the sun, and the plain paled into tone without contour, except for a distant cliff smouldering red. Quiet palpably settled on the flattened land. Only the children playing beside the road were briefly more boisterous, knowing they'd soon be called in to those grey drowsing houses; two women talking over a garden fence among the creepers seemed to grow there themselves, entwined in an endless conversation about the roots and branches and sprigs and sprouts of life in their town.

Looking up from the fading world, I saw with a shock that the sky was still burnished, radiant. The day had been clear; dusk was the whimsical exhibition of every colour inconsistent with enamelled blue – clouds bloomed like roses, and above the hills the light was citrous. Around a corner suddenly there was Mount Wellington, still far to the south and in jumbled perspective. For once I felt it to be a cosy totem: a big dog stretched guardingly on the doormat, its head down, its slopes of rubble and seared wood now a blue fleece of shadow. The river in its valley was also pacified by light, polished to silver. The interim of evening beautifies but saddens everything. It is a passage between ages, between eternities – that scorched, vital brilliance; this calm, resigned numbness. You are lullingly rubbed out, relieved of existence. I left the bus at Elwick, and stepped onto the crossroads of my previous life. To the right, the hulking sheds of the showground, one of which was once my cave; to the left, on the race-course ineffectively blessed by the Pope, the memory of that white rectangle on which the celluloid phantasms played; across the choppy bay, the hissing zinc works. A full moon slid out from behind Mount Direction, and hovered yellow above an avenue of throbbing violet street lights. I'd never seen this happen before, I realised; never known that Mount Direction, so shaggy and obdurate by day, contained the moon; that this rough barricade blocking off the view looked over the edge of the earth. Moonlight made me a spectre, invisible though audible as the dry grass of the paddock scratched underfoot. When I crossed the road into the suburb, there were laughing voices and trickling hoses in the gardens. This, I thought, was my privileged second chance: I had been allowed to trespass on the past, and to see it for a moment freed of fear and rage and the hungry yearning which had made this gap between two mountains, bordered by the drive-in's wall of illusion and the blaze from the factory chimneys, a prison to me. There was no sense of confinement now. Instead of bulk and fixity – the barbed wire of the showground fence, the blistered paint on the pavilions, the houses with their batteries of appliances kept alive by the torrents churning through turbines in the highlands – only a flotsam of lights drifted in space. Tasmania might have been unmoored, left to bob around in the ocean of chartless sky. What did it matter where you were? I remembered the sputnik I'd stayed up late to see once, blinking across the blankness above Mount Wellington: a dot incomprehensibly containing a brief life, glimpsed in transit. What did it matter who you were? We are all convocations of atoms – personified by proper names, lent importance by possessions, loyal to our little acreage, but nonetheless atoms, dancing particles of dust.

How fictitious home was: a magic circle scraped in resistant rock, as at Tiagarra; a consecrating allusion, as at Jericho or Bagdad; a house-shaped mail-box propped on a garden fence, to which I had been addressing letters for almost twenty years. Yet the improbability of the idea made it precious. I arrived at that mail-box, with its sloping red roof and its tiny twisted padlock, a diminutive replica and symbol of the house behind it; I walked up the path between the trees my parents had so proudly raised, each one an instalment in their modest campaign to outlast life; I let myself into the house. They weren't expecting me, and didn't hear me. I wished I could stay peacefully suspended there, disturbing no one. But our atoms are glued into a solid object, a character, a history. I opened the door of the room where my parents were watching television. They jumped, startled to see me. Was this the ghost of the child they'd once had, who left them? The shock on their faces rearranged itself to affection.

Soon I was eating my supper, and had forgotten about the sun's pyromaniac end in the midlands, about Mount Direction disappearing as it disgorged the moon, about precarious Tasmania itself, a raft of rock buoyantly adventuring through nowhere. The vagrant molecules hardened, like the pillars of concrete on which the house's timber frame was founded. Reality resumed for a while.

First words of my mother to me on my return to Tasmania after a decade, jerked from her by the emotion of the moment when I invaded her field of vision at the airport and tapped her on the shoulder: 'This isn't Peter,' she said. No, it wasn't. But I lied, and assured her it was.

Last word of my father to me when I telephoned from Sydney to say goodbye, before I got on the plane to New York: 'Tooroo.' Careless, or matily jaunty? I'll never know.

The Main Land

The day I left Tasmania the woman from next door came out to say goodbye to me. She hadn't yet said hello, so she must have thought the occasion was significant; she leaned across the fence in the morning summer sun and remarked with an air of baleful prophetic gravity, 'You'll be going to a cold place, Peter.' She didn't specify, and didn't need to. For her it was an abstract destination – unknown, chilling, not a home; an ice-death like Sir John Franklin's in his search for the North-West Passage.

To leave Tasmania, for those who remain behind sadly waving, is to quit the earth. People knit their brows to conceive of the looming mainland, or the still more outlandish worlds believed to be 'over there'. A neighbour who taps on my parents' kitchen window with a bottle most nights questioned me closely about drinking habits on this other planet. 'Is the beer you drink over there weaker than ours then?' he asked. No, stronger, I said. 'Then how can they drink pints of it?' he demanded. My father, showing off a new television set, warned that the local technology wouldn't be intimidated by comparison with the world upstairs: 'They reckon our TV is up with anything you've got over there,' he said. Between outer space and earth, metaphors try to mediate. 'What's Oxford *like*, then?' asked one of my cousins. I had no way of answering, because there was no peg for the cloudy similes: all I could say was that it wasn't like anything here. For all its incorporation of manifold elsewheres – inscribing its map with an Exeter and a Derby, a Perth, a Dublin and a Carnarvon, an Interlaken, a Florentine River and a River Don, a Jericho and a Styx – the island is an unattached, self-referring place.

Nor are there equivalents to it on the mainland. Leaving Hobart for Melbourne, you cross an invisible border into another age. Tasmania dwindles into the distance, lost like childhood, forgotten like the original sin of Australia's founding. Pastorally respectable, enriched by the gold rush, Melbourne never knew Tasmania's guilt and shame. The prisons with their flogging yards and manacles and smothering cowls seem here medievally, congenitally ancient. The

Tasmanian landscape dates from when time began, and has been scathed and battered ever since, broken into form – the drowned pinnacles of the Tasman Peninsula, the ejected clumps of Cape Grim, Mount Wellington with its core of fire and its ploughed field of sterile clods, the Edgar Fault finely stitched like a surgical scar through the button grass. After this punitive place of origin, Melbourne lodges you safely in the mid-nineteenth century.

Tasmania belongs to the beginning of that century, with its Gothic terrors and its Grecian temples, its sedate Georgian sandstone terraces and its cult of exhilarating, ennobling mountains. It stands for both a romantic dream and a romantic nightmare – the dream of revoking history and reinventing the world, of being the first man on earth and the busy indexer of creation like Hugh Germain; the nightmare of incarceration by your fears, of being the accursed last man in an empty world like Marcus Clarke's gobbling cannibal Gabbett or Fanny Cochrane gamely announcing herself to be the end of her race or Nevil Shute's characters computing the odds on Tasmania's holding out a few weeks longer. In Melbourne the solitude of Germain and the dejected solipsism of Clarke's Rufus Dawes are left far behind. Its makers were Victorian worthies, secure in their conviction of citizenship. The world has been rendered solid for them, as it never is in Tasmania; the city proudly drops anchor.

Melbourne's banks fortify money, or build palaces for it to live in. One of them in Collins Street has the swank of a grand hotel, with a ceremonial staircase in its foyer; gryphons guard the porch of another and the hall inside is a castle of polished wood and gold paint, hung with heraldic shields. The columns sprout ears of corn, to honour the landed source of the wealth coffered here and to show how cash is a crop. The banks speak for a society rich in material contentment. The heir to the bourgeois grandees of Collins Street is the Fletcher Jones man, posing in relief on the side of a shop in Queen Street. He personifies the Melbourne I always imagined across the water. He's there to advertise a brand of trousers which were my initiation into adolescence: stiffly military, dowdy grey, pressed to a knife-edge and with turn-ups (adjusted every January to allow for your growth in the year ahead) which collected a museum of musty souvenirs – pebbles, dust, buzzies, paperclips, the occasional button and blob of chewing-gum. The Fletcher Jones man models them in nicotine-coloured stucco, with glossily varnished hair and jewelled cuff-links, one hand on a pleated hip, the other propped in the air before him in a hieratic Egyptian attitude. This, I thought, was what being adult would consist of: rigid deportment; learning to be worthy of your Fletcher Joneses. Melbourne was where you got wisdom. The country which had its raw, unpropitious youth in Tasmania grew up to prosperity and smugness here. It's a Victorian city with optional palm trees. The railway station has a triumphal portico of clocks conserving the bourgeois regime of punctuality. Behind the main streets are narrower alleys, for stocking the emporia: the machine's workings are kept out of sight. The state library houses the brain which rules the system, in tiers of filed and stacked grey matter under a cranial cupola. Yet Melbourne is also the place where my cherished Anglo-Australia – the culture I pieced together from transplanted books – now goes under. In the years I've been away, the outpost of England I imagined we were has become a polyglot digest of Asia and the Mediterranean. Along Sydney Road in the suburb of Brunswick, nationalities collide: Gentiluomo Viaggi and Turismo shares the pavement with the legal firm of Numikoudis Ogilby; the Seattle butchers' shop evokes the meaty American west while Ali Baba's Variety Store displays a flurry of Greek, Lebanese, Turkish and Australian flags; tabouli salad and *baba gannouj* alternate with sugared Balkan snowballs, the Vietnamese sweets of Hông-Ngoc and indigenous 'Freshly-cut Sangers' (sandwiches in Ocker slang); the Bombay Club advertises its exclusive 'Crush Club (a Club within a Club)'. English literature with its gentle elegiac pastorals, against which Australia used to measure itself, retreats before other, more exotic mythologies. The Dedalos Garage on Sydney Road repairs hubristic high-flying autos gone astray in the urban labyrinth, and Dante's Espresso Bar boasts a fierily infernal Italian *rosticceria*. My main road back home in Hobart could manage no such supernatural diversions.

Outside the Brunswick post office, a municipal drinking-fountain set there in 1910 plaintively recalls the past. The little basilica of marble columns has four spigots under a copper canopy; around the pediment are twined art nouveau letters spelling out A N A – it was a gift of the Australian Natives Association. Façades of Victorian brick scowl above the hubbub of the street. One of them is fretted with urns, shields and acanthus leaves, but beneath this brave skyline of classical icons the Fatih Taekwondo Academy of Kick Boxing has broadcast its emblem, with a Bruce Lee lookalike soaring laterally, arms and fists extended. Next to it, a palsied sign propounds the virtues of woolly Imperial blankets, and of something else now illegible which was guaranteed to be PROMPT AND SECURE. Anglo-Australia makes its last shabby-genteel stand at the Spotlight Manchester store, among starchy lengths of linen and bolts of floral drapery; in the local Fletcher Jones, elderly mannequins flout the ethnic fashions of the street in Scottish blouses and tartan skirts primly fastened with bobby-pins.

If Melbourne meant to me the upright adulthood of the Fletcher Jones man, Sydney, even more elusively far away, offered the bliss of release from those responsibilities. Branded with a profanation when Nino Culotta in *They're a Weird Mob* was sent to King's bloody Cross, Sydney stood for whatever raffish sins I could imagine. Looking at Brett Whiteley's paintings of the harbour, I see my dream of it before me: a balmy pool to float or drown in, blue as midnight. Melbourne effortfully overcame the Tasmanian past; Sydney blithely forgot it. In Darlinghurst, on a chiselled ridge of rock which supports a row of cottages, someone has spray-painted the immemorial Australian graffito – the crow's foot of the government arrow, inscribed on all those instruments of travail at Port Arthur. But the three black blades wound no one here. In this city of joggers, with its kaftans and wine coolers and acrylic spa baths, people live for the heedless sensual present, or for the acquisitive future. A lanky youth beside whom I waited at a traffic intersection had been to a fortune-teller in Dee Why the night before. 'She was cheap, only twenty-eight bucks,' he told his companion. Did she look far ahead? asked the girl. 'She told me I'd have a career-change,' he said, and strode off across the street in quest of it. That seer knew what magic spells Sydneysiders want to hear.

Sydney predicts a career-change for Australia too. Melbourne was the sentry-post of stolid, imperial, English Australia; slick, image-infatuated Sydney gazes out towards California. Its twin icons, the harbour bridge and the opera house, sum up two phases of Australian identity. The bridge is a wire coat-hanger buttressed by salt and pepper cellars, lovably functional as the metaphors declare. I got to know it in this form: my parents had some salt and pepper shakers – a wedding present I think – in the shape of its thick squat towers; the bridge was a monument to their meagre, domestic

Australia, with its hard work and its square meals. The opera house, unfunctional and ornamental, belongs to a different world. It flaunts a life of extravagance and pleasure, to which my parents never felt they were entitled. It is pure form, less a building than a cluster of images – bunched like a colony of shells, each containing words or music as shells bottle up the reverberant sea; the symbol for a navigable city, its sails of tile angled to take the wind; sculpted from the same illusory stuff as my white, gleaming drive-in screen at Elwick, on which the sacred monsters came out to play at night. I saw it for the first time on this return journey, and realised that Australia itself had become the place I went overseas to find: a society where you could perpetuate childhood in the earnest playfulness of art. My cave of crumbling plaster extroverts itself to shine on Bennelong Point. The occult light the cave concealed flashes back at the sun from those spread wings.

Yet didn't this flock of ceramic gulls or fleet of billowing spin-nakers poise here at the water's edge in readiness to quit Australia? I couldn't help comparing the opera house with another Australian icon, which doesn't perch rootlessly on the shore but is plugged into the umbilical mid-point of the continent – Uluru, or Ayers Rock. The two monoliths measured the gap between landscape and society here, or between stern reality and the wishfulness of art. A knob of somnolent stone, against a brittle, brilliant assembly of images; a mass kneaded into shape after geological traumas, against a fantasy engineered by gravity-defying science; a boulder which glows like a coal from within, against a chandelier of glittery reflections and partial, multiplied facets; a cosmic tablet with history encoded on it – since every cleft and ridge of Uluru marks the advent of some fabled ancestor – against an acoustic hollow trapping echoes; a wart of earth against a vessel of air, which can only listen to the singing wind as it passes through.

The rock, unseen, belonged to the Australia I still didn't know, and perhaps never would. It was the ultimate rebuff to European impositions on this land, which set up fences, raised walls and nailed down roofs to keep the land out; its perils when climbed made it the place of ultimate trial, determining whether you deserved to be truly at home in this country. In its company were the gaunt storm-flayed mountains I had seen in the Tasmanian south-west, the trees cut down in the Lemonthyme forest which grew again to be felled once more by the sons of the axemen, the bituminous water of Macquarie Harbour: irreducible substance or impervious surface, on which human beings can do no more than scratch their insignia as the tribesmen at Tiagarra once did.

I remembered dimly the day when the field of mud around our house was concreted over to lay our paths through a notional, hopeful garden. My father got his work-mates to help, with the bribe of some beer. When the job was done, with the yards of grey mortifying sand ruled at intervals to look like flag-stones, or like the map of outback Australia arbitrarily sliced into states, my father's friends took a stick and wrote their initials into one of the squares. Their jokiness couldn't disguise the solemnity of the ritual. They were present, as you often are in Australia, at the inauguration of the world, the start of history; and the request they made as they passed the stick around was that time should remember their names. After thirty years, the little scrawls are already wearing away.

The gales which shake the island in the summer treat men and trees and the roofs of houses as air-borne litter: the wind is in a hurry to be rid of us. The Victorian pomp of Melbourne couldn't charm away my frightened sense of temporariness in Tasmania; Sydney's pursuit of pleasure couldn't stop me remembering the Tasmanian story of hardship and pain. Its people have always been battlers, and the strain of their lives is carved into their faces like the stick's intrepid scratch marks in our backyard cement or the brand on the convicts' irons or the incisions at Tiagarra. I saw it in the faces of my parents, where the lines were mute, questioning mouths. But they don't complain, and translate despair into indigestion. Such is life is their creed too.

To me, Tasmania itself was the cold place. It's a prison, but then so is the world. It's a castaway, adrift in a liquid nowhere, but then the world is too. It's a sundered, solitary, disowned infant; aren't we all? By creepy coincidence, around the corner from my house in London is a small roadside myth which dramatises and atones for Tasmania's orphan status. The sign advertises a firm called Tasman Nannies. From the north-western tip of Tasmania, redrawn to resemble the puffy foetal profile of a baby, a boneless hand extends across Bass Strait to stroke the promontory on the southern tip of Victoria. That severed coast is reshaped into a maternal face: furry eyelashes, curved nose, puckering lips. The prodigal island is rejoined to the body which in bearing it expelled it. The myth, like all myths, tells a lie to manoeuvre round an impossibility. Though I smile with happiness every time I pass the sign, I can't quite persuade myself to believe in this homecoming, with its promise to heal all geological and emotional wounds.

Instead, Tasmania reminded me that we are all still pioneers, required to colonise the piece of ground which chance assigns us, to make it our own by shaping it into a small, autonomous, intelligible world. Everything I had seen there enforced that moral – the homy relics enshrined by the museums at Queenstown or Wybalenna; the colonial paintings which strove so ingeniously to turn views of Hobart into visions; my own childish effort to see the main road as a narrative, a topographic story of gulfs and peaks, its pavements aswarm with marvels. The island has transformed itself into a universe, complete with gardened heavens and a penal hell. Its short history extends from the world's beginning, with the Old Beach reptiles bathing in the river and the megafauna prowling the bush, to foreknowledge of its end, when machines supplant men: those singing pylons in the mountains, the dam which has drunk the forests, the turbines underground. Yet despite Jane Franklin's temple in the scrub, despite Gustav Weindorfer's luring of the animals into his peaceable kingdom, despite the tallying of mementos in Eric Thomas's archive, Tasmania teaches you how briefly human history has interrupted the time of earth, and reveals how frail are all our efforts to make ourselves at home. Looking down on the seismic south-west from the plane, I saw that what we take for a floor, a stage we can tread with confidence, is a turbulent, unsupporting, unfounded sea.

I left Tasmania for limbo. Clouds denied that the place had ever existed. They parted now and then on stray fractions of terrain – the baked, cracking, mustardy pastures of northern Victoria; the grey surge of ocean at the Heads in Sydney, settled by accident when the navigators mistook that opening for Botany Bay; half a day later the same ocean, tropically torpid, at Honolulu; after more hours of obliteration, a sudden vent to show the Rockies, stiffened by snow and bluely frost-bitten; the oblongs and trapezoids and parallelograms of pulsing orange which are peopled America, and Manhattan aflare on the black water of another ocean; finally the countryside of England with its smooth flanks and bowery hollows and its kind, deceptive habitability.

As if by parachute, I was able to plunge into one or another of these excerpts from the globe revolving below. Like a spy for whom an alias has been prepared, I could find on the ground a door with my name on it, a closet with clothes which fitted me, a shelf with books I seemed to have read, a window which was my aperture on life. But reassembling those possessions, reassuming those characteristics, I felt an impostor. Everything that constituted me had been made by the place I left long ago, where I would never live again.

It was the landscape inside me: the space where I spent my dreaming time. Back there I recognised the random objects which staked out my borders, the totems which still accompanied me. The immitigable mountains and their stark, eldritch trees; coasts where earth abruptly snapped off, never to be continued, or beaches which gnawed it to bright dust and sucked it gently away. Also, preparing a defence, some conceptual animals sketched onto rock, and a bridge which hid secret thoughts under its arches; the hollow papery cave of light in its dark shed, and the metal screen cut out of the sky for projected fantasies. Reality, and the art of contradicting or augmenting it. Tasmania had set the terms of my life. The home you cannot return to you carry off with you: it lies down there at the bottom of the world, and of the sleeping, imagining mind.